EUROPE BETWEE
1815-

Professor JACQUES DROZ was born in Paris in 1909 and educated at the Lycée Louis le Grand and the Sorbonne. He taught at the University of Dijon from 1946 to 1947 and then became Professor of History at the University of Clermont-Ferrand. In 1955 he was appointed Dean of Studies there and held this post until 1962. He then became Professor History at the Sorbonne. Among his publications are *Restaurations et Révolutions and L'Allemagne et la Révolution Française*.

Fontana History of Europe
General Editor: J. H. Plumb

Jacques Droz

Europe between Revolutions
1815–1848

FontanaPress
An Imprint of HarperCollinsPublishers

Fontana Press
An Imprint of HarperCollins*Publishers*
77–85 Fulham Palace Road,
Hammersmith, London W6 8JB

Published by Fontana Press 1985
13 15 17 19 18 16 14

First published in Great Britain by
Fontana 1967

ISBN 0 00 686066 4

Set in Garamond

Printed in Great Britain by
HarperCollinsManufacturing Glasgow

CONTENTS

INTRODUCTION

In the period 1815-1848 two great social forces were pitted against each other: the traditional ruling class whose roots lay in the Ancien Régime, and the new men of the Industrial Revolution who made their bid for power in the name of Liberalism.

To all appearances the year 1815 set the seal on the triumph of reaction. Its traditions, resources and inclinations seemed everywhere in the ascendant. Yet the French Revolution could hardly have vanished into thin air. It had overturned the political and social structure of France. Through the wars which it had unleashed over Europe and through the victorious advance of the soldiers of the Revolution and the Empire, it had introduced its new ideas into the most hermetically sealed States. The victors wished to re-draw the map of Europe under cover of the Restoration; but the Congress of Vienna did not succeed in giving back to Europe the stability on which the sovereigns were counting. International diplomacy, with an appearance of unity in its political conceptions, was expected to establish universal peace, but it did not suppress the conflict of ideologies. Once the common danger was over, interests clashed and appetites were sharpened, harbingers of bloody disputes.

It was not enough to stop the hands of the clock and turn them back to 1789; the new ideas had infiltrated everywhere, and men's minds had opened to a new vision of the world. National identities had been asserted. Along with the ideas of social emancipation and freedom, the French invader had spread the concept of nationalism.

In the ruthless ideological struggle between the supporters

7

and the opponents of liberalism, the liberals carried the
day. But their victory was to be one of brutal egoism. The
bourgeois, in command of the economy and with power in
his hands, built his fortune on the misery of the greater
number. His contribution was to spread poverty. The
Industrial Revolution which had been in progress since
1785 moved even faster with the coming of the railways.
This rapid development of modern industrial capitalism
created a huge proletariat whose moral and physical
wretchedness found ever more articulate expression in
specifically anti-bourgeois movements, especially after 1840,
in the countries that were being industrialized. This
double antagonism is the context of European history between 1815 and 1848.

Chapter I

THE PHILOSOPHY OF RESTORATION

Unquestionably the year 1815 aroused great hopes among the governing classes of Europe. The diplomats gathered together in Vienna not only thought that they had put an end to the revolutionary and imperial adventure, but they also sought to restore respect for established power, together with the principle of legitimacy, and the sense of hierarchy and authority. The sovereigns who were taking up the reins of state again after twenty years of tribulation could in fact depend on a general movement of reaction against individualism, a movement which called upon the élite of Europe to rebuild unity of thought and to revive the taste for tradition as a bastion against the progress of free inquiry. In fact, this reaction against the Enlightenment had become apparent in the course of the last decades of the eighteenth century: it was in 1775 that Claude de Saint-Martin, the so-called 'unknown philosopher', published *Des erreurs et de la Vérité*; in 1790 that Burke wrote his *Reflections on the Revolution in France*; in 1796 that Joseph de Maistre wrote his *Considérations sur la France*; and in 1799 that Novalis planned *Christenheit oder Europa*, the first demonstration of German Romanticism. But it was about 1815 that these works began to bear fruit.

In France traditionalism was born of reflections on the Revolution of 1789, which was regarded as a conspiracy between Freemasonry and Illuminism, and of the experiences of exile, which had brought the aristocracy back to the religion of their forefathers. Joseph de Maistre, a nobleman from Savoy, and the Vicomte de Bonald, a gentleman from Rouergue, both *émigrés* and after 1815

9

the theoreticians of Ultramontanism, recognized that the Revolution, and later Napoleon, had been sent by Providence to punish the crime of unbelief; they ridiculed the rationalist pretensions of the eighteenth century, against which they set the lessons of experience; and they were united in demonstrating the inability of man to create a government, the vanity of written constitutions, and the superiority of empiricism over logical reasoning. Man, they said, could not create anything in the political world, any more than in the physical world: 'He can no doubt plant a pip, grow a tree, improve it by grafting, and prune it in countless different ways, but he has never imagined that he had the power to make a tree; how then can he have supposed that he had the power to make a constitution?' Thus Joseph de Maistre; while de Bonald wrote: 'Man can no more make a constitution for political society than he can give weight to bodies or extension to matter.' The former insisted in his book *Du Pape* on the theocratic origins of the legitimate rulers, who held their power on the authority of the sole true sovereign, the infallible Pope; and the latter stressed the absolute character of divine Revelation, which excluded free discussion, and even tolerance from social life.

In Switzerland in 1816, the Swiss Ludwig von Haller began publishing his *Restauration der Staatswissenschaften*. 'The legitimate monarchs,' he announced, 'have been restored to their thrones, and we are likewise going to restore to its throne, legitimate science, the science which serves the sovereign master, and whose truth is confirmed by the whole universe.' Taking his stand on Natural Law, he too reacted violently against eighteenth century rationalism. He compared the State to a family, the national territory to the sovereign's private estate, authority to property, the law to the monarch's grace, taxation and military service to voluntary assistance, and politics to the science of private law. In Haller's eyes the sovereign reigned, not by virtue of delegated authority, but by a right conferred upon him by his strength; he did not administer the common weal, but his own private affairs. The only limit on his power was the respect he owed other landed proprietors; thus he had before him a pyramid of liberties and privileges, but there could be no question of any contract between his subjects and himself.

This was likewise the opinion of the German Romantics. Reacting against the universalism of French Institutions, the School of Legal History also reacted against the tendencies of the men of the previous generation, who had lacked 'a sense of history'. Thus its founder, the jurist Savigny, protested in his book *Vom Beruf unserer Zeit* against his colleague Thibaut's pretensions to endow Germany with a uniform Law: according to him, the creative element of Law, like that of language and customs, was the spirit of the people (*Volksgeist*); it was therefore ridiculous to try to fashion it in accordance with the arbitrary caprices of men. From 1815 onwards, in the *Zeitschrift für geschichtliche Rechtswissenschaft*, Savigny and Eichhorn attacked the champions of Natural Law, in the name of custom and tradition. Moreover, falling to an increasing extent under the influence of Catholicism, and in many cases themselves becoming converts, the Romantics provided theological justification for the ideas of legitimacy, hierarchy, and obedience. It was against political liberalism and a materialistic economy that Adam Müller, the theoretician of the 'organic' State, directed his last works; after establishing that land cannot, like chattels, be the object of financial profit or commercial transactions, he proved that work had no value except as a service to the community, that credit was an act of faith in the State, and that taxes were sacred dues which ought to be paid with pious devotion. Going even further than Müller, Baader, the opponent of a liberal economy, pointed to the evolution of a society in which capital would accumulate in the hands of a few, leaving outside it a proletarian army filled with revolutionary passion. As for Friedrich Schlegel, his last works were inspired by the concept of a Christian State. These Romantics had the feeling that, if the values on which the old society had lived were to be saved, the Church alone was capable of doing it, and for that purpose ought to be given as much freedom as possible. The group of Viennese Catholics which had formed around the Redemptorist Hofbauer devoted its energies to the task of eradicating the last traces of Joseph II's enlightened legislation. As for Joseph Görres's 'Round Table' which had been formed among the professors of the new University of Munich, with the support of Ludwig I of Bavaria, it had prepared in the review *Eos* the weapons which, twenty years later, would restore its freedom to the German Church.

That the forces of conservatism should base themselves on strong religious feeling and a popular ultramontane Catholicism was also the opinion of the Frenchman Lamennais, who, in his *Essai sur l'Indifférence en matière de religion* (1817) tried to gather support for a new system of apologetics, founded on the certainty that 'there can be no peace for the mind except when it is sure of possessing the truth'. The admiration felt by Lamennais for the Christian Middle Ages, when all the peoples of the West were united by common convictions, led him to a radical condemnation of free inquiry, dear to Luther and Descartes, and to a rehabilitation of the principle of authority, essential for orderly consciences. 'The world,' he wrote, 'is a prey to opinions; everyone wants to believe only himself, and consequently obeys only himself. Restore authority and universal order will be born again.' The question of certainty was therefore in his eyes the chief problem of the day, and he saw it expressed in phrases such as 'the consensus' (*sens commun*) and 'universal agreement' (*consentement universel*). Now, the Catholic religion was the sole repository of this unanimity, its universality serving as a guarantee of its truth. Lamennais concluded that, since the Church was the only source of absolute authority and absolute certainty, it was essential that the states of the world should submit themselves to it, and that the temporal power should once again be subservient to the spiritual power. It was the function of the Popes to guide or depose the faltering princes of the world. These theocratic ideas awakened a vast response, both in France and abroad, especially in Belgium and Germany. While Alsatian figures such as Liebermann and Raess introduced the writings of the French theocrats to the German public through the Mainz review *Der Katholik*, Baron d'Eckstein, a great friend of the German Romantics, spread German ideas in France, first through the Ultra-Royalist press, and then through the review *Le Catholique*, which he published in Paris from 1826 to 1830. It seemed essential to the beneficiaries of the Restoration that Catholicism should envelop the lives of nations, like those of individuals, with its vast network of connections and obligations, without which authority could not acquire that absolute, priestly character which made certain of its subjects' obedience and devotion.

Admittedly Protestantism, sapped by the spirit of free inquiry, and fiercely attacked by the theocrats, could not offer the same guarantees as Roman Catholicism. But the revivalist movement turned it towards orthodox and even pietist ideas, which were in line with the demands of conservative thinkers. The services rendered in this respect by the Methodist sects in England are common knowledge. In the German States, remarkable results were achieved by the pietist movements and by the Moravian Brothers, who never ceased fighting the good fight against the Enlightenment, and who identified the French Revolution with the Beast of the Apocalypse. In Prussia, the most eminent representatives of the aristocracy grouped themselves in

1815 around the Gerlach brothers, in the *Maikäferei*, a religious and patriotic body which was the first embryo of the conservative party. It was this group which, immediately after the 1830 revolutions, was to bring out the *Berliner Politische Wochenblatt*, edited incidentally by a convert to Catholicism, the Bavarian Jarcke, the best theoretician of the Christian State; against the solvent of free-thought, nothing less would do in fact but a union of all believers.

In Germany, however, it was from Hegel that political philosophy was to receive its greatest stimulus. His teaching, which ran counter to the ' constitution-makers ' of the revolutionary period, demonstrated that there could be no freedom save in the State and that the latter, the sole source of Law, was defined simply by its sovereignty, and therefore could not recognize any other will than its own. According to Hegel, it was only in the State that man could attain the highest morality. The State in fact educated the individual, submitting him to a collective discipline which freed him from the contingencies of his animal nature and from sterile ratiocinations : far from reducing his stature, it enabled him to fulfil his personality by identifying himself with a superior moral organism which helped him to make progress in the direction of universality and ' concrete liberty '. The State was a permanent, unanimous community which was not simply a General Will formulated as the result of a contract emanating from individuals; it existed before them and endured after them; it was reality in its absolute primary form, and the individual himself had no ' substance ' or liberty except as a member of the State. Hegel's *Grundlinien der Philosophie des Rechts* (1820) gave a description of the State according to which the monarch, who was the incarnation of universality, made his decision with the help of his officials, the representation of the *Stände* serving simply to explain to the people the decisions taken at a higher level. Was this an apology for the Prussian State of his time? Hegel's dialectic doubtless forbade him to stop at the idea of a 'good state' where there could be no question of anything but successive imperialisms. But it is undeniable that by using the formula 'all reality is actual', Hegel gave support to those who were trying to justify their attachment to the existing systems. As he grew older, he, the admirer of the French Revolution, adopted an increasingly conservative philosophy. At the same time, scorning International Law, he provided justification for the policy of 'Might is Right': a State which possessed a superior organization and culture was entitled to enslave 'inferior' nations, for the victorious nation had, by its very victory, proved its superiority. Similar inferences can be drawn from the works of the great German historians of this period—Niebuhr, whose *Römische Geschichte* extolled the virtues of the Roman peasant, and above all Ranke, the father of 'scientific historiography' who presented the history of nations as a struggle between great political personalities and emphasised the need for each State to be actuated by a desire for power, as a surety of its independence: this was the thesis of the primacy of foreign policy which he formulated in his vast studies of diplomatic history, believing as he did that international life conditioned the political organization and the very institutions of the State.

The man who, in the eyes of his contemporaries, personified the policy of the Restoration was the Austrian Chancellor Metternich, who for many years was to stamp his mark on European politics. In fact, Metternich was more a rationalist than a Romantic; he shared little of his contemporaries' enthusiasm for the ideas of legitimacy and divine right, and even less for the theories of ultramontanism, which his mind, imbued with the anti-clericalism of Joseph II, found somewhat shocking. He was a man of the eighteenth century. The basic idea of his 'system' was that of equilibrium, which he owed to his collaborator Friedrich von Gentz, the theoretician of the struggle against revolutionary and imperial France. To begin with, according to Metternich, there existed an equilibrium inside each State, where the social order had to be defended against the forces of destruction. Next there existed an equilibrium between States, for the latter could not be left to their individual devices, but had to be made subject to a supranational community. And if it was true that 'only order produces equilibrium', nothing could be more dangerous for the existence of these States than the development of national liberal movements. Metternich therefore set his face against any constitutional change. Comparing Revolution in turn to a hydra ready to swallow everything up, to a fire, to a flood, and later to the cholera, hostile to the sovereignty of the people and constitutional government, which he regarded as nothing but the application of the principle: 'Get out of there so that I can take your place', he considered that the salvation of society depended on the preservation of the monarchies and respect for an aristocratic hierarchy, 'an intermediary class between the throne and the lower strata of the social body'. It was this faith in national and international equilibrium which was responsible for his sensitivity to European interests in general and his belief in the need for a concert of Europe, as something superior to the individual interests of each State. Reason therefore demanded that the monarchs should join together to save society from total subversion. As it was governments which were responsible in the last resort for revolutions, they had to be prepared to take preventive measures. It was necessary not only that the sovereigns should be in agreement among themselves and take counsel together frequently in congresses as to what measures to take, but also that they should be able to intervene in a neighbouring State to restore order when it was threatened; they had to form themselves into political supreme courts to maintain an international police force against revolution. Of the Holy Alliance—a document which Tsar Alexander I in a moment of mysticism invited the sovereigns of Europe to sign, as ' members of a single Christian nation ', in token of their readiness to rule in a spirit of brotherhood and charity—of the Holy Alliance Metternich wanted to make a union of governmental police forces against all innovators. In giving the European alliance its anti-revolutionary, anti-liberal character, he had a very clear sense of serving first of all the interests of Austria, the power most vulnerable to popular attack, but as a man aware of the solidarity of the destinies of Europe, which, he wrote in 1824, ' has acquired for me the quality of one's own country.'

Did the governing classes attain their objects? Besides the general atmosphere of exhaustion and boredom, they counted on the submission of the rural masses, and on the narrowness of urban and industrial life. But it was precisely the fact of economic growth which was to send the whole Restoration system sprawling. The forces of order would find themselves opposed by those of movement. The development of heavy industry, spreading from England to the Continent, would break the social structure of the Ancien Régime and make the middle class the chief element of the new political life. Now, this middle class, whose emancipation had been ensured by the French Revolution, was deeply attached to liberalism, in which it saw the guarantee of its influence in the State. The props supporting the Restoration were to be knocked away by the moral forces that sprang from the Industrial Revolution.

Chapter II

THE ECONOMIC DEVELOPMENT
OF THE GREAT EUROPEAN STATES

Profound as was the economic transformation of Europe
in the first half of the nineteenth century, the Continent
remained essentially as it had been under the Ancien
Régime. True, there were considerable technical advances
in industry : the development of the steam engine, of the
power-loom, the use of coke in the manufacture of cast
iron. A revolution was also in progress in transport :
the improvement of the roads, the application of steam to
ships and railways soon exerted a decisive influence on
the lives of the nations. However, between 1815 and 1848
the traditional features of the economy remained pre-
eminent : the superiority of agriculture over industrial
production, the absence of cheap and rapid means of transport, and the priority given to consumer goods over heavy
industry.

It was in the sphere of credit that the delay in development was most obvious. Admittedly, a financial oligarchy
had gradually been formed, which the governments of
Europe could not do without. The web which international
finance was weaving around the various States seemed
tighter and tighter. The international character of the
banks could be seen from the fact that it was the Barings
and the Hopes, of London and Amsterdam, who had made
the loans required for the liberation of France. The
Rothschilds were typical of this high finance. Sprung from
the Frankfurt ghetto, the five brothers, Amschel, Solomon,
Nathan, Jacob and Karl managed respectively the banking
houses of Frankfurt, Vienna, London, Paris and Naples.

Their fortune was founded on the transfer of funds between England and her allies at a time when the transference of large sums over great distances was still extremely dangerous. After 1820, most loans passed through their hands, the sovereigns of Europe could no longer ignore them, and Francis I of Austria raised them to the rank of barons. Metternich and his secretary Friedrich von Gentz contracted a marriage of reason and business with them at the Congress of Aix-la-Chapelle: 'The Rothschilds,' wrote Gentz, 'are vulgar Jews who are ignorant of good manners, but who possess an admirable flair which always enables them to do the right thing at the right time. Their enormous wealth (they are the richest men in Europe) is entirely the result of their instinct, which the public is in the habit of calling luck.' Anxious to maintain a peace which suited their business, they did their best to prevent war, for example in the Belgian Affair of 1830, or in the Egyptian Crisis of 1840, and to encourage agreements between the ruling monarchs. While taking an interest in the fate of their persecuted co-religionists, they worked in fact for the consolidation of the established order. Their profits were invested in fruitful enterprises: they laid their hands on the mercury mines of Idria and Almaden, obtained control of the Austrian Lloyds, equipped railway undertakings of some importance, and, in order to establish their political or economic influence, made use of the financial difficulties of various governments, as when Belgium was confronted with the laborious liquidation of the Dutch debt. Owning luxurious mansions and country houses, they entered high society, and some of them even succeeded in obtaining a measure of parliamentary power, though without entirely succeeding in overcoming the anti-semitism which accompanied their success, as evidenced by the pamphlet by the Fourierist Toussenel entitled *Les Juifs, rois de l'époque*. The fact remains that this aristocracy of money remained hostile as yet to the idea, which would be dear to the Saint-Simonians, of the diffusion of credit. Except in England, credit banks were so far unknown. Admittedly, limited partnerships were developing, but they would have to wait for more favourable times in order to expand, and the formula of the joint-stock company corresponded to a phase of widespread capitalist expansion which only a few people could dimly foresee. Generally speaking, the development of credit continued to be characterized by a prudence and sometimes a timidity, evidence of the stubborn resistance put up by habit of mind as well as by established practices. This was because the echoes of the old controversy about the lawfulness of usury had not yet died away; and even after 1830, it is possible to find certain prelates expressing indignation at the indulgence of the Curia's instructions in this respect.

In any case, the general situation of the money market was scarcely favourable to vast economic expansion. The period 1817-1850 was marked by a fall in the price of gold. The production of precious metals had slowed down; and the tendency for prices to rise which had existed since the second quarter of the eighteenth century had stopped shortly after the general restoration of peace. Contractors accordingly wished to reduce wages, all the more so in that there was an abundant supply of labour; and they did not hesitate to resort to tariff protection. What is certain is that the economy was affected by crises which recurred roughly every ten years, with periods of recovery in between: the principal dates were 1817-1818, 1826-1829, 1836-1839, 1840-1850. Usually due to bad harvests, these crises produced steep rises in agricultural prices, upset the living conditions of the agricultural labourer, and led in succession to the closing of the peasant market, a drop in industrial production, first textile and then metallurgical, commercial stagnation, unemployment, a fall in wages and industrial unrest. Be that as it may, these disturbances in the economy did not fail to have a direct influence on social or political agitation, which, to a certain extent, was the outward form they assumed.

Just as the economy did not undergo a complete revolution between 1815 and 1848, so there was no radical transformation in the sphere of demography. The population of Europe continued to grow, rising in fifty years from 167 to 266 million; although it is true that the French increase, still remarkable at the beginning of the century, slowed down as a result of a fall in the birth-rate, which was henceforth higher in England and Germany. The surplus population was directed towards the towns, which needed an ever-increasing labour force: in 1800 there were only twenty-two towns in Europe with more than 100,000 inhabitants, while in 1850 there were forty-seven (twenty-eight of them in England); the population of London rose from 960,000 to 2,000,000, and that of Paris from 550,000 to 1,000,000; Cologne doubled its population in half a century. But the drift in population from the country to the towns was still only slight; the France of 1848 was three-quarters rural. The expectation of life in this Europe of the first half of the nineteenth century remained short, and the bulk of the population consequently very young. In the great industrial centres, the average expectation of life was little more than twenty years; and it only required a bad harvest for thousands of poor people to die. Huge epidemics—of typhus, bubonic plague, and especially cholera—continued to claim hosts of victims. Coming from Russia and facilitated by the military operations between Russians and Poles in 1831, the great cholera epidemic which spread to Europe between 1831 and 1837 wrought havoc everywhere, claiming 100,000 victims in France, including 18,000 in Paris, killing Casimir Périer, Cuvier, Sadi Carnot, and taking its heaviest toll in the poorer districts. Why then bring into the world so many creatures doomed to a speedy death or a wretched existence? This was the question put by Malthus at the end of the eighteenth century, when he had shown that subsistence increased in an arithmetic progression. His ideas, opposed in certain quarters, obtained considerable success with the liberal economists, such as Say and Dunoyer; and a Malthusian League was formed in England to combat the terrifying proliferation of the poor.

Finally, the Industrial Revolution had not yet been able to abolish the old rural supremacy. However great the progress made by capitalism in Great Britain, the balance between landed interests and moneyed interests, had not been finally upset in favour of the latter. In France, under the Restoration, more than three-fifths of the nation's wealth lay in land, and this proportion was exceeded in most of the other continental countries. Even when a man did not live by working on the land, the problem of eating his fill remained an everyday pre-occupation, and the fear of famine disappeared only in the very rare years of exceptional abundance. Moreover, the towns, which were generally of moderate size, were closely associated with the surrounding countryside with which they exchanged their products. Admittedly agriculture, already much improved in the eighteenth century, made fresh progress in those regions where the big landowners took an interest in farming their estates and invested capital, not in the acquisition of more land—the dream of the small French landowner—but in the purchase of machines, fertilizers and seed. It was Great Britain above all which was notable for this class of big farmers who were able to apply the new agricultural methods thanks to the redistribution of land and the enclosure system. Some progress, due either to drainage, or to the liming of siliceous land, or to the improvement of the plough, could be noted in certain privileged zones, in Lombardy and Piedmont, amongst the country gentry of North Germany, and in such parts of

France as Flanders, Normandy, Limagne and Poitou. Regions began to specialize in particular kinds of farming : hop-growing in Bavaria, vine-growing in the Mediterranean areas, and stock-farming in the vicinity of large towns. But the majority of European farmers remained faithful to the traditional methods, with land left fallow for long periods, preference given to cereals, stock-farming regarded as a subsidiary source of income, and cattle neglected so that they remained subject to epidemics. Finally, the pattern of land distribution was not greatly changed; France remained a country of small peasant landowners, who continued to divide their land into small-holdings and became increasingly attached to individual property. From the North Sea to the Appenines, the manorial system was on the decline as a result of the upheavals of the revolutionary and Napoleonic periods, but without any consequent improvement in the lot of tenant farmers or the agricultural labourer; the big estate remained the rule in the Mediterranean countries as a whole.

These are simply general indications. But it is impossible to generalize about the European economy between 1815 and 1848; the development of each country differed so much from that of its neighbours.

In 1815 Great Britain enjoyed a considerable start over the Continent, although as yet only the technique of cotton-spinning had been radically changed by the Industrial Revolution. Geographically, specialization was only just beginning; small workshops were still powered by hydraulic engines; hand-looms were still in general use. The domestic system, which involved the employment of scattered craftsmen, remained in force for weaving and for cloth manufacture in Norwich, Leeds and Bradford, for hosiery in Leicester and Nottingham, for silk manufacture at Spitalfields, and for light industry in Birmingham and Sheffield. The development of these industries still had a long way to go, and yet the total value of English production remained higher than that of the Continent.

Alone among the countries of Europe, England already possessed an agricultural system of a capitalist type. During the second half of the eighteenth century, the great landed proprietors, taking advantage of the theories made fashionable by the economists, obtained permission from Parliament to appropriate and enclose on a large scale the waste land which belonged to the village communities; the concentration of the aristocratic estates, run by rich farmers, resulted in the triumph of large-scale farming, treated as an industry, practising four-course or five-course rotation, and notable for the development of chemical fertilizers, drainage and new grazing crops. True, the middle class of freeholders or yeomen farmers tended to disappear, leaving the gentry faced with a proletariat of small tenant farmers and agricultural labourers, often poverty-stricken, who, about the 1830's, tried to rise in revolt and break the agricultural machines. The development of the manufacturing industries tended to eliminate rural craftsmanship. There can be no doubt that the landed proprietors tried to secure the national income for themselves and it was against landlordism, protected by high taxation on imported foreign corn, that the Free Trade movement, originating in commercial and industrial circles, was to be directed.

It was between 1815 and 1850 that the manufacturing industries took shape in England. By the middle of the century, Watt's steam engine was no longer a laboratory instrument; taking the place of the hydraulic engine, it had transformed first mining and the iron and steel industry, and then textiles. Hand weaving in its turn was doomed as a result of the application of the Shrap and Roberts patent. Small industrial undertakings tended to disappear, ruined by the progress of mechanisation and successive economic crises. At the same time the old craftsman class broke up, some elements finding a place in the manufacturing industries, but the vast majority joining the proletariat. The factory system won the day in Wales and the North of England. It was the transport system in particular which was transformed: until 1824, what railways were laid were used for horse-drawn vehicles, but after Stephenson had built the first locomotive in 1814, steam trains started running between Stockton and Darlington in 1823, between Liverpool and Manchester in 1830, and between London and Birmingham in 1837. The technique of railway construction was perfected by two Frenchmen, Brunel and his son, who built the tunnel under the Thames; and iron bridges linked Anglesey with Wales and Chester with Holyhead. The railways were financed entirely by private enterprise, the State merely giving permission for the laying down of lines, neither underwriting loans nor paying for the purchase of land. By the middle of the century, as the result of an unparalleled orgy of speculation, nearly seven thousand miles of railway had been laid, and were being operated by a variety of companies. What is more, it was English capital which gave the original impetus to the development of railways on the Continent; it was an Anglo-French company which undertook the construction of the Paris-Le Havre line, it was the London and South-Eastern Railway which financed the Amiens-Boulogne line, the eight directors of the French Nord Company included two Englishmen, both Barings; and W. Mackenzie, one of the great figures of international capitalism, was involved in a great many continental railway undertakings. Finally, in answer to the competition of the railways, the canals, which were also in the hands of private companies, were improved and modernized, while the roads were transformed thanks to the metalling process invented by the Scot Macadam. Everywhere, the improvement in communications made possible the establishment and concentration of industries in the most suitable sites.

As for credit, it became more widespread and more easily available. Already in 1815, the Bank of England was the biggest depository of capital in the whole world; the concentration of capital was evidenced by the founding of large banking houses like Baring's, linked with the biggest banks in Amsterdam and Hamburg. The prestige of the Bank of England was increased still further in 1819 when the House of Commons voted for a return to payment in gold. It took part, incidentally, in a great many speculations, to such an extent that a law passed by Parliament in 1844, separating the monetary department from the banking department, fixed a limit to the issue of notes, in proportion to the bank's capital and gold and silver reserves. The private banks gave place increasingly to joint-stock banks, whose basic function was to receive deposits, open accounts, and re-invest their available capital at very short notice. Crashes, accompanied by a succession of bankruptcies, occurred repeatedly in 1825, 1836, and 1847, but production always recovered quickly as consumption and orders rose steeply.

Thus English capitalism triumphed between 1815 and 1851 over the unfavourable conditions due to the fall in the price of gold; on the basis of the rate of industrial production, of the volume of trade, and even of real wages, the historian is obliged to recognize that this was a period of extraordinary development, such as England has never known at any other time. Coal production more than trebled, and the production of iron increased eightfold. England was coal merchant to the world, and the zenith of her power seemed to coincide, at the beginning of the Victorian era, with the peak of her coal exports. It was, of course, the ports handling shipments from the colonies and exporting manufactured goods which benefited most from the new prosperity; their expansion was favoured too by the progress made in steam shipping : the building of iron clippers with four or five masts; the use of composite ships; the substitution of the screw-propeller for the old paddlewheel, thanks to the discoveries of the Swede Ericsson; and the formation of big companies such as Cunard, whose ship *Britannia* crossed the Atlantic in 1840 in fourteen days. Business was greatly helped by the use of the telegraph, and by the reform of the postal system carried out by Rowland Hill, who introduced the penny stamp paid for by the sender. Was this development greatly assisted by the progressive establishment of Free Trade, which was in the air, and then by the repeal of the Corn Laws (see p. 139)? Certainly the supporting role played by Free Trade was considerable; but it must be remembered that, as a result of persistent protectionism, continental markets did not give reciprocal treatment to English goods.

It was in the Belgian provinces, subject to the Netherlands until 1830 and independent afterwards, that the influence of English methods and techniques was the most potent during the decades following 1815. The existing coal and iron resources and the quality of a labour force with centuries of experience in spinning and weaving behind it were favourable conditions. Considerable help was provided by King William I, through government orders placed with industry and the granting of subsidies. Coal production developed thanks to the use of steam engines; the textile industry at Ghent and Brussels was transformed by mechanization; and the metallurgical industry made enormous strides at Namur, Charleroi and Liège. In 1839 great aristocratic landowners such as the d'Oultremonts and Cockerill employed over two thousand workers; and the d'Arenbergs were to be seen taking an interest in industrial development. Everywhere, English technicians were at work. Interrupted for a moment by the 1830 Revolution, this movement quickly recovered its impetus, helped by the rapid building of railways intended to provide Belgium with new economic outlets: this was a matter of linking Ostend with the Rhineland and Holland with France, the two main lines crossing at Malines. The government decided to build railways itself. In the overall movement of economic expansion, special mention must be made of the basic role played by the Société Générale, founded by William I, which began to establish its hold on industry and the coalfields at this period.

The development of capitalism was much less advanced in France than in England; progress was slower and on a smaller scale. France remained an essentially agricultural country, where in 1848 seventy-five per cent of the population still lived on the land. While the big estate predominated, France was a democracy of small farmers, living poor lives in a closed economy, victims of their 'hunger for land'. But the need felt by farmers to cut their costs resulted, especially after 1825, in a sort of 'Agricultural Revolution', in accordance with the principles laid down by Mathieu de Dombasle and taught in the Agricultural School at Grignon: the improvement of farming techniques, the abandonment of the fallow land system, the use of fertilizers, the specialization of crops, the care of cattle, and the extension of areas of cultivation. These reforms led to a general increase in yield; but there were still too many regions absolutely hostile to agricultural progress, so that France was like a mosaic of agricultural areas at completely different stages of economic development. A major factor in the process of change was the extension of the road system, both on a national and local level, for which a vast national plan was laid down by the Highways Department in 1837. Progress, incidentally, helped the big landlord or farmer more than the day labourer who suffered as a result of the abandonment of collective rights.

As for industry, it was subject to the system of tariff protection, and even of prohibition, which was the basic obstacle to French industrial development, and which, in spite of a few timid efforts by certain statesmen, it proved impossible to abandon (cf. p. 124). Contrary to what was happening in England, smelting in charcoal furnaces remained predominant, although it is true that blast-furnaces fired by coke began to be introduced on a small scale about 1840. However, the fall in the price of gold obliged manufacturers, if they wished to keep their profits, to mechanize and rationalize their factories: the number of machines increased, but faster in spinning than in weaving, faster in the cotton industry than in the woollen industry. Horizontal concentration, which was far advanced in cotton-spinning in the Mulhouse region, was still unremarkable in weaving and metallurgy, where the possessions of the Wendels in Lorraine and the Compagnie des Mines de la Loire were exceptions; vertical concentration was only just beginning. Generally speaking, industrial undertakings remained family affairs, sometimes bringing together a few near relations in what were known as *sociétés en nom collectif*, and less frequently resorting to limited partnerships. The textile industry in particular remained in the control of merchant-manufacturers and governed by the methods of commercial capitalism. On the other hand, there was a significant decline in domestic and rural industry, although this had not yet entirely disappeared. In short, while in the France of the mid-nineteenth century the small shop and the workshop still predominated, and large undertakings were still the exception, a monopolistic capitalism, favoured by the government, was gradually developing.

Industrial progress was moreover ill served as yet by the communication system. The building of railways owed its progress to the active propaganda of the Saint Simonians (cf. p. 70), products of the École Polytechnique such as Enfantin and bankers such as Pereire, who saw it as a sort of pledge of economic prosperity and universal brotherhood. However, railway construction, neglected for a long time, exposed to the hostility of the stage-coach companies and of certain statesmen, and slowed down by the difficulty of finding capital, was left at first to private companies, without any co-ordinating plan in spite of the appeals of the engineer Legrand. It was only in 1842 that a law was passed authorizing the State to repurchase the land—the permanent way and the rolling-stock being provided by the companies. From then on, as English money poured into France, the so-called ' railway mania ' developed in an entirely new business climate. However, this orgy of speculation led to a formidable waste of effort and money : by 1848, there were only about 1,200 miles of railway laid, which left France far behind England and Prussia.

The development of banking and credit houses was likewise slow, even though the Bank of France, under the influence of Deputy Governor Vernes, increased the number of its branches in the provinces. The link between banking and small savings had not yet been established; and the State was suspicious of joint-stock companies. True, there was no lack of people who realized the enormous advantages offered by a credit system built on a wider basis; and it was in this spirit that J. Laffitte founded the Caisse Générale du Commerce et de l'Industrie, which practised discounting and industrial investment; but its enterprises, often established on a shaky foundation, were to collapse in the economic crisis of the late 1840s.

Thus in France, economic life remained marked by the stamp of the past, and stultified by Protectionism, the prestige of property investment, and the absence of credit : a country very close to the Ancien Régime and in which the progress of a tentacular capitalism had not yet succeeded in shaking the nation out of its torpor. As Balzac's novels show, it was in a rather sordid atmosphere of monetary penury that the French economy developed, constantly threatened with bankruptcy and obsessed by the falling due of bills and the fear of usurers.

Certain special factors delayed in 1815 and for a long time afterwards the development of the economy of the German States. Agriculture, which was the basic economy, was dominated in the east by the *Gutsherrschaft*, in which the nobleman still lived essentially on the farming of his estate, and in the west by the *Grundherrschaft*, a system closer to the western economy, where the big land-owner derived his income from privileged rights on lease-holds and peasant labour. In the first of these agrarian systems, in which what Lenin called the 'Prussian way of capitalism' triumphed, the aristocratic reaction, by virtue of the legislation of 1821, confined the reforms laid down in 1811 to the 'cart-owning tenant farmers'; and everything seemed to combine here to strengthen the power of the Junkers, which rested both on trad-itional authority and a large speculative fortune. The second and more complex of the two agrarian systems was characterized by over-population and land hunger, which gave rise to large-scale emigration. As for the industrial economy, which as yet retained a local craftsman character, it suffered first of all from the multiplicity of tariff barriers. It was this problem of tariffs, pointed out as early as 1819 by the economist List, which was to govern the develop-ment of the German economy for three decades. The Customs Union or *Zollverein* was a remarkable achieve-ment, more physical than political in character, patiently brought to fruition by the Prussian bureaucracy, more often than not in the face of public opinion, which had remained particularist. The law of June 1816 abolished internal customs in Prussia, while that of May 1818 laid down a moderate tariff for the whole territory under Prussian rule. The protest made by the German States at the 1819 Diets did not succeed in shaking the determination of the Berlin government; on the other hand, certain little States entirely surrounded by Prussian territory allowed themselves to be absorbed into its new customs system. However, this system had still achieved only slight success when in 1825 von Motz was appointed Finance Minister and launched a customs offensive: in 1828, Hesse-Darmstadt entered into an association with Prussia on an equal footing. To begin with, this achievement provoked particularist reactions: Bavaria and Württemberg hurriedly concluded a customs union between themselves, while the Elector of Hesse-Cassel formed an Intermediary Union. Motz waged a merciless war against these leagues. Taking advantage of the weakness of the Southern Association (the two States had a similar economy), he succeeded in 1829 in concluding a treaty with them on the basis of a progressive reduction of the existing tariffs; then came the turn of the Intermediary Union which was split up by a series of treaties, the last of which was concluded in 1831 with Hesse-Cassel. In 1833 the negotiations for the creation of the *Zollverein*, skilfully conducted by Maassen, Motz's successor, were brought to a successful conclusion; on 1 January 1834, the Customs Union was formed with the two Hesses, Saxony, Württemberg and Bavaria; in 1836, after the adhesion of Baden and Frankfort, it included twenty-five States with twenty-six million inhabitants, the only outsiders, apart from Austria, being the Hanseatic ports and the States of the *Steuerverein*, grouped around Hanover.

The unification of frontiers and of customs tariffs was very quickly recognized as the necessary condition of the rapid economic development of the German States. But the means of bringing this about was the creation of a railway network. However, here as elsewhere, the building of railways, which the economist List, the engineer Harkort and the banker Camphausen wanted to make a ' national undertaking ', was hampered for a long time by lack of comprehension on the part of the various governments: the establishment of the first railways was the work of private enterprise. However, after 1840, Frederick William IV of Prussia became passionately interested in the question and gave effective support to the railway companies: in 1850, nearly four thousand miles of track were operating in Germany (the Rhineland Group, the Prusso-Saxon Group, and the Southern Group), and in 1847 the Union of German Railways was established at Hamburg. It was the construction of the railway network and the expansion of German markets which were the principal causes of industrial development, which showed itself in the increase of mechanization under the influence of figures such as Harkort and the Cockerill brothers, the inflow of foreign capital, the establishment of a system of free enterprise after 1845, and the remarkable progress of research (particularly by J. von Liebig in chemistry) and of technical training. The increase in industrial production, from 1835 onwards, was more rapid than that in France and sometimes in England. Borsig in Berlin and Maffei in Munich built the locomotives required by the railways; Silesia, Saxony, and especially Westphalia became important industrial centres for mining, metallurgy and textiles. However, their importance was still of a provincial order: German industry was not yet a serious rival to England, suffering as it did from a shortage of capital and a lack of joint-stock companies; the German merchant navy, based on Bremen and Hamburg, was still in its infancy. The new industries called for a rise in customs tariffs, which neither the Prussian government nor trading circles seemed ready to concede: the wealth of the *Zollverein* seemed in fact to be founded on the idea of Free Trade. The conferences held by the *Zollverein* led in 1846 to only a sligb' increase in customs dues. However, in spite of everyt'ing, the clash of interests was to be forgotten in the face of the considerable advantages offered by the formation of a large economic bloc and a feeling of solidarity thanks to which the idea of a single fatherland assumed a concrete form for the Germans. Excluded, of course, from this group were the Habsburg States, whose industrial economy, highly developed in certain regions such as German Austria and Bohemia, and much less developed in Hungary (which, incidentally, was separated from Austria by a customs barrier), was in spite of everything behind that of the other German countries.

In Italy, although the country was not so divided as Germany, there were no arrangements similar to the *Zollverein*, creating a common economic region. Undertakings were generally financed by foreign capital from England, Switzerland and Germany. Agriculture was still in a precarious position, and good land remained very scarce, and the South was governed by the latifundiary system. This situation was aggravated for the peasants by the exactions of the *gabellotti*, the stewards of the big absentee landowners. However, some voluntary efforts were made by agricultural societies such as the Tuscan *Georgofili*. In industry one can discern the beginning of concentration based on improved spinning and weaving equipment from England and built up by powerful industrial dynasties such as the Sellas of Biella. Silk was particularly flourishing in Lombardy, Piedmont and Tuscany, while wool was firmly established on the slopes of the Alps. But the development of credit remained extremely slow (the Lombardy Savings Bank was the only really important credit house), and above all the building of railways came up against fierce political resistance: the King of Naples considered that the railways should serve 'for the rapid assembly of troops and the safeguarding of his rule, but under no circumstances for the convenience of the public', while Pope Gregory XVI expressed the fear that they 'would carry fewer goods than ideas'. The railways built in 1848 were purely local lines linking Naples, Milan and Turin with their suburbs. However, thwarted by retrograde governments, the free growth of industry and trade was to be promoted by the entry into the business world of an active class of producers, who planned to create a large economic area with no tariff barriers or political frontiers. In an essay which he wrote in 1846, Cavour, himself a big Piedmontese landed proprietor, demonstrated that the railways, by freeing trade and spreading ideas, would make a vital contribution to the *Risorgimento*. This élite gathered together periodically at scientific congresses, and in 1842, formed itself into the Sub-Alpine Agrarian Association, which was also a centre of political revival.

The farther one went towards the east of Europe, the more clearly agricultural and feudal the economy remained. This was the case with Russia, whose economic and social structure had scarcely any points of comparison with western and central Europe. During the first half of the nineteenth century, while the rapid industrialization of Europe left scarcely any openings for the marketing of Russian goods, agricultural production was on the increase. But the supremacy of the agricultural economy did not lead to a parallel transformation of serfdom, even though the latter was regarded as harmful from the technical point of view. In this respect only fragmentary reforms were achieved : the confirmation of the rights of peasants to the plots of land granted to them; improvement of the lot of the State peasants, thanks to the reforms introduced by the minister Kisselev; and permission given to the landowners to sell land to ' tied ' peasants; but there could be no question of the abolition of serfdom under Nicholas I. Only the massive use of serf labour could make up for poor techniques and poor yields. Moreover, in spite of exports, the market was incapable of absorbing the whole of the country's production : hence . a state of overproduction which did not exclude terrible famines in some years. These various causes led to a constant fall in agricultural prices. Currency depreciation, which the Minister Kankrin hoped to prevent in 1839 by stabilizing the rouble, the almost complete absence of a banking system and the lack of capital, and finally the difficulty of recruiting workers, all contributed to the backwardness of Russian industry. However, the fall in agricultural prices attracted a large labour force to the towns; a great many landed proprietors built factories on their estates: moreover, free labour tended to take the place of serf labour in industry, and a law of 1840 permitted the serfs employed in factories to buy their freedom for a small fee. But—and this is a feature peculiar to the Russian economy—industrial development did not take place at the expense of domestic and rural industry, on account of the difficulties of transport and the existence of a scattered market. There were a great many isolated workers or *kustarni*, especially in the weaving industry, which tended to be dispersed about the countryside; they usually worked for merchants who provided them with looms and raw materials. Contrary to what happened in the rest of Europe, Russia's factories in the first half of the nineteenth century were scattered far and wide, a phenomenon connected with the relatively slow development of mechanization. However, Russian industry needed high protective tariffs; prohibition, established in 1822, was later slightly relaxed; but it failed to prevent the development of foreign trade, the massive exports of wheat to other countries producing a uniformly favourable balance. Unfortunately, the internal market was absolutely unorganized; the consumption of industrial goods was insignificant; Russia remained a conglomeration of little isolated economic units. In the building of roads, military consideration came before economic requirements; and before the Crimean War, the railway network, for want of capital and labour, scarcely existed.

Chapter III

LIBERALISM AND THE BOURGEOISIE

The period 1815-1848 was characterized, in all countries of
Europe, by the steady rise of the bourgeoisie. A human
type was to appear, whom literature has popularized under
the name of Joseph Prudhomme, César Birotteau or Pod-
snap, who prided himself on his respectability and good
manners, and even, despite his fear of the common people,
on a certain humanitarian idealism, yet who has been constantly denounced as hypocritically scrupulous, devoid of
all artistic sensibility, and ridiculous in his self-satisfaction.
This was a type we can recognize in the portrait of the
founder of the *Journal des Débats,* the elder Bertin, whom
Ingres has seated squarely in his armchair, his hands rest-
ing firmly on his knees, and his gaze magnificent in its
assurance. The great writers who have depicted the bourgeoisie in the first half of the nineteenth century have been
struck by the contrast between, on the one hand, that
passion for money and that ambition to climb the social
ladder which endowed the bourgeoisie with a conquering
character, and on the other hand a ridiculous vanity, a
strict, narrow conformity, and a mistrust of anything new
which confined it to a sort of mediocrity from which it was
powerless to escape.

In every State in Europe the pattern of development was
the same: everywhere money assigned a place to the individual inside the bourgeoisie and in relation to it. True,
there was no comparison to be made between the English
middle class about 1830, a class which was already imprint-
ing its character on England, and the few individuals who
ran factories in Russia. The former were men who were
already applying to the political problems, over which they

had control after 1832, the methods which had brought them success in the economic sphere; men whose desire for independence and whose highly developed will-power had endowed them with an individualistic character; men in whom a sense of realism and business experience had strengthened the utilitarian instincts of their race. The Russians, on the other hand, were a small group of merchant-manufacturers, sprung from the class of peasant serfs, often remaining serfs themselves in spite of being in control of a factory labour force, and only after years of work succeeding in buying their freedom, as well as the factory in which they had toiled. Between these two extremes, there was, of course, the greatest variety of types, depending on the degree to which the economy had developed; but in a country like Germany, where the economy had been making great strides since 1835, the change from the hierarchy of the pre-revolutionary states to a class system founded on work and wealth was a long way from being complete in 1848; outside the Rhineland, where the influence of French legislation had had its effect, it was very difficult to find any sign of a Third Estate ready to become that 'totality' to which Sieyès had referred in 1789; and even then, these contractors, factory-owners, businessmen or bankers were nearly all of Calvinist origin. Friedrich Engels observed that in the middle of the century it was impossible to make any comparison between the impotent, poverty-stricken German *Bürger* and the powerful bourgeois of the western States. 'Its lack of numbers and above all its dispersion,' he wrote, 'would prevent the German middle class from acquiring that political supremacy which the English middle class had possessed since 1688 and which the French bourgeoisie had won in 1789.'

It was in France that the rise of the bourgeoisie was most spectacular. It was there that it distinguished itself most clearly in relation to the aristocracy from which it had seized power in the 1830 Revolution, and to the 'common people' from which it felt separated by its wealth and its occupations. The July Monarchy can be regarded as the most typical example of a régime in which money became the basic factor of social discrimination. It is therefore the formation of this French middle-class that we shall consider first of all.

Under the Restoration (1815-1830), the rise of the bourgeoisie was still taking place. In the society of that time, still very close to that of the Ancien Régime, everyone was trying to climb the social ladder, by means of work and patronage; the artisan aspired to set up in business on his own; the petty bourgeois, who sent his daughters to a convent school and his sons to a private school where they were given an exclusively classical education, dreamt of their obtaining a fine match, a solicitor's practice, a barrister's gown, or best of all a public office. For the power of the civil service, inherited from the Empire, caused a rush for the bureaucratic professions, on account of the authority, respect and security which went with them : a career in the civil service came to be regarded as the chief means of social betterment. But there were also a great many petty bourgeois who laboriously worked their way up in business; the number of registered tradesmen rose from 847,000 in 1817 to 1,163,000 in 1830. The dream of every shopkeeper who was a member of the National Guard, paying for his uniform and his equipment, was to fulfil the property qualification for the franchise, and thus enter the ' pays légal ', something which made him a ' notability ' enjoying local prestige. The bourgeoisie used its savings to buy land, which it leased out in return for payment in money or kind, or else to buy house property : a new social type appeared, the landlord who let out flats in tenements. But so far it was rare for money to be invested in companies or industrial undertakings, for the risk was regarded as too great.

For this bourgeoisie Paris had a real fascination. The dullness of provincial life, in which the hard-working, money-grubbing middle class seemed to be enslaved to conformist public opinion and obsessed with fierce petty intrigues, contrasted with the capital, which attracted not only the working class but also the more ambitious elements of the provincial bourgeoisie, such as Balzac's hero Rastignac, who as he first set foot on Parisian soil exclaimed: ' It's between the two of us now, Paris!' Thiers, an ambitious young journalist from Aix-en-Provence, would be helped to enter the drawing-rooms and the newspaper world by Talleyrand, whose sarcastic smile paid knowledgeable tribute to his frenzied *arrivisme*. All the provinces of France contributed to this rejuvenation of the capital, the consequences of which could only be favourable: there was nothing stiff or stuffy about the Parisian bourgeois milieu, where the desire to climb the social ladder was general. To force one's way into the different bourgeois circles of the capital did in fact call for a great deal of talent, ability and courage, and there were countless cases of exclusion and failure. But there can be no doubt that the drift from the provinces gave much of its character to the Parisian bourgeoisie; fifty-five per cent of the electors registered in Paris between 1815 and 1830 were emigrants; among tradesmen and civil servants the proportion was above sixty per cent; it was slightly lower for the liberal professions and the unemployed.

This Parisian bourgeoisie, at the time of the July Monarchy, was a long way from offering a homogeneous appearance; it was divided into an infinite number of groups, whose interests, aspirations, standards of living and degrees of prosperity were profoundly different, if not opposed. Right at the top there was a limited élite, the *haute bourgeoisie*, a small minority of rich men which tended to merge into the landed aristocracy; lower down was the *bonne bourgeoisie*, which included some of the notabilities, more down to earth than the *haute bourgeoisie*, but resembling them in their wealth and occupations, and the bulk of the liberal professions and the business world; then came the *moyenne bourgeoisie*, largely consisting of the shopkeepers of Paris; and finally there was the *bourgeoisie populaire*, which was rather hard to distinguish from the common people, except by its occupations, which were not of a manual character. Between these various groups, the frontiers were vague and the exchanges constant; the bourgeois categories overlapped, as someone remarked, 'like the tiles of a roof,' and there were countless links between the different layers. So far there was no segregation of districts in the capital, of the kind which is so marked in nearly every great modern metropolis.

However, the new feature of the 1830s was the establishment of the supremacy of the *haute bourgeoisie*. Naturally exclusive, it had no wish to be absorbed into a social order it considered out of date, and it succeeded in creating a new hierarchy; an aristocracy of money, office and responsibility, which in its turn tended to become an aristocracy of birth. These bourgeois were able to base their supremacy on a threefold power, economic, political and social; in other words, by means of money, by which they obtained political position enabling them to favour their own interests by legislation, and to mould public opinion as they wished. They were the 'great notabilities' of the July Monarchy, the representatives of those 'bourgeois dynasties' which for a long time would turn power into a profitable monopoly under the banner of Orleanism (see p. 117). At the height of their success they appeared as a meritocracy consisting of individuals with a sense of innovation and a love of power, but without magnanimity or nobility of character; individuals who pursued their objectives with unimaginable ruthlessness, and who showed themselves to be incapable of subordinating their personal aims to the general interest, as was evidenced by the economic policy of the July Monarchy.

The 1830 Revolution thus substituted the *grande bourgeoisie* for the aristocracy as the principal governing class of the country. With the 1830s, the Industrial Revolution brought to the fore a series of phenomena—mechanization, industrialization on a large scale, and concentration—which were doubtless not new, but which had a new amplitude, and which would stamp their character on the society and the economy then emerging in France. Admittedly this transformation was only in its early stages under Louis-Philippe; and it would not be until after the middle of the nineteenth century that the keynote of the French economy would be really capitalistic. All the same, as early as the period 1830-1850, it became clear that the first effect of the country's economic development would be to enrich the *grande bourgeoisie* more than the other classes. Among the various sources of income, the upper middle class would retain control of those likely to give the best return.

On the other hand, the landed aristocracy became a 'declining class' in France after 1830. Many noblemen retired to their estates and gradually became ' *émigrés* inside their country and their century.' True, this political abstention could in certain cases be accompanied by a strengthening of their influence on their peasants in so far as they taught them new agricultural techniques and allowed them to join in their enterprises; but for one Forbin-Janson or one Duc de Montmorency-Laval, scores of heirs to large landed fortunes abandoned all interest in the development of their estates and confined themselves to dissipating the family heritage in their Faubourg Saint-Germain mansions or simply in the nearest town. The breaking-up of the great landed estates continued : a process which, during the Restoration, had already caused considerable concern to the

Ultra party and to those who, like Balzac, dreaded the economic and social consequences of such a development. However, this decadence had not reached its conclusion in 1848 : at the end of the July Monarchy, the aristocracy still represented a force to be reckoned with in many parts of France—in the west of course, but also in Provence, in the south of the Massif Central, and in the regions of the Parisian basin notable for large estates.

The fact remains that the *grande bourgeoisie* was the 'conquering' or 'rising' class. But this term comprised a great many different categories. At the summit was the *grande bourgeoisie* of the business world, whose strength and cohesion were reinforced by the rapid development of industry and trade: the upstarts of finance and banking, like Laffitte, Gouin, Hottinguer, and Mallet, or leading manufacturers such as Delessert, and Casimir Périer—the latter a native of Dauphiné, enriched by both industry and banking, who combined his famous political career with the offices of Governor of the Bank of France and President of the Anzin Mining Company. It was in the drawing-rooms of the Chaussée d'Antin that most of the politicians of the régime gathered together, and the bonds between the business world and the July Monarchy were tightened. In the provinces, merchants and ship-builders, enriched by the development of sea-borne trade, reigned over the society of Marseilles, Le Havre and Bordeaux. In the manufacturing regions, large-scale industrial development was often the work of self-made men, such as those who founded at this period the great undertakings in Dauphiné. This upper middle class also included the great industrial dynasties : the Wendels in Lorraine, the Peugeots and the Japys in the Montbéliard region, and the great families of Mulhouse, the Miegs, Dollfuses and Schlumbergers.

However, this *grande bourgeoisie* of the business world did not make up the whole of the governing class. In the middle of the nineteenth century, land still remained the principal source of wealth. Income from land formed a great part of the fortune of many manufacturers or financiers: to be convinced of this, one has only to study the electoral registers giving the taxes paid by each elector, and their nature: the landed proprietors far outclass the owners of small factories or modest businesses. Finally, it was common practice for these rich landed proprietors to add to their ground rents the income from a liberal profession or a public office: if the notabilities in Paris included lawyers and University professors (such as Guizot), in the provinces it was the magistrates who played an essential role, as did the notaries, the chief advisers and bankers to the peasant masses.

On the other hand, this *grande bourgeoisie,* which was the principal beneficiary of economic change, was careful to keep its distance from the *moyenne* and *petite bourgeoisie.* The latter had joyfully welcomed the 1830 Revolution and had made up the bulk of the National Guard, that essential bulwark of the régime. But they had never been accepted by the governing classes and their bitterness, sustained by the systematic refusal of any reform of the franchise, finally resulted in their turning against the régime. Moreover, social advancement became increasingly infrequent, the closer one came to 1848: the richer bourgeois tended to close their ranks as their positions were consolidated, and by the end of Louis-Philippe's reign it was difficult for a man of humble birth to get to the top of the social ladder. All the same, it would be incorrect to see the *grande bourgeoisie* as a monopolistic class whose large-scale undertakings ruined the small businesses and workshops of France. In fact, the movement towards concentration was only beginning before 1848. What was striking was rather the frenzied individualism of every kind of bourgeois confronting each other inside one and the same social group: the existence of coteries engaged in a fight to the death. The sense of class was sustained only by the desire to keep the common people outside the quarrels of the bourgeoisie.

The rise of the bourgeoisie was matched by a certain concept of the world known as liberalism, which in the last analysis was simply the expression of its economic and political interests. The bourgeoisie, while industrial development was enabling it to increase its income slowly but surely, declared itself to be satisfied with the normal operation of supply and demand. Unaffected by the growing misery of the masses, it contented itself with preaching charity, thrift and celibacy; besides, it believed that technical advances would make possible a progressive improvement in general well-being. As for forms of government, the best was that which disturbed the bourgeois least in his accumulation of wealth. In short, the bourgeois considered the State as the guardian of freedom; its function was confined to the protection of individual interests; it had no business to interfere in economic relations, still less in the organization of society; its role was entirely negative.

Not that the advocates of the *laisser faire, laisser passer* policy were all necessarily ' optimists '. Economists such as Malthus and Ricardo no longer believed, as did Adam Smith and the physiocrats, in a spontaneous order due to the kindness of Providence and the free play of individual liberty. On the contrary, they discerned disturbing conflicts explained by economic laws; but since these laws were ineluctable, there was nothing to do but regret them and bow before them. The pessimistic Malthus observed that the population of the world was increasing faster than its subsistence, and that mankind was advancing towards famine; but to deal with this state of affairs, all that he proposed, (putting aside the natural operation of epidemics, famines and wars) was voluntary birth control and conjugal chastity, firmly opposing any measure of assistance and any State interference in social matters. ' The common people,' he wrote, ' must regard themselves as being themselves the principal cause of their misfortunes.' As for Ricardo, he formulated the theory of differential ground rent, showing that ground rent would tend to increase on account of the rising cost of farming land newly put under cultivation, while the price of food would also rise to the detriment of the masses, whose wages would remain at the minimum required for subsistence. But according to him, this regrettable situation could not be changed by State legislation; the only way of combating this rise in ground rent was to allow foreign corn to enter Britain freely, especially from younger nations with lower production costs.

The position of the French representatives of the classical school seemed more logical, for they were liberals and advocates of State abstention in economic affairs because they considered that everything was for the best in the best of all possible worlds. J. B. Say, an admirer of England, a country that had inspired his *Traité d'économie politique* as early as 1803, a manufacturer, a professor of political economics and a man of the Left in his political sympathies, who had consistently defended mechanization and exalted the role of the contractor, gave pride of place in his economic theories to the mechanism of the market: according to him, there was no reason to fear that markets would ever be choked for any length of time by economic activity, for 'goods are exchanged for goods.' Money was simply an intermediary which one accepted only to get rid of it straight away. Goods found openings on a reciprocal basis; a country which manufactured one object created the possibility of buying another. The greater the variety of goods produced, the easier it would be to sell them. There could not be any general crisis of overproduction. At the very most, some partial crisis of overproduction might occur when the productive services had been badly organized; but these crises would be only temporary, provided that trade remained free, and provided that the working of prices enabled contractors to know what was in demand

and what they should manufacture. An even more radical figure, the economist Bastiat, whose advocacy of free trade brought him into conflict with political circles under the July Monarchy (cf. p. 126), believed that he could discern a pre-established harmony in the economic world, and gave his principal work the characteristic title: *Les Harmonies économiques*: 'It is not simply the celestial organization which reveals God's wisdom and shows his glory.' This was because Bastiat, like Charles Dunoyer, denied that poverty was on the increase: a poverty, incidentally, which they considered inseparable from civilization, like a necessary evil, because it 'gave encouragement to the difficult virtues' of economy and continence.

The accuracy of these opinions was scarcely questioned under the July Monarchy by the theoreticians of political economy, the elder Blanqui, Pellegrino Rossi, and Wolowski. In England, the middle class, strongly influenced by the utilitarian philosophy and the doctrine of the happiness of the greatest number which Jeremy Bentham had inculcated into it during the preceding generation, and to which the electoral reforms of 1832 had given a place among the governing classes, now followed the guidance of McCulloch and Nassau Senior. McCulloch and Senior argued that irresistible natural forces doomed any sort of social intervention to failure and, while they had to accept in principle assistance to the poor, hoped that it would be organized in such a way as to make it unacceptable.

On to this economic liberalism there was grafted a political liberalism which in France at least, after it had managed to disentangle itself, from its attitude of opposition to the Restoration, from its penchant for secret societies, from its anti-monarchical and anti-clerical fanaticism, and from the contributions of the Napoleonic Legend (as seen, for example, in the works of Béranger and Paul-Louis Courier), became a doctrinaire liberalism of the happy mean, re-

conciling order with liberty. This was the liberalism of
those 'bourgeois dynasties' which had rallied to the
Empire and then to the different régimes which had succeeded one another in France, and which throughout the
nineteenth century still retained a dominant place in industry, banking and the Academies.

It was Benjamin Constant who defended most ardently
the liberalism which placed him between the partisans of
the Ancien Régime and the supporters of democracy. Introduced to eighteenth century philosophy by the Ideologues
and Madame de Staël, he became, first of all against
Napoleon, and then against the Ultras under the Restoration, the apologist of the "happy mean'.

In no other writer were the preoccupations of the bourgeoisie made so manifest. His system was opposed to 'the
authority which would like to govern by means of
despotism', but also against the masses which claim the
right to subordinate the minority to the majority'. Equality,
he said, was 'oppression of each man by his neighbour';
while democracy was not liberty but 'the vulgarization of
despotism'. It was 'the great achievement of the Revolution to admit the middle classes to the administration of
political affairs': it was this conquest which had to be
consolidated. That was the object which he set himself in
his *Principes de Politique* (1815).

The dominant idea of this work was systematic mistrust
of the State. Constant attributed to the State a desire to
destroy freedom by constantly encroaching on the rights of
the individual. Therefore, before anything else, it was
necessary to define 'a part of individual existence' which
was 'outside the jurisdiction of society': these were the
'natural rights of man', namely individual freedom,
religious freedom, freedom of opinion, and the enjoyment
of property. Man was a 'temple', and in that temple he
carried something divine: freedom, inviolable and in-
accessible. All that he needed to be happy was 'to be left

completely independent' with regard to everything concerning his occupations, his enterprises, his sphere of activity and his private whims. This essential reservation in respect to the State could only be obtained under a representative government. Power was doubtless lodged in the people, but on condition that the people did not exercise it themselves, but immediately relinquished it in favour of their representatives. The chief concern, in fact, of the modern citizen was not so much effective participation in the government of the country as that 'individual independence' which the ancients had sacrificed: the representative system, therefore, had to be organized in such a way as to ensure an extended sphere of individual freedom. To this purpose Constant distinguished between four powers: the royal power, the ministerial power, the representative power shared between two chambers, one hereditary and the other elected, and the judicial power: a division aimed at reducing as far as possible the activity of the executive, which should 'be above and apart from human unrest'. But above all, anxious to defend the individual in the exercise of his natural rights, Constant saw any interference by the State as a set back for the individual. He was fond of referring to England, where public order was all the better ensured 'in that it was entrusted to the reason and interest of each person'. It was maxims of this sort which led him to adopt a position, in economic matters, against State interference in the industrial sphere, and to advocate the separation of Church and State, as well as widespread municipal decentralization under the name of federalism. 'A matter concerning only a small section of the community,' he wrote, 'must be decided by that section.' The supreme guarantee of political liberalism remained, in his opinion, the property qualification for the franchise: property alone gave a citizen sufficient interest to share effectively in government; just as property alone provided him with the necessary leisure to 'acquire understanding and sureness of judgement'. This shows how far Constant regarded freedom as a privilege which had to be sparingly distributed.

The philosophy of natural law, which according to the writers of the eighteenth century had been a call for the emancipation of the citizen had become, according to Constant, a justification of the political supremacy of the bourgeoisie. This deviation from liberalism was continued by the 'Doctrinaires', those bourgeois of the 'happy mean', who during the Restoration, first in the *Globe* and then in the *Revue Française*, defended the Charter against both left and right. The philosopher Royer-Collard saw it as the 'fixed point' which marked the end of the revolutionary era, 'the indissoluble alliance of the legitimate power from which it emanates with the national liberties which it recognizes and consecrates'. According to him, sovereignty was lodged in neither the king nor the people, but in the Law, which should not be a matter of force but of reason, and which was the result of an anonymous agreement between king and nation. This agreement would be established if the balance of powers was perfect, in other words if neither the legislative nor the executive predominated. In contrast to Benjamin Constant, however, Royer-Collard believed that the king should not only reign but rule: in this respect it was not possible to transfer the British Constitution to France. As for Parliament, it was not the mandatory of the nation; it represented only certain 'interests', some of which were common to all the citizens of a country, the others peculiar to a particular group. Thus the citizen who, by virtue of his financial position and his supposed attitudes, seemed most capable of expressing those interests should alone be called upon to vote. Hence the restriction of the franchise to certain 'political qualifications'. In other words, the franchise was not a right inherent in human dignity, but a duty and a function which required a minimum of understanding and experience for their performance.

To this political philosophy, Guizot would later contribute the fruit of his historical studies. What in fact was the meaning of French history, if it did not consist of the gradual rise to power of the bourgeoisie? After the downfall of the aristocracy, the bourgeoisie was the only class with sufficient education and wealth to be interested in the government of the country; moreover, as a class open to all, it was still close enough to the common people to welcome the superior elements which wanted to better themselves. Consisting of citizens who were neither overworked nor indolent, and controlling public opinion, it possessed both a sense of progress and a sense of authority. Freedom, in other words the necessary participation in the government of the country, consequently had to be confined to the middle classes; they alone constituted the ' pays légal '. Thus, in the writings of the Doctrinaires, Orleanism would be defined as a parliamentary monarchism with a property qualification, for the use of the new ' notabilities ' produced by the Industrial Revolution, yet open to intelligence and talent: in other words, government by an élite, as close as possible to that which ensured the prestige of the English governing classes.

The absolute confidence which Guizot displayed in his system was to bring about the collapse of the bourgeois monarchy in 1848. His mistake had been to think that the social inferences of the Revolution had been exhausted and that nothing remained but to draw the political inferences; he had failed to appreciate the importance of the strong egalitarian feelings which had existed in the spirit of the French people since 1789. That was something which Alexis de Tocqueville had understood, although he too was a liberal, and which he explained in his *Démocratie en Amérique* (1835). Profoundly impressed by the New

World, he observed that democracy was neither a 'bright dream', nor 'an upheaval synonymous with anarchy, robbery and murder', as its supporters and opponents imagined; it was a fact which could not be denied in modern society. And its strength lay in the sense of equality, which was stronger in the masses than the sense of liberty. On the other hand, it was undeniable that democracy held formidable evils in reserve: anarchy, which made governments unstable, and servitude, which resulted from an increase of the powers of the central authority. With the equalization of social status, the individual, de Tocqueville observed, became smaller and smaller, while society became bigger and bigger; and the individual turned his gaze towards that huge Being, the State, which alone rose above the general abasement. A hateful tyranny covered society with 'its network of little complicated, pettifogging, uniform rules'. In short, 'the unity, ambiguity, and omnipotence of society formed the salient features of all the political systems produced in our time'. This was an inevitable process, made still worse by industrial development and the resulting State control of economic life. Thus the number of government officials grew enormously, as did the taste for public office and the field of government interference: nothing remained but the isolated individual face to face with an omnipotent State. De Tocqueville also observed that as a result of their egalitarian fervour, a spirit of selfish materialism developed among the majority of citizens, who were convinced that the providential, tutelary State would attend to all their needs. He saw them as satisfied with the condition of the servitude that they had given themselves, and increasingly incapable of making proper use of the 'great and unique privilege' which was the possession of power. But, however distressing this spectacle might be, he was convinced that there existed remedies for these evils, provided that men did not look for them in the formulas of the past, but 'encouraged the growth of liberty in the heart of the democratic society in which God has placed us '. It was towards America that de Tocqueville turned his gaze in search of a corrective: he found it in the development of local liberties, which had been brutally stifled in France by the Ancien Régime and then by the Revolution, and which it was essential to restore: for ' it is in the *commune* that the strength of free peoples is lodged '. A remedy was also to be found in the development of the idea of association, which would reduce State interference by taking the place of the intermediary bodies of the past. No one has extolled more than de Tocqueville the feeling of solidarity, whose function he saw as bringing home to the individual the idea ' that men's duty is to make themselves useful to their fellows '.

Looking as he did towards the future, de Tocqueville was aware that liberalism could not confine itself to the bourgeois individualism which Constant and Royer-Collard so admired.

Nothing, however, would be more misleading than to reduce the entire thought of the new governing classes to liberalism. Without questioning the principles behind the development of the industrial society of their times, there were many who were struck by the abuses which had arisen in that society, by the injustices of which it was guilty, and by the crises which shook its economic structure, and who believed that it would be impossible in the future to prevent growing State interference in economic and social relations.

In this respect Sismondi showed himself a forerunner. The author of a liberal treatise (*Richesse commerciale*, 1803), he was so overwhelmed by the poverty and economic crises which he observed in England, that, disavowing his first work, he answered Ricardo with his *Nouveaux Principes d'Economie Politique* (1817). Sismondi was in no way a revolutionary; the historian of the Italian republics was an aristocrat by his environment, by his attachment to the past, by his patriarchal tendencies, and by his links with Romantic circles; his preference was for a society of small peasant landowners using intensive farming methods with the help of a government concerned to maintain order and efficiency. The essence of his culture he owed to Coppet, where he was often a guest of Madame de Staël. Now he insisted that the point of view adopted by the liberal economists was completely mistaken. In the technical sphere, he inveighed against the evils of mechanization; he cited the warning example of the sorcerer's apprentice and called upon the State to reduce the flow of inventions. In the economic sphere, he denounced the crises in industry, which he attributed (and was probably the first to do so) as much to the abuses of competition as to underconsumption by the workers. The basic evil in the social sphere seemed to him to be the division of society into two antagonistic classes, one of which was the 'exploiter' of the other. If the solutions which he proposed still bore a reactionary stamp—whether it was a case of a peasant smallholdings system or industrial 'guaranteeism'—he had the merit of defining property as a 'social right' and of strongly advocating State intervention.

Somewhat similar conclusions would be reached by the German economist Friedrich List, who incidentally played a considerable part in both the organization of German Customs and in the building of the country's railways. Strongly influenced by Fichte's *Der geschlossene Handelsstaat* and by political romanticism, but even more by his business experience and by American writers on economics, notably Raymond and Carey, this Swabian economist, whose career was linked with the rise of German liberalism, expressed the view in his *Das nationale System der politischen Okonomie* (1841) that the fundamental mistake of classical economics was not to take sufficient account of the concept of nationalism. For nations were natural units which could not be disregarded. Referring to England, List wrote: 'It is a rule of elementary prudence, when you have reached the top, to kick away the ladder you have used, in order to deprive others of the means of climbing up after you'; for the English, 'the cosmopolitan principle and the national principle are simply one and the same thing'. But in a period of nationalism it was important that a people should know that in order to obtain true independence, it must exploit the whole of its resources and not simply 'its exchangeable goods and values'. The ideal at which all countries should aim was to produce a 'normal nation' with a complex economy; and that nation needed temporary, limited customs tariffs in order to reach the stage where all its productive forces would be harmoniously developed. The industrial development obtained by these means would, according to List, solve in particular the problem of rural overpopulation, which at the time was resulting in harmful and constantly increasing emigration to the United States.

During the same period, England, reacting against orthodox economics and the utilitarian philosophy, witnessed the appearance of a literature of 'social remorse'—a sign of the awakening of the people's deepest instincts. The breaking of the old social links, the disruption of the political and economic order, and the relaxation of habits and traditions, all combined to substitute for the old beliefs a vision of society and the relations between its parts that was cold, dull and uninspiring. With the triumph of the middle classes, beneath a sky darkened by the smoke from factory chimneys, in the midst of the vulgar display of tasteless luxury and the degrading pursuit of profit, the charming, colourful features of traditional English life seemed to have disappeared. Men of sensibility found in the fundamental fact of economic evil, denounced by Dickens with a moving sense of social justice, the necessary centre and point of departure for counter-attack. Before 1848, Carlyle, who had been brought up in the puritan tradition, had been influenced by Saint-Simonism, and in describing the vicissitudes of *Chartism* (1839) had taken up the cudgels against modern industrial civilization. He had indicted the governing classes, accusing the bourgeoisie of greed and the aristocracy of frivolity. Arguing that it was necessary to substitute the agreement of men for the collisions of the economic process, he had proposed reconstructing society by restoring the principle of authority, in favour of industrial leaders conscious of their social mission. Economic life had to be transformed in its very principle; the obligation which services rendered by the worker imposed on the employer was not to be recognized merely by payment of a wage; a deeper and more effective solidarity accepted by the industrial leaders would bind them to the men under their orders. On the pattern of the army, man-to-man relationships would be restored between individuals; competition would no longer bring together human atoms, simply to scatter them a moment later; and life would inter beneath a carpet of flowers the bare bones of economic laws. In submission to necessary authority, society would recover the health which it had lost in the dizzy pursuit of liberty. The same hostility towards liberal individualism inspired the social novels of the young Disraeli, who in *Coningsby* and *Sybil* laid the foundations of a rejuvenated Toryism, the first manifestations around 1848 of the Christian Socialism of F. D. Maurice and Charles Kingsley. Finally the first works of Ruskin, disgusted like Carlyle by an industrial and commercial civilization, horrified by the ugliness of his time, sought to reawaken the sense of beauty in his contemporaries. Taking the Middle Ages as his model, he advocated a hierarchical, patriarchal society of craftsmen. For if the Middle Ages had succeeded in creating beauty, it was because the medieval craftsmen had found joy in the act of creation: the machine and the division of labour had killed that joy and led to a servitude worse than that of the past. Political economy did not remain deaf to these anathemas: John Stuart Mill, though regarded as the master of the liberal school, thought it necessary in 1848, in his *Principles of Political Economy*, to reconsider certain judgments: he now advocated State intervention, which would develop co-operative enterprises, collect the profits from ground rent, and reduce inequality by limiting the right of inheritance.

The very essence of bourgeois liberal thought was expressed by Auguste Comte, a pupil of both the Comte de Saint-Simon and of Joseph de Maistre. Although he published his *Plan des travaux scientifiques nécessaires pour réorganiser la société* as early as 1822, his system of positive politics was to exert its full influence only on the next generation. Politics for Comte were bound up with his overall doctrine of positivism. Before reaching the positive age, politics had passed first through the theological age, then through the metaphysical age; the doctrine of the divine right corresponded to the former, that of the Social Contract to the latter. But those times were over: positive politics founded on observation were based on a very simple proposition, namely that the social system, at any stage of the development of mankind, was the necessary consequence of man's organization; it was absurd to think that scientific effort could determine the political constitution by itself.

Starting from these premises, Comte showed that with the French Revolution a profound and ever spreading anarchy had taken hold of men's minds; for while the revolutionary maxims and methods were excellent for destructive purposes, they were a hindrance to reconstruction. Their fundamental error lay in the affirmation of freedom of thought, which was as ridiculous in politics as in astronomy or physics. It was 'the western disease', according to Comte, to 'recognize no other spiritual authority than individual reason': a disease for which Protestantism was originally responsible, but of which the revolutionary philosophy was the most formidable manifestation. It was necessary for men to renounce once for all 'their absolute right to individual examination of subjects which were beyond their understanding and whose nature required a real and stable communion'. Politics, like the other positive sciences, should be a matter of competence.

To remedy the existing situation, it was necessary to substitute for the critical principle and arbitrary caprice something which would regulate and 'rally' minds, and to develop a body of doctrine which everyone would accept. Everything would be put to rights, according to Comte, if it were possible to substitute a 'demonstrable faith' for the 'vague ideals' on which mankind was living at the moment. It was here that Comte turned for an answer to his philosophy of history. In his eyes the Middle Ages represented a particularly remarkable period in the history of the human race because it had succeeded in distinguishing between the spiritual power and the temporal power; it had managed to create at the centre of the world a universal moral authority, the Papacy, which submitted all human thought to an admirable discipline and which, in excommunication, had at its disposal a weapon which put an offender outside the pale of humanity. The creation of an exclusively moral power which worked out principles and gave advice without orders had to be regarded, according to Comte, as the greatest advance ever made in the organization of society. It was to the 'eternal honour' of medieval Catholicism that it had created a 'government of souls' which, thanks to the organization of the priestly caste, had conquered the whole of mankind, and outside which there had been no salvation. The result had been the construction of an 'eminent masterpiece of human wisdom.'

Was it possible to bring mankind back to the medieval Catholic organization? Comte declared that this was out of the question. Catholic morality seemed to him to be incompatible with progress. Ascetic and retrograde, it was out of keeping with modern times. On the other hand, the part of Catholicism that ought to be preserved was its social philosophy. The 'religion of mankind' which Comte was to endeavour to define would be nothing else than a deconsecrated Catholicism or, as he aptly described it, 'Catholicism minus Christianity'. It would be designed in such a way as to satisfy the supreme requirement, which was to provide a rallying point for consciences to meet and harmonize. This religion of the Supreme Being would teach men in particular that the individual, who was an 'abstraction' to himself, assumed significance only in so far as he participated in mankind. Men were not to be regarded as so many separate beings, as so many individualities endowed with rights, but as organs of the sole reality which was mankind. The latter was the product of 'an immense co-operation', of an existing solidarity and a historical continuity. Mankind did not mean simply those alive at present, but also the dead endowed with a subjective life in the memory of the living, and those still to be born, who together made it up. 'Mankind,' wrote Comte in a striking phrase, 'consists of more dead than living persons.' Hence a new morality and a new religion. What would be the way to obtain salvation, if not an attempt to seek subjective immortality, an effort to incorporate oneself in mankind by means of a life of altruism? What would be the external forms of religious life, if not, in public, commemoration of the great men who had been the benefactors of mankind, and in private and in the very heart of the family, worship of the gentle sex, of woman, who, by her virtues of love and devotion, represented 'the best type and example of humanity'? This was a philosophy which led Comte to forbid divorce and demand perpetual widowhood.

As for the positivist political régime inherent in this

religious reorganization of mankind, it would be based, as in the Middle Ages, on the separation of the spiritual and the temporal, and the subordination of the second to the first. To organize the State, according to Comte, meant establishing first of all the moral authority which would impose itself upon one and all, upon the leaders as upon the humblest members of the community. The moral power centred in the hands of the 'Western Pontiff' would work out a doctrine to which everyone would have to submit; while the temporal authority would exercise a dictatorship sufficiently powerful to enforce the application of the positivist principles. Comte rejected not only the metaphysical principle of the sovereignty of the people, but also every sort of representative system : 'Parliamentarism,' he wrote, 'is a system of intrigue and corruption where tyranny is everywhere and responsibility no-where'; while government on the English pattern 'disguised with metaphysical trappings the theocratic idea of royalty'. Unlike the liberals, the founder of the positivist philosophy refused to regard the government as 'a natural enemy installed in the middle of the social system', towards which society ought to maintain itself 'in a permanent state of distrust and defensiveness' : it was not a necessary evil, a mere police institution, but the real organizer of social life.

It was with the help of such an organization that Comte considered it possible to solve the social problem which had always obsessed him, as it had obsessed Saint-Simon. Here too he inveighed against the abstentionism of the liberals, which he described as 'a solemn resignation' and 'an admission of social impotence.' 'The bourgeoisie,' he wrote, 'is building dungeons today for those who ask for bread'. However, Comte was not prepared to bow down before 'communism' : refusing, in the name of the historical continuity of the family, to attack the principles of property and inheritance, he depicted the landowner as 'a functionary responsible to society' and possession as 'the indispensable social function, intended to accumulate and administer the capital by means of which each generation prepares the work of the next.' This meant that, in a positivist State, property would become not a privilege but a source of duties. It also meant that the spiritual power would have to impose a common moral education on the nation. In Comte's eyes, the solution of the social problem belonged to the sphere of politics.

Chapter IV

SOCIALISM AND
WORKERS' MOVEMENTS

Seen from an economic point of view, society during the first half of the nineteenth century was afflicted with a terrible contradiction. Taken as a whole it grew richer; the value of agricultural production, and above all of industrial production, rose. And yet the majority of the population grew poorer: wages fell, and at certain times dropped steeply. This was an international phenomenon: the whole of Europe experienced the same difficulties, the same crises, the same fall in prices, and the same reactions on the part of the employers—reactions which were no more deliberate than the economic circumstances which produced them: many employers, indeed, deplored them, but were forced by the laws of competition to take them into account; it was essential to produce goods at a lower price than your competitor, and the weakest had to go to the wall. Admittedly, the antagonism of rich and poor was nothing new, and down through the ages it had been the theme of countless exhortations and harangues. But now for the first time the problem was going to arise in the industrial sphere; for the first time it was going to be a problem of machines and men, of material wealth rapidly rising and workers' wages rapidly falling. A whole school of economists and reformers was going to study this state of affairs and ask themselves whether it was inevitable, or whether the entire structure of the economy ought not to be changed.

If until 1830 there was little talk of working-class poverty, this was no longer true after that date, when a great many investigations, such as those of Villermé, Morogues, or Villeneuve-Bargemont in France, and that of Buret and Engels in England informed an ever-increasing public about what was happening in the big industrial towns. The conclusions of these investigations might differ according to the political ideas of their authors : some might stress the need for close co-operation between capital and labour, others insist on the moral and religious education of the working class and refer to the principles of Christian charity, and yet others put forward the notion of class warfare. But all recognized that poverty was keeping step with capitalist concentration, and that it was a poverty of an entirely new character, utterly different from that of the previous periods; all condemned the idea of unbridled liberalism and drew attention to the need for social legislation.

The countryside still supported various minor trades which it could not do without; a host of things were still manufactured in the country, which required time, care and experience, and even if low wages were the rule, the countryman frequently regarded them as a useful and often indispensable contribution. However, it was noticeable that the situation of the textile workers scattered among country villages was often worse than that of the craftsmen who, grouped together to a greater degree in the towns, maintained the fine traditions of their artistic work—cabinet-making, bronze, pottery, luxury glassware, printing—and formed a real working-class élite. No one was poorer than the domestic weaver in Britain, Flanders or Silesia. But wherever a certain concentration was already beginning—in the mines, the cloth mills, and the iron and steel works—the worker who had to make do with his industrial wages was just as seriously affected by competition from the machine and from a large labour force. The liberal economist Auguste Blanqui remarked in 1848 that ' in-

dustry is organized in huge factories which look like bar-
racks or monasteries, and the workers are crowded in
hundreds, sometimes in thousands, inside these grim
laboratories, where their work, carried out under the orders
of the machines, is exposed like the machines to all the
vicissitudes resulting from the variations of supply and
demand '.

Although living conditions varied a great deal from one
place to another and from one trade to the next, there
can be no doubt that, generally speaking, they did not improve during the first half of the century. The general fall
in prices led to a reaction on the part of the employers
which was identical everywhere, and which was determined
by economic circumstances : the producer tried to cut down
his costs, and among the factors over which he had some
control, wages struck him as the easiest to reduce. The
annual expenditure of the French working-class family
rose until 1825, then levelled out or even went down; the
cost of living index rose far more rapidly than that of
real wages. In the mines, a wage of 100 units in 1892
represented a wage of 36 units in 1805, 42 units in 1830
and 49 units in 1850: that was a favoured sector of industry, but there was no denying the fall in wages in
textiles: 80 units in 1800, 65 units in 1820, 40 units in
1827, and 45 units in 1850. There is abundant testimony
to the recession in this last sector : the silk weavers in
Lyons, employed by merchants who provided the raw
material and fixed the purchase price of their finished work,
saw their wages fall by half during the period of depression
from 1825 to 1830. In England, the domestic weavers
earned only seven or eight shillings a week about 1840
instead of thirty shillings about 1820; they continued to
eat oatmeal, but their consumption of wheatflour and
butter fell by half; as for meat and beer, they disappeared
from their tables. In Germany, the index of real wages,
which stood at 86 units between 1820 and 1829, fell to 82

units between 1830 and 1839, and 74 units between 1840 and 1849, with even steeper falls in the crisis years (65 units in 1846 and 57 units in 1847).

For the worker in Nantes, 'living meant not dying', Dr. Guépin noted in 1845. Contemporary records stress the difficult conditions in which work was done: the excessive heat or cold, the lack of light, the constricted or damp premises, the harmful effect of the products handled, or the promiscuity of sexes and ages. In the Croix-Rousse suburb of Lyons, Auguste Blanqui observed that the working girls earned 'three hundred francs a year working fourteen hours a day at looms where they were hung from a strap in order to be able to use both their hands and their feet, and whose continuous and simultaneous movement was indispensable for the weaving of braid.' In the spinning-mill at Annecy, according to a petition of 1848, 'infamous foremen treat the male and female piecers with obscene cruelty and many of the latter succumb under their blows'. But what sort of home did the workers go to when they left the mill? There were few employers who took the trouble to build decent houses for their employees. Home was therefore the cellars of Lille or Liverpool, the hovels of Whitechapel, Reims, or Rouen, and the towering tenements of Lyons with their stinking courtyards; inside, whole families slept on matt-resses, sometimes without sheets or blankets—the 'indescribable beds' described by Martin Nadaud, a mason from Creuse, in Paris, by Auguste Blanqui in Rouen, and by an inspector of the lodgings of Flemish weavers. During the famine of 1846, the latter dug up dead horses, and fought over dogs and cats. Several travellers observed that the faces of the working women in England were bloated by gin, and their hair thick with grease; while Blanqui came across children in Rouen who were 'premature invalids, stunted to such a degree as to cause strange misconceptions as to their age', and in Lille 'skeletal, hunchbacked, deformed and for the most part half-naked'. Scrofula, rickets and tuberculosis ravaged these sections of the population, who drank more as they ate less, and who regarded the prostitution of a daughter almost as a normal source of income. One child in three was illegitimate in Paris, one in five in Mulhouse, and one in three died before the age of five in certain districts of Lille; most workers, incidentally, saw their children die with indifference and sometimes with joy. Beggars and vagabonds were as common as ever: in 1833 the French department of Eure-et-Loir alone contained 17,000 paupers and over 8,000 beggars; in 1845, assistance had to be given to over 1,100 people out of 7,000 in the little town of Nogent-le-Rotrou. In *Past and Present* Carlyle described an England bursting with wealth with two million people in the workhouses and 1,400,000 paupers. In Cologne, on the eve of the 1848 Revolution, no less than one citizen in four was in receipt of public assistance.

It was these disturbing elements which gave the big towns of this period their abnormal and even frightening character, especially as there was no clear division yet between the working-class and middle-class districts. In Berlin, a town of over 400,000 inhabitants in the 1840s, where about 20,000 bourgeois practised recognized professions, there were 10,000 prostitutes, 6,000 people in receipt of assistance, 4,000 beggars, 10,000 criminals behind bars, and as many 'vagabonds'. In the opinion of both bourgeois and peasants, the working classes rapidly acquired a reputation as 'dangerous classes': these proletarians, who in many cases had never known a family environment, who lived indescribable lives, and who aged and died prematurely, were regarded as creatures apart; they only had to rise in revolt to be called 'new barbarians' by public opinion. Violence was extremely common in the urban societies of the time, where people felt a sort of fascination for crimes 'shrouded in horror and haloed with a sombre glory'.

Paris in particular gave the impression of a city sunk in poverty and crime; and in 1840 a high official at the prefecture of police could declare that in that city of one million inhabitants there were 60,000 who had declared war on society and represented a danger to it. The influx of immigrants on the one hand, and the degeneration of the working class on the other, account for the opinion of contemporaries that a 'new city' had arisen in Paris, different from the traditional city and living apart from it, not only from the economic point of view, but even in a biological sense; and it is interesting to note that the great mass of workers had a similar opinion of themselves, as can be seen from their songs and melodramas. Physical sickness and moral corruption helped create 'that cadaverous, diabolical appearance' which struck all those who approached the 'dregs of the common people'. The Memoirs of Vidocq (a former convict who became one of the chiefs of the secret police), the works of Balzac and Victor Hugo, and Eugène Sue's *Mystères de Paris* bore witness to the danger presented by the lowest strata of society. In the face of unhygienic conditions and the physical and moral ills that resulted from them, the authorities' attempts at town-planning were pitifully inadequate; and Prefect Rambuteau's efforts were confined, for want of funds, to the opening of a few roads.

Economic freedom, discredited by the use which its principal supporters made of it, was the object of a chorus of criticism directed against the whole economic and social system founded on individual freedom. Systems were proposed in opposition which called for a rational organization of society. In the meantime, this intellectual movement, which was not yet a mass movement, brought together thinkers who believed in the supreme power of the human will to transform society and who in that respect often appeared as heirs of the eighteenth century. Imbued with ideas of justice and legality, they advocated a gradual transformation of economic institutions. Faith in the power of ideas, reforming zeal, and confidence in the power of the human will were the characteristics common to all these idealistic socialists, and this led their opponents to label them 'Utopians'. In point of fact, these authors were not entirely agreed as to the ideal form of social organization, especially with regard to the role of the State in economic life, with the result that some laid emphasis on production, others on association, and yet others on a sort of anarchy. It was only in Germany, with Marx and Engels, that the first outlines of a scientific socialism appeared before 1848.

Socialist ideology was born after 1815 in France, where the weakness of the working class movement was offset by a remarkable profusion of doctrines of social emancipation. The important part played by France in this sphere can probably be explained by the fact that the French were able to draw a certain number of lessons from the Revolution of 1789, and that close links were established between socialism and Romanticism after 1830. There were a good many themes common to these two movements, if only such affirmations as that society tended to corrupt, that the passions tended to ennoble, and that women should be given their rights. It would be unthinkable to isolate Sainte-Beuve, George Sand and Victor Hugo from the contacts they had with the Saint-Simonians, Lamennais and above all Pierre Leroux, who as a literary critic, a philosopher, and a democrat exercised a threefold influence.

It is hard to classify Saint-Simonism among the socialist systems: it was in fact an authoritarian, State-exalting technocracy, but by its criticism of industrial anarchy it provided countless arguments for those who believed that society had to be organized on strict lines. The Comte de Saint-Simon served as an officer in the American War of Independence, and was a lavish patron of the arts under the Directory. But after speculating in national property, he was ruined and obliged to become a copying-clerk to a pawnbroker. However, he remained faithful throughout an adventurous life to the idea of codifying all the exact sciences in a vast encyclopedia which would be the introduction to a 'positive' social science. As early as 1814, when he published *De la réorganisation de la société européenne*, in collaboration with Thierry, he conceived the idea of a European federation with a parliament composed of savants and intellectuals which would draw up a code of general morality based on freedom of conscience, with institutions and an educational system common to the various peoples.

Under the Restoration, he turned his attention permanently towards questions of an economic nature, with an emphasis on production rather than consumption. In the four volumes *De l'Industrie*, and in the numerous periodicals which he published at this time, such as *Le Producteur* (1819-1820), he stressed the evolution which led mankind towards the industrial era. In the meantime, reading the works of the theocrats such as de Maistre and Bonald, he was influenced by their ideas of organization and hierarchy, by the notion that there had been an organic period, the feudal and Christian Middle Ages, followed by a critical period, the Revolutionary eighteenth century : it consequently remained for him to open a new organic period based on work. He confronted the 'international' party (nobles, priests, landowners, and persons of independent means) with the industrial or 'national' party (farmers, workers, manufacturers, and savants); and in 1819 he published his famous parable, in which he compared the harm the State would suffer, on the one hand, by the deaths of its savants, artists and manufacturers, and on the other hand, by the disappearance of its princes of the blood, ministers and bishops. The government of men ought, according to him, to be replaced by the government of things, brought about by a technocratic body in three chambers (dealing with the three phases of invention, examination and execution): 'Power' should give way to 'abilities'. To his eyes, the form of government was not as important as the organization of the economy: 'The philosophy of the last century,' he wrote, 'was revolutionary: that of the nineteenth century must be organizational.'

However, after 1821 his chief preoccupation was the problem of solidarity; and at the end of his life he recognized the importance of a 'New Christianity', intending to reform religion by introducing a new morality allowing the development of the human 'passions' and the pursuit of well-being; a religion without any miracles, without any supernatural belief, but which, like Catholicism, would have its own morality, creed and dogmas, and which would comprise the supreme requirement of social life: 'the fastest possible improvement of the lot of the poorest class'.

The Saint-Simonian ideas, by stressing 'the exploitation of man by man', the need to put an end to competition by means of the organization of credit and industry, the elimination of parasitic idlers, the suppression of inheritance, and the sanctification of labour and talent, and by providing the formula: 'to each according to his abilities, to each ability according to its works', opened the road to socialism. On Saint-Simon's death, his chief disciples, Eugène and Olinde Rodrigues, Enfantin, a product of the École Polytechnique, and Bazard, who had been a member of the Carbonari, set about applying his ideas to the problem raised by the existence of the industrial proletariat. In their *Exposition de la Doctrine* (1829), they showed that the social evils caused by the dispersal of effort, the predominance of selfish greed, and the abuse of competition, could only be cured when industry was organized in accordance with a comprehensive plan. The *Exposition* was in effect a criticism of the private ownership of productive capital, which, according to them, consecrated ' the exploitation of man by man '. Although it was expounded from 1825 onwards in newspapers such as *L'Organisateur*, this analysis became widely known only after the 1830 Revolution, thanks to the *Globe* which Pierre Leroux put at the disposal of Saint-Simon's disciples. As for their lectures, they were addressed to an élite, particularly economists, students at the École Polytechnique and the École des Mines, foreigners like the musician Liszt and the poet Heinrich Heine, and rich Jews, while a great many women were attracted by the mystical character of the system. Gathered together in the Rue de Monsigny in a Family which rapidly took on the appearance of a religious sect and chose Enfantin and Bazard as its ' popes ', the Saint-Simonians quarrelled over the question of marriage. But in 1832, at Ménilmontant, Enfantin founded a community of love, a sort of socialist convent, thus arousing the hilarity of the public which made fun of the inmates' weird rites, as well as of their coats buttoned down the back to remind men of the great law of human solidarity. The government took offence and lost no time in breaking up Sainte-Pélagie. Enfantin left for Egypt with a few disciples, announced the marriage of East and West, and prepared a project for a Suez canal which attracted the interest of the young French consul in Cairo, Ferdinand de Lesseps. Soon a commercial Saint-Simonism was to take the place of the cloudy sect of 1830, but without the former denizens of Ménilmontant abdicating their belief in progress and humanity. As early as 1842, Michel Chevalier had outlined in the *Globe* a vast programme of major works; the banker Pereire, the engineer Talbot, and Enfantin himself were involved in the first great railway undertakings. All of them considered that they should no longer 'worry about the distribution of wealth, but only about its increase'. Equipping the country with means of transport and credit facilities became the chief object of the new practical Saint-Simonism.

In stressing like their master the importance of the role of a technocratic state in the economic and social life of the country, and in proposing the organization of a 'strong, beloved, revered power' which would embrace the entire social order, the Saint-Simonians were far ahead of their time. The first theoreticians of socialism, on the other hand, remained faithful to individualism, which they sometimes pushed to the most paradoxical extremes; they felt the same mistrust of the State as the doctrinaires of Liberalism.

Charles Fourier, a humble shop assistant, a poor, unknown dreamer who had waited for years for the rich patron who would finance his great enterprise, put all his trust in the one idea of association. This discovery, in his view as important as Newton's discovery of gravity, cleared the way for that pastoral, innocent, no longer fallen world in which, far from the Saint-Simonian factories and loco-motives, and sheltered from speculation and usury, he in-vited mankind to take refuge. Certainly no one criticized the incoherence of the existing economic system more severely than he, notably in *Le Nouveau monde industriel* (1820). Trusting in the natural goodness of man, wishing to give free rein to the passions and the instincts, and seeing association as the highest human activity, he ad-vocated the foundation of 'phalansteries,' where the 'séries passionnées', gathered together in 'phalanxes' of 1620 people, would joyfully engage in attractive work, which would be rewarded in accordance with the capital invested, the labour expended and the skill employed; the Fourierist society would therefore retain an agricultural, artisan character. But if this co-operative system appealed so strongly to Fourier, it was because the organization of economic units seemed to him to make possible the suppression of the State. There was no place in his system for political power; the phalanx consisted only of individuals linked together by the phenomenon of attraction; and at its head there was no machinery of government, but simply an economic administration composed of the series' leaders, endowed moreover with purely moral authority imposing no restrictions on the interests of the group, and therefore strong enough, according to Fourier, to take the place of a government. He solved the problem of authority in the simplest possible way: by abolishing it. It was obvious that such a utopian scheme could only lead to disaster, as in the phalansterian project at Condé-sur-Vesgres in 1833. However, the Fourierist school was skilfully managed after Fourier's death (1837) by his disciple Victor Considérant, who had expounded his ideas as early as 1832 in his paper *Le Phalanstère*, and who abandoned his master's visionary dreams to retain, in *La Démocratie Pacifique*, nothing but the idea of consumer co-operatives. Thanks to him, Fourier's system made several converts, in France where Godin founded the workers' phalanstery at Guise, and as far afield as America and Russia. Considérant was undoubtedly one of the most perspicacious socialist authors writing before the 1848 Revolution: in his *Principes du Socialisme*, his theory of concentration and his description of economic crises foreshadowed Marx's revolutionary vision.

Proudhon was even more of an individualist than Fourier. A native of Franche-Comté, and the son of poor artisans of peasant stock, employed as a printer in Lyons and an accountant in Paris, he educated himself entirely by his own efforts. His often lyrical, sometimes misty style was full of a Rabelaisian verve, the shock of which sometimes stops the reader in his tracks. An egalitarian after the manner of Rousseau, he won notoriety in 1840 with a pamphlet entitled *Qu'est-ce que la propriété?* in which like Brissot in 1780 he replied ' Property is theft.' He expressed the egalitarian aspirations of the ordinary humble artisan, deeply attached to his independence, and extremely hostile to all authority, to the State, to the Church, and to large-scale enterprises. Although his doctrine was only defined later on, he already appeared as the theoretician of mutualism, making exchange and barter the basis of the economy. He looked forward to the time when ' the workshop would replace the State', a state of affairs which he called anarchy. He dreamt of a federation of autonomous communes, composed of associations of small landowners who were masters of their fields, their tools and their families, and accordingly he condemned the female emancipation advocated by Saint-Simon and Fourier. As early as 1846, in connection with *La Philosophie de la Misère*, he expressed strong opposition to Marx whom he knew at that time in Paris. There can be no doubt that Proudhon, whose diatribes against the Church failed to conceal his underlying religious feeling, could not be attracted, despite his alleged Hegelianism, by the dialectical materialism which the author of the *Communist Manifesto* was in the process of formulating; but there can also be no doubt that, in the century of the great manufacturing industries, Proudhon expressed the anachronistic attitude of the artisan class.

The campaign in favour of association, which Saint-Simonians and Fourierists had made fashionable, was joined by socialists with religious tendencies. Pierre Leroux, a former member of the Carbonari, foreman and founder of the *Globe*, had gone through a phase of Saint-Simonism and had never succeeded in ridding his social-ism of pantheistic and esoteric speculations. Gathering enthusiastic disciples around him he made contact with the world of letters through Sainte-Beuve, George Sand and Eugène Sue. More specifically Catholic in his convictions,

Dr. Buchez, who in his *Histoire Parlementaire de la Révolution Française* endeavoured to reconcile the Revolution with the teaching of the Church, felt the need, in his periodical *L'Européen*, to advocate the accumulation, through productive co-operatives, of an inalienable and indivisible capital administered by the workers themselves; his great merit was to have founded, in *L'Atelier*, a working-class paper produced by working men. Finally there was Constantin Pecqueur, who came to similar conclusions, and who was chiefly remarkable for the description he left of the industrial concentration of his time. From the formation of the great monopolistic companies which were taking the place of individual ownership, he deduced a materialistic theory of history; but he too relied upon the self-sacrifice of the capitalists to restore on earth a system more consistent with divine morality, with the 'Republic of God' which he chose as the title of his principal work.

These authors do not seem to have realized the part which the State was bound to play in the emancipation of society; they failed to see that only State intervention could solve certain problems created by the formation of the proletariat. It is interesting to note that the reaction against this hostility toward the State displayed by the first socialist thinkers should have come from a number of bourgeois who, disturbed by the evils of competition, began to concern themselves with the moral and physical conditions of industrial labour. Encouraged by reading Sismondi, a remarkable precursor in this sphere, Villeneuve-Bargemont, the Prefect of the department of the Nord, published in 1834 his *Économie Politique Chrétienne*, in which he advocated the 'official and public' organization of charity: governments were the 'visible ministers of Holy Providence'; they were 'the common centre of light, effort and power, whose rays could reach the farthest ends of the kingdom'; and he concluded: 'The principle of government intervention seems to us to be called for equally by religion and politics.' The same conclusions were reached in Eugène Buret's work *De la misère des classes laborieuses en Angleterre et en France* (1842), an arsenal of arguments for the opponents of capitalism, in which 'the government of industry' was advocated as the true *raison d'être* of the State. On the eve of the 1848 Revolution, it was increasingly recognized in socialist circles that the State was 'an instrument of progress', a 'guiding force' furnishing man with the conditions of his improvement. Associationist socialism was followed by the authoritarian socialism of Louis Blanc, who in his *Organisation du Travail* (1840) recognized that it was for the State to bring about freedom. 'Failing to take power as an instrument means meeting it as an obstacle.' The emancipation of the proletariat could not be achieved by a series of partial efforts and isolated attempts, but only by 'the omnipotence of the State'. As the supreme director of production and the banker of the poor, it would raise the loans necessary for the creation of national workshops, co-operative working-class organizations which, by concentrating the workers of a single trade, would rule out competition and end up, after a transitional period, by proving their superiority over capitalist enterprises. Louis Blanc praised the Saint-Simonian school for 'having rehabilitated the authoritarian principle'; on the other hand, he condemned the Charter for having 'deprived the State of its noblest, most natural and most necessary prerogative'. However, Louis Blanc's socialism remained attached to the idea of individual freedom, the philosophy of the rights of man: what he passionately admired in the men of 1793, whose history he wrote, was their effort to bring about 'real freedom', that is to complete the individualist revolution by a social revolution. And it was in the name of that 'real freedom' that he now called for an authoritarian government: the socialist State was to be based on the democratic will of the nation; the exercise of power would be entrusted to a single assembly, elected for a brief period, to which the executive would be subordinated. Louis Blanc clearly had no doubt that the nation's will, expressed in this way, would found on its own authority the 'fraternal' régime which would be the government of the future.

Another example of authoritarian socialism was provided by Étienne Cabet's *Voyage en Icarie* (1841). In the country of his imagination each citizen was an official who had chosen his post from among the various activities open to him, for which the remuneration was identical: work was therefore a 'public office'. The communist State, which did not recognize individual ownership, would leave no freedom to the individual: 'Give me absolute power,' the State seemed to say, 'and in return I will guarantee you every material satisfaction.' Thus in Icaria any criticism would be regarded as an offence; there would be no room for freedom of belief. Society submitted every individual will and every individual action to its rules, its orders, its discipline. Cabet, who believed in the natural goodness of man and the virtue of education, supposed that citizens would conform easily to this Spartan régime. On the eve of 1848, he gave his 'Icarism' the mystical character of a Church; and he counted on his disciples' enthusiasm, not on violence, to bring about the triumph of his ideas, which he was to try out in 1848 in Texas.

With its utopian character, Icarian communism is not to be confused with the Babeuf brand of communism, as handed down by Buonarotti. The latter had published in Brussels in 1828 his *Conspiration pour l'Égalité*, which, although it is hard to say whether it was a faithful expression of Babeuf's ideas, had considerable influence in working-class circles after 1830, both inside and outside France. Buonarotti, who played a major rôle in the European Carbonari, inclined Freemasonry towards the working-class and the republic, and thus as a corollary inclined the working-class and the young republicans towards Freemasonry.

True, those who grasped the full implications of this French 'scientific socialism'—men such as the publicist Lahautière, the historian of the French Revolution, Laponneraye, and the materialist Dezamy—formed a tiny band. However, during the July Monarchy these ideas penetrated into the secret societies after 1836 and inspired Blanqui's activities. For Blanqui, whose contant preoccupation was to point to the antagonism between rich and poor, and between luxury and poverty, co-operative enterprises for consumption or production were a 'dangerous trap' set for the proletariat; all that mattered was the conquest of power and its inexorable use by the revolutionaries; he believed in the creative force of revolt and insurrection.

However, these were not the writers who, on the eve of the 1848 Revolution, exercised the profoundest influence in working-class circles. The most widely read author was probably Lamennais, whose *Le Livre du Peuple* (1837), written after his break with the Church (cf. p. 197) preached in an apocalyptic style social democracy founded on the teaching of the Gospels. He supported neither communism nor socialism, which he accused of reducing man to the level of an animal; and he saw no solution to the social problem except in a return to brotherly love and the democratization of property. In his book *De l'esclavage moderne* (1839), he showed that slavery still existed in modern times, and had indeed become the condition of the whole nation, with the exception of 200,000 privileged persons. But this was not in order to preach recourse to violence. He counted on the law alone to bring victory for the just cause of the people: it was in men's minds that social regeneration had to take place first of all. In any case, political emancipation was the first condition of permanent emancipation: for it was power which made the law: democracy led inevitably to socialism.

England, where the working-class movement was extremely

strong in the 1830s and 1840s, was a long way from being able to produce a socialist school comparable to that existing in France. Its most influential exponent, Robert Owen, who was by turns a manufacturer, a philanthropist, and a trade union organizer never stopped insisting, in the same spirit as Fourier, on the principle of association. Convinced that human nature, which was neither fixed nor unchangeable, was greatly influenced by the environment in which a person was brought up, he tried to change that environment, in his New Lanark spinning mills, by eliminating selfish profit and by substituting work vouchers for money: he attempted to bring about the realization of his ideal in small self-sufficient agricultural communities; and, like most of the French socialists, he rejected both violence and class warfare. Believing that society could be reformed by the example of a model community, he tried to put his ideas into practice first with his ideal city at New-Harmony in the United States, which failed for lack of initial capital, confidence and discipline, and then, on his return to England, with the creation of an 'equitable exchange bank' founded on a mutualist, co-operative socialism. His trade union activity inside the working-class movement (cf. p. 88) was just as unsuccessful. However, he died with the conviction that he had been ahead of his times and that in his dreams of socialistic messianism he would be understood one day. Greater realism was shown by William Thompson and above all by Thomas Hodgskin, an egalitarian Ricardian whose hostility to capitalism was based on anarchistic philosophy of natural law. Their social philosophy, which is somewhere between Ricardo and Marx, stressed above all else the idea that since work was the only measure of value, the worker had an absolute right to the product of his labour. They found the remedy in productive co-operatives, in which they wished to retain the competitive system, in order to raise the level of productivity. These theorists were admittedly capable of levelling effective criticism at the society in which they lived, but their isolation from the masses led them to look for a solution in purely rational terms. Devoid of any sense of history, they saw socialism as an idea which could be grasped and applied at any moment in time, as soon as it was expressed with sufficient force and clarity so that everybody was forced to admit that capitalism was essentially unreasonable and unjust. Thus while the writings of the ' egalitarian Ricardians ' helped to shape Marx's ideas, they had little immediate influence. True social philosophy was created by the English in working-class action itself.

Far more than in France and England, socialism and communism were the object of theoretical speculation in Germany. It was by the roundabout route of ideology that the faults in the economic and social structure would finally affect the course of events. On the eve of the 1848 Revolution, socialist writings were influencing a growing section of the German intellectual élite, but their effect on the masses was as yet only imperfectly understood.

There were two main channels by which socialist ideas penetrated into Germany: first, the influence of the Utopian writings of French and English authors; and secondly, the interpretation in a social sense of left-wing Hegelianism, and especially of Feuerbach's philosophy.

Most of the great works of Western socialism had already been written when socialism began to arouse a certain curiosity in Germany, in circles which, limited as they may have been, generally possessed a wider culture than Owen or Fourier could draw upon. Only slight importance, confined to his town of Trier and some other parts of the Rhineland, can be attributed to young Ludwig Gall, who after trying to found a phalanstery in the United States, published his Fourierist writings in Germany: ' The privileged rich and the working classes,' he wrote in 1835, ' are fundamentally opposed to each other by contrary interests; the situation of the former improves in the exact proportion in which the situation of the latter worsens, and becomes more precarious and wretched.' The work which did most for the accurate diffusion on western socialism was a treatise written by an agent of the Prussian government in Paris, Lorenz von Stein, *Der Socialismus und Communismus des heutigen Frankreichs* (1842). In this work he showed that the springs of history lay in the struggle between the bourgeoisie and the proletariat. The modern form of the production of wealth, industry, brought about by its basic principle of competition a fall in wages and an increase in poverty, with the result that the proletarian could never under any circumstances become a property-owner. His conclusion was that the necessary reforms should not only lead to the establishment of a constitution, but also result in a new division of property between the members of society. If the capitalist State did not take the initiative in this respect, the revolution would be carried out by the class most directly concerned, namely, the proletariat. As it happened, Stein himself was not a socialist; and his book was an appeal to the governing classes as much as to the government of each country. As a good conservative, he saw the monarchy as the only institution capable of rising above class conflicts and promoting a policy of reform. None the less, his book became the breviary of the German socialists.

It was France once more which helped to mould the ideas of Wilhelm Weitling, a tailor by trade and a native of Magdeburg, but who had lived a long time among the German colony in Paris: a member of the *Bund der Gerechten*, an association which brought together the communists among the German craftsmen in Paris, he had published in his first book there: *Die Menschheit wie sie ist und wie sie sein soll* (1838), in which he depicted the working class as the instrument of the emancipation of mankind and communism as the ideal society. Moving to

Switzerland in 1841, he founded various associations there, and published *Die Garantien der Harmonie und Freiheit* (1842), as well as pamphlets and periodicals which his correspondents distributed in Germany. His great service to the revolutionary movement was to have linked that movement to the proletariat's awareness of its own poverty : in his eyes. this proletariat was the class of the future, destined to bring greater justice to the world. However, this socialism remained more humanitarian than scientific, for the simple reason that he was a representative of a dying social class and could not imagine the possibility of a revolution actually engendered by the development of large-scale industry. Finally, convinced that the Gospel was nothing other than communism, he remained attached to a certain mystical messianism, as was shown by *Das Evangelium eines armen Sünders* (1843): here Jesus was depicted as the prophet of love and liberty, the first great revolutionary, whose fight against the Pharisees and the rich gave the Gospels their real significance. Weitling's influence extended over a good many groups of German comrades* in correspondence with Switzerland; but after his arrest by the Swiss authorities in 1843, while his faithful disciple Becker continued his communist activities, others such as Marr moved towards Feuerbach's humanism and in 1848, Weitlingism was on the decline.

At this period, 'true socialism', taught by a whole school of thinkers deriving more or less from Neo-Hegelianism (cf. p. 84), had obtained much greater credit among the left-wing German intelligentsia. In point of fact, while the Hegelian left was compromising its cause in risky speculations and while Bruno Bauer was attacking communism with increasing violence, another group of Neo-Hegelians, following a contrary course, held that Hegel's criticism could lead to a philosophy of action, and prescribed for this action an aim which was no longer political but social. It is here

* Gesellen

that mention must be made of Ludwig Feuerbach, whose book *Das Wesen des Christentums* (1841) was a positive revelation for the post-Hegelian generation. According to Feuerbach, man, in creating in his image a God without any independent existence, externalized and alienated in him the loftiest qualities of the human race, and at the same time impoverished himself and became a selfish creature cut off from collective life. Liberation could never come to him unless the illusions of religion were dissipated and qualities attributed to God alone, reabsorbed in his own self. Thus the criticism of religion produced a social philosophy which tended to combat the selfish individualism of society and to represent the collective love of mankind as a sociological imperative. To enable man to live a life in conformity with his 'true nature', it was necessary to reintegrate him in the human community by abolishing religion with its tendencies towards isolating the individual : that was the requirement of 'humanism'. However, if that doctrine had the merit of putting the problem of alienation in a new way, might it not also, by turning it into a question of metaphysics, divorce the problem from its economic and social context? It was on this point that the criticisms of 'true socialism' would bear.

As early as 1841, a young Rhenish Jew, Moses Hess, who had likewise mixed with the Berlin *Freien*, remarked in his book *Die europäische Triarchie* on the inability of liberalism to solve the social problem. Showing that three countries in succession had worked for the emancipation of mankind, Germany by giving it intellectual liberty, France political liberty and England economic liberty, he declared that the end of this development was bound to be the abolition of private property : this was using the Neo-Hegelian dialectic to prove the need for communism. However, it was Feuerbach's philosophy which shortly afterwards opened his eyes to the fact that religious alienation was simply the effective expression of the alienation of the human essence which took place under the capitalist régime; for the weak were forced to alienate their labour to create wealth, which ceased to belong to them and which took the form of money, that god of modern society, a god which was foreign to them and enslaved them in its turn. To abolish this alienation, Hess advocated a sort of communism, which alone would allow a man to lead a life in conformity with his true nature and re-establish collective relations on the basis of altruism and love. Expounded in numerous Neo-Hegelian periodicals, these opinions, which were complemented by the observations of the Proudhonian Karl Grün in *Die soziale Bewegung im Frankreich und Belgien* (1845) gave birth to ' true socialism ', which claimed to restore to man's nature its real meaning, namely altruism. In point of fact, in most cases, ' true socialism ' was a purely ideological concept, which condemned all political activity as sterile and directed its attacks against liberalism, accusing it of camouflaging the selfish purposes of the bourgeoisie: a retrograde attitude in the practical sphere and also far too abstract to interest the working masses. However, it should not be forgotten that certain ' true socialist' periodicals, like Elberfeld's *Gesellschafts-spiegel*, provided information of inestimable value on the social question in the 1840s. And Joseph Weydemeyer, in the *Westfälische Dampfboot,* showed that constitutional reform could be equally useful for the working class, who by means of political action could obtain certain immediate improvements, such as the right of association. Already Marxist language was being spoken.

Before arriving at historical materialism the young Karl Marx was, in the years before 1848, to chart his course by the criticism of every movement of his time: criticism of the left-wing Hegelianism which he had met in the course of his university studies in Berlin, and which in his opinion was too inclined to consider the effect of ideas on morality; criticism of Feuerbach, who saw mankind out of the context of its historical development; and criticism of Hess, whose communism, with its reasoning about the human essence was utopian and abstract. In Cologne, in 1842, he served his apprenticeship as a controversialist by editing the *Rheinische Zeitung* (see p. 151-2); in Paris he published in collaboration with Ruge the *Deutsch-Französische Jahrbücher* (1844), in which he pointed to the need for an alliance between socialist philosophy and the industrial proletariat. He then abandoned the Hegelian idea according to which the State was the constituent sphere of society: the State, he maintained, was determined by society, and consequently the pursuit of political emancipation implied a preliminary disruption of the economic relations between men. In his *Die Heilige Familie*, directed against Bruno Bauer and his associates, and in his *Karl Marx über Feuerbach* (1845), he tried to show that the sole revolution which was both social and political could only be the work of the proletariat; and by the same token he rejected not only reformism and State socialism, but also the apolitical communism of Blanqui's disciples, who were satisfied with attacks on the machinery of the State.

However, the chief event in his life was the friendship of young Friedrich Engels, a Rhinelander like himself, but the son of a well-to-do merchant, who in his book *Die Lage der arbeitenden Klasse in England* (1845), written in course of a business trip, taught him that communism would be produced by the very evolution of capitalist society. From then on, Marx deduced history, not from ideas any more, but from reality, in other words from economic contradictions and class conflicts. Expelled from Paris on account of his contributions to the newspaper *Vorwärts*, he went to Brussels where, after clarifying his ideas by writing *Die deutsche Ideologie*, he broke first with Weitling, then with Proudhon, whom he attacked in *La Misère de la Philosophie*, helped to provide the Communist League (cf. p. 74) with its ideology, and at the end of 1847, at its request, wrote the *Communist Manifesto*. Here, on the basis of historical materialism—the belief that in every period economic production and the resulting social structure formed the basis of the political and intellectual history of that period—he developed the theory of the class struggle, the concentration of capital, and the inevitable final 'catastrophe'; he showed that while the bourgeoisie had played a revolutionary role in the past, its historical mission was over, and that now only the proletariat was a revolutionary class. 'The sole essential condition for the existence and supremacy of the bourgeoisie,' he wrote, 'is the accumulation of wealth in the hands of private individuals, the formation and increase of capital; the condition for the existence of capital is wage-earning. Wage-earning depends on competition between the workers. Industrial progress . . . is replacing the isolation of the workers, due to their rivalry, with a revolutionary union by association. Thus the development of the manufacturing industries is taking away from under the feet of the bourgeoisie the ground on which it has established its systems of production and appropriation. The bourgeoisie is providing its own grave-diggers. Its downfall and the victory of the proletariat are equally inevitable.' Accordingly Marx called upon the workers of the whole world to unite in readiness for a revolution which he announced as imminent. In the development of his thought, the *Manifesto*, without being a definitive statement of his position, was intended to reveal the general tendency of the historical process and to provide the elements of a strategic policy for the working class. It would be a mistake, however, to exaggerate the influence of this work: Marx's ideas, which to a great extent were a forecast of the future, were scarcely known in Germany when the 1848 Revolution broke out, except in a few limited circles connected with the Communist League. It was not the *Communist Manifesto* which was to give socialism its original character in 1848.

With the ideological factors thus defined, how did the working-class movement in Europe develop between 1815 and 1848?

By its scope and efficiency, the English working-class movement easily surpassed the continental movements. But powerful though its activities were, it established no link between the ideas of trade-unionism and revolution.

At the end of the Napoleonic Wars, a 'Luddite' movement had grown up in Britain, organized to protest against starvation wages and intolerable working conditions: as the workers at that time rented the machines from their employers and used them at home, the only way of ensuring that production came to a stop was to make them unusable. Until 1817 Luddism of various sorts remained the primitive form of the social struggle, to such a degree that neither the dispatching of troops into Nottinghamshire—12,000 men, a force greater than Wellington had used in Spain— nor the threat of the death penalty for breaking machines (a law against which Byron protested in the House of Lords) could overcome it. Moreover, in spite of the Combination Acts of 1797, there still existed in 1815 trade organizations which escaped the inefficient supervision of the English police. During the crisis of 1817-1819 (see p. 131), thanks largely to figures such as Cobbett and Hunt, the workers were drawn into action behind the radical bourgeoisie; but there was no question yet of an autonomous working-class movement. The latter would come into being only after the Act of 1824, passed thanks to the influence of the Tory reformers, which laid down the principle of the right of combination. There then began a period of rapid progress for trade unionism, as solidarity was established across local and professional boundaries. During the period 1829-1832, when the example of France proved contagious and disturbances were frequent, a revolutionary trade-unionism developed. In 1829 John Doherty, a progressive employer, organized the General Union of Spinners and Piecers, then in 1830 the National Association of United Trades for the Protection of Labour, which catered for every trade and helped strikers; it disappeared the next year, but in 1832 the Builders' Union was revived. In 1833 Robert Owen, the philanthropic manufacturer and the prophet of the co-operative movement, founded the Grand National Consolidated Trades Union. But the employers answered these movements with the 'lock-out'. In 1834 six Dorsetshire day-labourers were sentenced to seven years' transportation for illegal activities; and in spite of the indignation aroused by this sentence, the over-ambitious Grand National Union gradually disintegrated. The force of revolutionary trade-unionism petered out in sporadic demonstrations which were promptly abandoned.

This check turned the militants back to political action. Chartism was only possible through collaboration with the radical party, which provided the leaders of the movement. The trade unions as such generally held aloof, considering that the political struggle did not come within their province. Yet Chartism, even if it did not claim to be 'socialistic', was basically a mass movement, a primitive revolt against poverty, which reached its highest point at times of crisis—in 1838, in 1842 and 1848—and its numerical strength was due to the adherence of the workers, especially the domestic weavers, who had been ruined by industrial mechanization. Such people looked back nostalgically to a more prosperous past when the hand-weavers belonged to the working-class élite; and they still hoped for a reversal of history which would enable the manual worker to recover his former prosperity. However, Chartist agitation had been provoked in the first place by the passing of a new Poor Law in 1834 which obliged the unemployed to work in workhouses, controlled by 'Unions' of neighbouring parishes, and made out-door relief the exception instead of the rule. In 1836 the Working Men's Association laid down the six points of the People's Charter (universal suffrage, a secret ballot, annual Parliaments, etc.) drawn up by the cabinet-maker Lovett; certain Benthamite radicals gave their support to these peaceful demands. But the partisans of 'moral force' were rapidly left behind by those who, especially in the industrial areas of North West England, joined with the Irishman Feargus O'Connor in pressing for a general strike, the idea of which had been put forward by Benbow. Supporting them, James Bronterre O'Brien, the remarkable journalist of the *Poor Man's Guardian* and the *Northern Star*, presented the social concepts which had been those of Robespierre and Babeuf in the French Revolution. But the Chartist Convention of 1839 hesitated between these two tendencies and fell into discredit. On the other hand, in November 1839 the Government put down the Newport rising led by John Frost, and imprisoned the leaders: the movement seemed to be over.

The distress of the winter of 1841-42, however, brought about renewed agitation led by the National Charter Association, and the drawing up of a fresh petition to the Commons: but O'Connor, a militant of unrivalled energy and force of character but without any profound grasp of politics or strategy, was unable to develop the strikes and meetings into the hoped-for revolution. After this fresh setback the moderate elements turned in preference towards the Free Trade Movement led by Cobden and Bright (cf. p. 138), while O'Connor, after the elimination of Joseph Sturge and the 'political' elements, published his Land Scheme for the breaking up of large estates into allotments. When, after the French Revolution of February 1848, O'Connor, who had been elected a

Member of Parliament, tried to present the Commons with a monster petition in favour of the Charter, he came to grief before the organized repressive action of the police. The day of April 10th ended in confusion.

The story of Chartism would therefore seem to have been a tale of utter failure. The fact remains that Chartism was the first example in the world of a national political working-class movement and that it evolved all the battle tactics and techniques which contributed to the experience of the international working-class movement. The later Chartists, such as Ernest Jones and George Julian Harney, found it easy to assimilate the ideas of Marx and Engels, who for their part had learned a great deal from Chartism.

The trade unions had frowned upon the revolutionary character of the movement. Abandoning politics, the working-class élite returned to its occupational activities, trying to reconstruct the union bastions—the Miners' Association of Great Britain in 1841, and the National Association of United Trades in 1845—or else turning towards the co-operative movement, like the ' equitable pioneers ' of Rochdale in 1844. A new generation of realistic militants, such as Allen and Newton were foreshadowed by this new trade-unionism, which was more individualistic than socialistic in character. The romantic period of working-class agitation was over.

The working-class movements on the Continent could not be compared with that which was evolving in England.

In France it was a matter of an infinitesimal minority. Until 1830 the only type of organization, apart from a few Friendly Societies, was the *Compagnonnage* or association of trade-guilds, which had its own secret masonic rites and its own *Tour de France*, but which, on account of irremediable internal divisions between rival ' obligations ' (such as those to Father Soubise, Maître Jacques and Salomon), was no help to the workers; Agricol Perdiguier's attempt, in his *Livre du Compagnonnage*, to awaken a feeling of class-consciousness ended in failure. After 1830, however, the working class, which felt that it had secured the triumph of the revolution, became conscious of its own existence. It was then that the first working-class papers made their appearance and what were tantamount to resistance groups were formed under the cover of Friendly Societies. The riot of the Lyons silk-weavers (20–22 November 1831) was a movement to secure a collective contract and showed for the first time the revolutionary strength of the French working-class. 'The Lyons Revolt,' observed the *Journal des Débats*, 'has laid bare a grave secret: that of the struggle between the class with possessions and the class without. The barbarians who are threatening society are not in the Caucasus or on the steppes of Tartary; they are in the suburbs of our manufacturing towns. It is not a question of the Republic, nor of the Monarchy, but of the safety of society.' The failure and suppression of the Lyons insurrection did not interrupt the process of organization engendered by the introduction of the socialist doctrines; little by little the principal trades in Paris and Lyons formed fraternal societies: as from 1833 strikes were organized in collaboration between one town and another.

However, after the events of 1834 (see p. 120), the integration of the workers in the republican organizations slowed down the progress of the working-class movement, which developed inside secret societies (the Société des Familles, the Société des Saisons). It was only in 1839-40 that the economic crisis, producing a series of strikes, led to a revival of agitation. It was then that the workers began to demand a ten-hour day; in the union of the Paris printers there appeared a really effective resistance group. Appeals to class-consciousness became more and more frequent, the *Riche Populaire* and Corbon's *L'Atelier*, widely read by the printers, defended the strikers' interests, advocated co-operation and showed an interest in Chartism.

Like Buchez, *L'Atelier* was fond of repeating that the Revolution was the daughter of the Church, and that democratic ideas were simply a modern transposition of Christian ideas; it thought that the revolution ought to be 'rechristianized' and 'the Church made as revolutionary as it could be'. Consequently the paper dwelt less on the organization of the struggle than on the Christian idea of the dignity of man; in its opinion, the social question was essentially a moral problem. It was a woman, Flora Tristan, who proposed in her *Union Ouvrière* (1843), a national and international union of workers; convinced that the workers ought to achieve their own emancipation, she tried, in the course of a long tour of France, to communicate her gospel to them.

However impressive certain strikes may have been, such as the one which led to the massacre of Rive-de-Gier in 1844, it would be a mistake to think that there was a coherent feeling of working-class solidarity in France before 1848. Besides, the heterogeneous quality of the French working-class movement would have prevented any such feeling. It was not in fact the factory hand, generally a man of no education, who thought about his working conditions, but the craftsman, the tailor, the cobbler, the carpenter, or the printer. And this working-class which was beginning to become aware of its unity and strength only existed so far in the big towns, in Paris and Lyons, and only to a limited extent elsewhere. This was because in France the working-class movement was above all a legacy of the *Faubourgs* and their place in the Revolution, a tradition handed down from the Jacobins and Babeuf.

The working-class movement did not acquire the same amplitude in Germany during the *Vormärz*, although the spectacular revolt of the Silesian weavers in 1844 attracted the attention of the entire civilized world. The weavers, domestic labourers who were forced to sell their work to middlemen who then disposed of it at a profit, were burdened with heavy household rates not to mention State taxes. Their situation had been aggravated during the 1840s by the closing of the American market and the creation of a textile industry in Poland, which put a lot of people out of business and showed how frightening the prospects were for those who could not keep abreast of improved techniques of production. The revolt, which started on the estate of the Zwanziger family at Peter-swaldau, had nothing premeditated about it, and was the product of extreme poverty. None the less it provided an opportunity for bloody repression by the army. This re-pression, apart from evoking countless literary reactions, such as the famous request sent to King Frederick William IV by Bettina von Brentano, had at least the advantage of enabling Wilhelm Wolff, in his book *Die schlesische Mil-liarde* (1845), to make a detailed study of the workers' problems, which had profound repercussions on the socialist movement.

The years of economic crisis would be marked in Ger-many by a great many working-class riots, sparked off by the despair aroused by famine and unemployment, and in-flamed by the hatred felt for the army everywhere. The abundant supply of manpower, the working conditions, the wandering life, and the number of itinerant workers or homeless labourers explain the existence of a latent agita-tion, especially on the railways, where repeated strikes broke out before 1848. Much more important for the future of the working-class movement was the creation of numerous workers' study-groups (*Bildungsvereine*), some-times on the initiative of young intellectuals or well-mean-ing bourgeois who would soon be outnumbered by their listeners, and at other times as the result of a spontaneous decision taken by the workers. The printers founded a certain number of these groups; although they often con-fined themselves to occupational claims, some of them went on to general issues and political discussions. These

Bildungsvereine, which were in correspondence with the organizations of German workers abroad, and some of which—like the Hamburg group—had up to 450 members in 1847, produced a great many figures destined to play an important part in leading the working-class movement in 1848 : Stephen Born from the *Bildungsvereine* in Berlin, and G. Lessuer, later a member of the First International, from the one in Hamburg.

Finally, mention must be made, in this picture of the awakening of the working-class movement, of the important role of the *émigrés* and the growing awareness of the international solidarity of the workers.

The first manifestation of the workers' International was in fact the creation in 1836 of a group which called itself the League of the Just (*Bund der Gerechten*). To be precise, there had existed in Paris for several years a League of the Outlaws (*Bund der Geächteten*) which included a number of German intellectuals and workers, especially from the Fauborg Saint-Antoine; it published the paper *Das Geächtete* and maintained close relations with the German workers in Switzerland. It was inside this league, and with more clearly defined political aims, that the *Bund der Gerechten* was formed; Article II of its statutes stated its intention to free Germany from the subjection in which she was living and called upon the working classes of all countries to become aware of their situation. It regarded itself as linked to the Société des Saisons, which was then under the leadership of Blanqui and Barbès, and which, in the late 1830s, had precise revolutionary aims : under the influence of Buonarotti, it advocated seizing power in a surprise attack which would lead to the establishment of the dictatorship of the proletariat. But when the insurrection of May 1839 proved a total failure a great many members of the *Bund der Gerechten*, who had been compromised in the affair, had to take refuge in England.

These *émigrés* included a printer called Karl Schapper, a fearless revolutionary who had worked with Büchner in Hesse and with Mazzini in Savoy, and who had been one of the founders of the league. He helped to found in London a German Workers' Educational Association (*Deutscher Arbeiterbildungsverein*), which rapidly assumed an international character, taking the motto ' All men are brothers,' around which the *Bund der Gerechten* was soon reconstructed. However, the *Bund* now found itself confronted with two ideologies: on the one hand that of Weitling who, after playing a leading part in Switzerland, had emigrated to England in 1844, but whose utopian, sentimental outlook repelled Schapper; and on the other, that of Engels and Marx, who, as a member of a correspondence committee in Brussels, first made contact with Schapper in 1845. It was one of the members of the league, Joseph Moll, who invited Marx to London to give a lecture in November 1847 to the League of the Just, which had changed its name a few months before to that of the Communist League. After speaking to an audience composed of Germans, Belgians, Frenchmen and Englishmen, he was invited to write the famous *Manifesto* in which he based Communism on historical materialism and the idea of the class struggle. At that time the League constituted an embryonic international organization since it had a great many cells on the Continent, and particularly, thanks to the links created by emigration, among the German workers' study-groups.

The same spirit of international solidarity inspired the Fraternal Democrats, a group which had been formed in Chartist circles in London, and which recruited its members from among the political *émigrés* living in the English capital. The guiding spirit of this movement had been George Julian Harney of the *Northern Star*, who gave the Fraternal Democrats a fairly centralized organization, with a separate section for each nation and a central council which would later be adopted by the First International. Karl Schapper for the Germans and J. Michelot for the French, joined this organization, which maintained constant relations with the *Association démocratique* in Brussels, a body created by a number of Belgian, German and French radicals, on whose behalf Marx came to speak in London in November 1847 on the occasion of the commemoration of the Polish rising of 1830.

Thus links were formed in the world of the *émigrés* which the reaction following the 1848 Revolution finally broke, but which were to be re-established by the First International during the 1860s. To an increasing extent, thinking people in Europe were becoming aware of the solidarity which united the oppressed and the disinherited throughout the Continent. 'A blow against freedom on the Tagus', cried Harney at a meeting of the Fraternal Democrats in support of the Portuguese Revolution, 'is a blow against freedom on the Thames; a victory for republicanism in France would mean the end of tyranny in the world; the triumph of the English democratic Charter would mean the liberation of millions of people in Europe.' In fact, the idea of the Workers' International had not yet entirely emerged from the democratic and nationalist ideology which, under the banner of Mazzini's Young Europe, believed it could create an alliance of the peoples of the world against tyranny. However, Marx's growing influence in the active centres of European *émigrés* was beginning to set the European working class on the course which was to lead to its emancipation.

Chapter V

THE POLITICAL EVOLUTION OF
THE GREAT LIBERAL STATES

France and England were the two great powers which, after
1815, engaged in the experiment of a constitutional monarchy within which parliamentary institutions gradually
developed. The political forces involved were very much
the same : in both countries there was an aristocracy which
was the ruling class about 1815 but which was faced by a
rising upper middle class enriched by trade and industry
which, as from 1830, supplanted that aristocracy as the
dominant class. Again, in both countries the electoral
system, here by virtue of the property qualification for
the franchise, there as a result of ancient historical traditions, left unenfranchised the poorer classes—not only the
proletariat and the peasantry, but also the lower middle
class—[which wanted to bring the régime closer to democracy.] Bourgeois liberalism therefore found itself at
grips with opposition on both sides, right and left, which
often made the exercise of power difficult for it. And yet
the story of the years 1815-1848 was very different in the
two countries : while monarchical France had to endure
two revolutions, the régime in England adapted itself to
circumstances; and, despite the greater scale of economic
and social change in England, the consistent application
of parliamentary principles provided the stability that made
possible the reforms that, without jarring, shifted the
country towards democracy.

1. The Constitutional Monarchy in France

The constitutional Charter of 1814 had created a system which was a compromise with the society born of the Revolution and the Empire, and kept unaltered its essential institutions, from the Civil Code and the Concordat to the sale of *biens nationaux*, the University, and the Napoleonic administrative system. Thus the Restoration had been neither judicial nor social, but purely dynastic in character.

The Charter 'granted' by the King established in France a régime inspired by the British. There were three powers: the King, who initiated, sanctioned and enforced laws, convoked the Chambers annually, and could dissolve the elected Chamber; the Peers, nominated by the King on a hereditary basis, with no limit on numbers. The Deputies from the Departments had to be over forty and paying 1,000 francs in direct taxation; they were chosen by electors aged at least thirty and paying 300 francs in direct taxation—about 90,000 electors in all, who made up the *pays légal*. English customs were introduced into the system imposed on Parliament: an annual vote on the budget, a 'civil list' voted to the King by the Chambers, a speech from the throne at the opening of the parliamentary session, and an address from the Chamber in reply to that speech. Secret in the Senate and public in the Palais-Bourbon, the parliamentary sittings often gave rise to impassioned debates, and the forum provided by the Chamber helped to carry out the political education of the nation. Gaps in the Charter left unanswered important questions which dominated public life after 1815. Had the ministers any responsibility to Parliament other than a 'penal' responsibility for 'acts of treason or peculation'? In accordance with what electoral law were the deputies to be elected? How was the Press to be controlled? It was according to the reply given to these questions that the political parties were gradually formed.

As it happened, the régime was installed in an atmosphere of civil war. True, Talleyrand's Ministry, in which the most active figure was Pasquier, the Minister of Justice, urged the Prefects to follow a policy of appeasement; but it came up against violent passions. Although the King had promised an amnesty in his Cambrai declaration, a policy of proscription was initiated: nineteen generals were court-martialled. Immediately after the Battle of Waterloo, reprisals against the Bonapartists began in the valley of the Rhône and in Marseilles. Once the Restoration was an accomplished fact, an epidemic of acts of vengeance broke out—at Avignon, where Brune was killed, at Nîmes, where the massacres were extended to the Protestants, and at Toulouse, where the Verdets put General Ramel to death. The Government proved itself, if not inert, at least impotent: Fouché, the Minister of Police, was dismissed. It was in the midst of this 'White Terror' that the elections took place, for which the electoral colleges of the Empire were used, with the addition of Royalist notabilities. The result was the so-called *Chambre introuvable*, bristling with hatred for the Revolution; and the Duc de Richelieu, who succeeded Talleyrand in September 1815, formed a government of a more reactionary complexion. It put through a series of emergency laws, suspending individual freedom, punishing seditious crimes, and setting up *cours prévotales*, half military, half civil courts, from whose decisions there was no appeal: this was the 'Legal Terror'. Its principal victim was Marshal Ney, who was sentenced to death by the Peers. As for the administration, it encouraged widespread repression. Thanks to the activity of secret societies such as the *Association bretonne*, the *Association royale du Midi*, and the *Francs régénérés*, the whole of France bowed down under the Terror. Reactions such as Didier's anti-Bourbon conspiracy at Grenoble were insignificant.

However, this situation finally began to cause some anxiety to Louis XVIII's advisers, as well as to certain foreign ambassadors, such as Pozzo di Borgo, who represented Russia in Paris. The Chamber soon found itself at odds with the Ministry. The conflict between the two powers turned on the electoral question, which, by a curious paradox, the Chamber wished to settle by fixing the franchise qualification at 50 francs, in order to rally the electors to its side. In opposition to the Ministry, which upheld the Royal prerogative, the deputies stood up for the parliamentary system, which they saw as destined to give the Chamber control of the administration. This was calculated to annoy Louis XVIII, who was extremely sensitive on the subject of his prerogatives. Decazes, the Minister of Police, persuaded him to dissolve the *Chambre introuvable*; and the electors showed their approval of this attitude in October 1816, by returning to Parliament a majority in favour of the Ministers.

It was after these elections that a real public life began. Three parties gradually made their appearance, though without setting up recognized organizations as in England. Moreover, the distinction between them came out more often under the pressure of events than as a result of preconceived ideas, more through negative reflexes than on the basis of a positive programme.

The first to take shape was the Ultra-Royalist party, as its opponents called it. Its supporters described themselves as 'pure royalists', seeking to contrast in this way their unswerving loyalty with the dubious devotion of the men of the Revolution and the Empire, tardy adherents to the monarchy which they intended, so they claimed, to adapt to the new ideas. The Hundred Days had shown the Ultra party the dangers of this policy of compromise. They intended, not so much to go back to the Ancien Régime, as has been said too often, but to found a new monarchical and religious order, based on the ideas which had come to fruition during the emigration and which the Catholic and Romantic revival in France had developed. 'France,' wrote Chateaubriand, 'wants all the freedoms and all the institutions brought about by time, the change in manners, and the progress of understanding, but with everything which has not perished of the old monarchy, with the eternal principles of justice and morality . . . France wants the political and material interests created by time and consecrated by the Charter, but it wants neither the principles nor the men who have brought about our misfortunes.' However, this comparatively moderate position adopted by Chateaubriand, who in *De La Monarchie selon la Charte* (1816), as well as in *Le Conservateur*, stressed the impossibility of a complete return to the past, was outstripped by the Ultra press, which, giving prominence to the ideas of the Vicomte de Bonald, advocated in *La Gazette de France, La Quotidienne,* later *Le Drapeau Blanc,* and Fiévée's *Correspondance politique et administrative,* the close alliance of throne and altar. The party's principal asset, its great hope and its leader, was the King's own brother, the Comte d'Artois, who gathered around him the men of the *Pavillon de Marsan,* the Baron de Vitrolles, Jules de Polignac, and the Comte de Bruges : a real 'secret government' with considerable facilities at its disposal. As the Comte d'Artois had been appointed Colonel of the National Guard of the entire kingdom, with the right to choose his officers, it had been possible to exclude from that militia all who were opposed to their ideas and to make it an internal army at the service of their party. Finally, the secret society of the *Chevaliers de la Foi,* created to fight the Empire, and more or less put to sleep during the First Restoration, had come to life again to combat the Talleyrand-Fouché Ministry and its Orleanist schemes. Another royalist secret society, that of the *Francs-Régénérés,* was formed at this time by dissident freemasons, and competed with the Masonic movement for a while, but had only an ephemeral existence. It was the *Chevaliers de la Foi* who maintained the remarkable cohesion of the deputies of the Ultra-Royalist party in the Palais-Bourbon. 'The party stood up, sat down, spoke and kept silent like a single man,' said Molé. Tactics were decided upon in secret committee, and instructions were then given to the uninitiated in meetings which were held at the house of the deputy Piet, an individual whose insignificance protected him from jealousy. The real parliamentary leaders were the Comte de Villèle, a former mayor of Toulouse, who in the *Chambre introuvable* had shown himself to be an indefatigable debater and a cunning tactician, and who had considerable financial and administrative ability; his friend the lawyer Corbière, the deputy for Rennes, and in the Chamber of Peers, Mathieu de Montmorency, Polignac and also Chateaubriand. Many of these leaders were also members of the Supreme Council of the *Chevaliers de la Foi*. The chief supporters of the Ultra party were to be found in the bishoprics, seminaries and presbyteries, as well as in the country seats of the south and west of France; its electors were the great landed proprietors, but also the merchants of the big ports such as Marseilles, who had particularly suffered from the blockade; and through the activities of the clergy its influence was widely exerted on the peasantry and certain trade guilds.

The 'Constitutional' party was born of a reaction against the excesses of the Ultra party, just as the latter had come from a reaction against the policy of compromise of the first Restoration; the 1816 elections gave it consistency by grouping behind the Ministry all those who repudiated the methods and principles which had inspired the White Terror. Such a negative programme obviously left room for a great many shades of opinion, and this party never had the practical cohesion or the doctrinal unity of its opponents. The right wing of the party was represented in the Ministry by the Duc de Richelieu and Lainé, who had less distaste for the theories of the Ultras than for their methods; and the left wing by a small group of intellectuals, the *doctrinaires*, namely Jordan, Guizot, Barante, the Comte de Serre, the young Duc de Broglie, and Charles de Rémusat, who all recognized the influence of the philosopher Royer-Collard. In point of fact, they were tools in the hands of the Minister of Police, then of the Interior, Élie Decazes, the son of a Libourne notary, and a high official of the Empire who had come over to the Bourbons. Decazes was a clever politician, without any beliefs or principles, but who, by reporting the secrets and the gossip of the *cabinet noir* to the King, had managed to make himself indispensable, and who moreover knew all the currents of public opinion. The Constitutional party, whose supporters included an important section of the aristocracy and liberal upper middle class, had *Le Moniteur* as its principal organ, but intellectual circles preferred to read *Le Journal Général de France*, inspired by Royer-Collard, as well as the *Archives philosophiques, politiques et littéraires*.

The party of the Independents took shape and distinguished itself from the Constitutional party during the summer of 1817. This name concealed all the enemies of the régime, who however had not declared their true loyalties: Republicans, Bonapartists, and Orleanists. After the 1817 elections they formed an 'anti-ministerial' group with Casimir Périer, Dupont de l'Eure, and the banker Laffitte, who were joined by Lafayette, Manuel and finally Benjamin Constant. These various figures made up a 'guiding committee', opposed to the *Pavillon de Marsan* and the Supreme Council of the *Chevaliers de la Foi*, which corresponded with affiliated members and electoral committees in all the provinces; its programme was very close to that of the Masonic movement, of which most of the Independents were dignitaries; it was even more anti-clerical than anti-monarchist. The Bonapartists, by joining the party and gaining increasing influence in it, introduced into it a note of military nationalism and of revenge against the 1815 treaties, as well as a tendency to resort to violent methods foreign to the liberal spirit. The brain of the party was Benjamin Constant, its figurehead Lafayette, its financial backer Laffitte. Its press was constantly censored, and survived only by becoming positively Protean: a single editorial team brought out in succession a series of papers with different names, which were no sooner published than they were suppressed; thus the year 1818 alone saw 56 independent papers come and go. The best known, because they lasted, were to be *Le Constitutionnel*, *Le Journal du Commerce*, and finally the review *La Minerve* which, thanks to Benjamin Constant, was probably the finest product of French journalism under the Restoration.

The political history of the Restoration was characterized by two separate periods: an attempt at constitutional government which lasted from 1816 to 1820 and an Ultra period, more marked under Charles X than under Louis XVIII, which culminated in the 1830 Revolution.

After forming his Ministry following the elections, the Duc de Richelieu tried to win the support of the middle classes for the régime. He put through the electoral law of February 1817—the so-called *Loi Lainé*—which laid down that elections should be held at the chief town of each department and on the basis of a vote for several deputies out of a list, a system which favoured the liberals; he settled the financial question by starting a sinking fund to repay the National Debt; and he allowed Marshal Gouvion-Saint-Cyr, the Minister of War, to reorganize the army in accordance with the law of 12 March 1818, which enacted recruiting by voluntary enlistment and ballot (with provision for substitution), and contained rules for officer promotion designed to prevent arbitrary appointments. However, the progress made by the Liberals in the elections of September 1817 and October 1818 ended up by alarming him: he obtained the resignation of the Ministry, in order to bring right-wing elements into it; but the demands of the Ultras made this solution impossible, and the Dessoles-Decazes Ministry, formed in December 1818, moved in fact further and further left. After having Guizot appointed director general of departmental and communal administration, the Cabinet dismissed the Ultra Prefects, and then carried out a purge of the principal State institutions. Wishing to make public life more open, it put through the *Loi de Serre*—named after the Keeper of the Seals—which abolished censorship and preliminary authorization, prescribed trial by jury for press offences, and stipulated that caution-money should be the only obligation placed on the founders of newspapers: whence, for a short period, the remarkable rise of the liberal press. Decazes was planning a complete reform of the administration and of criminal law, as well as constitutional organization of ministerial responsibility. But the successes obtained by the left in the 1819 elections (typified by the election of the regicide Abbé Grégoire at Grenoble) led him to take his government further to the right, and even to review the electoral law. The murder of the Duc de Berry by a republican workman, Louvel (February 1820), a murder committed in the hope of putting an end to the dynasty, forced Decazes to resign and opened the way for a long period of Ultra reaction.

The Duc de Richelieu, who succeeded Decazes, suspended individual freedom and freedom of the press, and changed the electoral law, so that there was a double vote, in both arrondissement and department, the latter vote being reserved for the more heavily taxed electors (June 1820). Put into application straight away, this law brought an Ultra majority to the Chamber. Richelieu, who had thought he would be able to govern with the help of the right, but without a right-wing programme, soon found himself overwhelmed by the demands of the Ultras, represented in the Government by Corbière and Villèle: in December 1821 he had to resign, having lost the support of Louis XVIII.

The opposition, deprived of its legal weapons, then moved in the direction of revolutionary action. Liberal deputies, republican university students grouped together in the *Loge des Amis de la Vérité*, and Bonapartist officers on half-pay (although it is true that not all half-pay officers automatically became enemies of the régime), had already planned an insurrection under the tricolour flag for 20 August 1820; but it was discovered even before it could break out. The next year, they grouped together in the Carbonari, a secret society copied from the Italian *Carbonaria*, whose basic unit was the private or communal *vente* consisting of ten members, so that the members of the different *ventes* did not know one another and communicated only through their delegates—a cellular arrangement which was essential to foil infiltration by the police. Each member entered into four engagements: to observe secrecy, to pay a monthly contribution, to have weapons ready at all times, and to obey the orders of the *Haute Vente*. A powerful force in Paris, around Mulhouse and Lyons, and in the west where it was linked with the *Chevaliers de la Liberté*, the Carbonari were in favour of overthrowing the Bourbons and convoking a Constituent Assembly. If Lafayette, Manuel and Dupont de l'Eure controlled the supreme *vente*, which itself headed a centralized, hierarchical organization, the young members, students and officers, formed the really active element. Hopes of a general revolutionary movement throughout Europe led in 1821 and 1822 to a whole series of risings, at Belfort, Saumur, La Rochelle and Colmar. The most sensational event was the trial of the four sergeants of La Rochelle,

whose execution did more harm to the Restoration even
than Ney's execution. Repression, as well as internal dis-
agreements, resulted at the end of 1822 in the dissolution
of the Carbonari. In fact, it had never had more than
about 40,000 members and had never succeeded in pen-
etrating the working class.

The fears aroused by these movements favoured the reactionaries, who held the Villèle-Corbière Ministry in their
power. Villèle, a talented administrator who had continued
the policy of financial reform begun by Corvetto and
Louis, organized the State accountancy system, arranged
the voting on the budget by sections and ministries, and
made parliamentary control of public expenditure a permanent reality, he was much less at ease in the political
sphere—' He never sees the lofty side of things,' Pasquier
said of him—where he was the tool of the Ultra party,
whose excesses he tried in vain to control. The Press Law
of 1822 restored censorship, created a number of arbitrary
offences, and substituted trial by summary jurisdiction for
trial by jury: which accounts for the rapid decline of the
left-wing press. After the dissolution of the Chamber, new
Ultra-Royalist elections (resulting in the *Chambre retrouvée*)
and the accession of Charles X, who was both less intel-
ligent and less prudent than his brother, there was no
longer anything to obstruct the political and religious programme of the right. In the religious sphere, the University, under its Grand Master, Mgr. Frayssinous, was
brought under the influence of the clergy; the government
closed its eyes to the little seminaries, which had become in
fact secondary schools; as for the alliance between Church
and State, it was consecrated not only by the Coronation—
which evoked paeans of enthusiasm from Romantics such
as Lamartine and Hugo, but was ridiculed by the liberal
and Voltairean songwriter Béranger—but also by the passing of two laws, one authorizing the government to restore

by ordinance the religious communities of women, the other punishing the profanation of sacred objects with hard labour or death: a 'sacrilege law' which would concentrate liberal hostility to the 'priest party' and help to develop that anti-clericalism which would be one of the principal causes of the fall of the Bourbons. In the political sphere, the so-called 'law of the milliard *émigrés*' authorized the payment of indemnities to those *émigrés* whose property had been sold as *biens nationaux* by means of a conversion of Government stock which fell most heavily on the bourgeoisie (April 1823). On the other hand, the law restoring certain rights of primogeniture was rejected by the Peers (April 1826); while the Press Law, introduced by Peyronnet, the Keeper of the Seals, described as a measure 'of justice and love' and intended to gag the opposition press, was withdrawn by the Ministry to escape a hostile vote (April 1827).

Villèle's government was shaken by the defection of the extreme right (the so-called *Pointus*), supported by Chateaubriand, who had been refused the Ministry of Foreign Affairs, and by *Le Journal des Débats*, edited by the Bertin brothers. As for the liberal opposition, it occasionally disguised itself behind a Gallican mask, and found itself supported in 1826 by a *Mémoire à consulter* written by a nobleman from Auvergne called the Comte de Montlosier. This work, which denounced the Congregation, the Jesuits, Ultramontanism and the missionary zeal of the priesthood, created a confusion, which lasted a long time, between the very active but much reduced group of the *Chevaliers de la Foi*, and a huge secret society which, under the name of the Congregation, was alleged to be plotting the destruction of the Charter in order to found a theocracy, to control all public offices, and to dominate the Court, the Ministries, Parliament and the public services. A great many magistrates and a few members of the Chamber of Peers urged the government to enforce the law against the Jesuits. On the left, the new liberal generation, which had abandoned its clandestine airs, now read *Le Globe*, which provided it with a philosophic doctrine. After demonstrations by the National Guard, which was disbanded in April 1827—a step which further antagonised important sections of the Parisian bourgeoisie—Villèle, the object of concerted attacks, set up a censorship office in the Ministry of the Interior, and pronounced the dissolution of the Chamber (November 1827). But the Government came up against well organized opposition, due partly to Chateaubriand's *Société des Amis de la Presse*, and partly to Guizot's *Société ' Aide-toi, le Ciel t'aidera'*, which re-established relations between Paris and the provinces by means of a pamphlet campaign, and checked the electoral registers: in many constituencies the right-wing and left-wing opposition presented common lists of candidates. The election resulted in a defeat for Villèle, whose government had long been regarded as moribund, and who resigned in January 1828.

Was Martignac, who kept the Ministry of the Interior for himself in the new Cabinet, capable of governing? His task would be all the more difficult in that, in a hybrid Cabinet, he enjoyed neither the confidence of the King nor a definite majority in the Chamber. He was personally in favour of a conciliatory policy, allowed Guizot and Cousin to resume their lecture courses, and accepted proposed changes to the Press Law. He took up a position against the 'Priest party', by issuing an ordinance forbidding the Jesuits to teach, and by limiting the number of pupils in each seminary, though not without arousing lively opposition among the bishops. He then tried, by administrative reform, to obtain the election of municipal and general councils, without weakening the central authority. In fact, 'a shamefaced Villèle', he satisfied nobody. After he had suffered a parliamentary reverse, the King asked him for his resignation (August 1829).

The programme of Prince Jules de Polignac, a personal

friend of the King, who succeeded Martignac, was to establish a constitutional and aristocratic régime rather similar to the one which existed in England. But by appointing Bourmont to the Ministry of War and La Bourdonnais to the Ministry of the Interior (with their associations with Coblentz and Waterloo), he immediately aroused a strong current of opposition in the country, where he was extremely unpopular. A Republican party now appeared with Armand Marrast's newspaper *La Tribune*; others envisaged an Orleanist solution, which was advocated by the *Le National*. This paper was produced under the inspiration of Talleyrand by Thiers, Mignet and Armand Carrel, who tried to spread the idea that the constitutional régime which the nation desired was incompatible with the maintenance on the throne of the elder branch of the Bourbons; all the people had to do, they said, was to imitate what the English had done in 1688. Political discontent was aggravated by the unrest created, since 1827, by the intensification of the economic crisis. In some circles there was talk of refusing to pay taxes.

Faced with this situation, the Ministry was divided and powerless, but it acted all the more threateningly for that: on 2 March 1830, the speech from the Throne hinted at the possibility of a fresh dissolution. When the Chamber showed its lack of confidence with a reply, signed by 221 deputies, which raised the question of ministerial responsibility, it was first prorogued, then dissolved (16 May). In spite of the capture of Algiers which took place in the midst of all this, and in spite of the personal intervention of the King who implied that an opposition vote would be an offence, the July elections, carefully prepared for by the *Société 'Aide-toi, le Ciel t'aidera'*, were a liberal triumph: 274 members of the opposition were returned. However, the situation was not yet desperate for the monarchy: the opposition deputies were quite prepared to spare the King's feelings; moreover, as well-to-do bourgeois they were scarcely ready to open the flood-gates to a lower-class movement, and some of them even approached Polignac suggesting that he should take them into his Cabinet.

But the King, in his feudal simplicity, thought only of fighting, convinced that his just cause would eventually triumph. The government, invoking Article 14 of the Charter, which authorized it to issue what regulations and ordinances it considered necessary for the enforcement of the law and the safety of the State, signed four ordinances on 24 July, which had in fact been drawn up before the election results had come in. They provided for the suspension of freedom of the press, the dissolution of the Chamber, changes in the electoral law to take into account only land tax and property tax, and the calling of new elections. Resistance was organized, not among the deputies, but among the journalists, the first to be affected by the royal decisions, especially at the offices of *Le National*, where Thiers drew up a protest (26 July). Popular agitation, helped by the closing of the workshops, was rapidly taken in hand by the Republicans, (Cavaignac, Bastide, Marrast, Arago and Trelat). On the 27th, Marmont, the commandant of the troops in Paris, was still in control of the situation; but on the 28th, trying to take the offensive against the barricades which had been put up, he lost the eastern districts and fell back on the Tuileries; on the 29th, with the Louvre surrounded, he gave the order for retreat. But in the meantime the deputies had intervened, alarmed at the strength of the popular movement. On the 29th, at Guizot's suggestion, they appointed Lafayette commandant of the Municipal Guard and set up a municipal commission of five members. They did not believe yet that the régime was doomed, and their only concern was to bring the insurrection under control. It was on the 30th that, faced with growing Republican agitation—which the tardy formation of a Mortemart Cabinet at Saint-Cloud and the withdrawal of the Ordinances had been unable to stem

—they rallied to the candidature of the Duc d'Orléans, proposed by Thiers and supported by the banker Laffitte: they saw in him a means of avoiding a Republic. After coming to an agreement with the Peers, they offered Louis-Philippe the post of Lieutenant-General of the Kingdom. On the 31st, the latter appeared beside Lafayette on the balcony of the Hôtel de Ville, was acclaimed by the people, and promised to surround his throne with 'republican institutions': the insurrection died down, while Charles X left Saint-Cloud for Rambouillet, abdicating on 2 August in favour of his grandson, the Duc de Bordeaux. In point of fact, the liberal deputies had cheated the Republicans of their revolution. Really the Revolution was in no way inevitable: in the course of those July days, the deputies rallied to the Orleanist solution only because it limited as far as possible the consequences of a rising which had begun and developed outside their control.

The Paris Revolution of 1830 represented more than a change of dynasty. The emotional shock caused by the sight of a popular rising encouraged the development, after the *Trois Glorieuses*, of ideas and doctrines which had only existed in embryo before the Revolution: the Revolution, considered as a fact in itself, thus had important consequences which were to weigh heavily on the future of the régime. In the front rank of these ideas which had burgeoned in the July sunshine was the revelation of the common people, of the political force they represented, and of the obvious need to take them into account in the future. Rémusat, whose *Mémoires* expressed the opinions of the Liberal notabilities of that period, and who had thought until the last moment that the Revolution would be crushed, admitted: 'We did not know the people of Paris and we did not realize what they could do.' In the months following the Revolution, workers rubbed shoulders with bourgeois in the countless clubs which made their appearance; the National Guard even went so far as to present arms when working-class processions went past. The July Days thus played a decisive role in making the working class aware of its strength, and in revealing to other Frenchmen the existence of the social problem, as was evidenced in particular by the interest shown in the diffusion of the Saint-Simonian doctrine. However, the 1830 Revolution was even more than that: although, in the sphere of international affairs, it revealed the extent of national opposition to the 1815 treaties, the strength of French patriotism, and the conviction that France had a historic mission in Europe (cf. p. 229), it produced an absolute revolution in the French way of thinking, leading the Romantics, who had hitherto shown a penchant for the political forms of the Ancien Régime, to reconsider their attitude and to support the cause of national liberty and political and social revolution. From then on, Victor Hugo would devote the bulk of his work to the defence of the humble and the victims of society—the *Misérables*. Similarly, George Sand would give expression to the revolt of her sex and of the underprivileged of all sorts, in her private life as in her novels—another example of the extraordinary 'moral explosion' which followed the *Trois Glorieuses*.

This, then, was the question: would Louis-Philippe take account of the aspirations of this 'young France' which had carried out the Revolution and wished to continue it? And could such aspirations be fulfilled in conflict with the interests and ideas of those who had put the Duc d'Orléans on his throne.

In fact, the revised Charter which Louis-Philippe swore to respect on 9 August changed the régime only very superficially. No longer granted by the King, it had become a contract between the monarch and the nation. Article 14 had disappeared; Catholicism had lost its status as the State religion; the censorship had been abolished. The election by the deputies of their president, discussion of the budget by sections, the right of interpellation, secured *de facto* if not *de jure*, increased the parliamentary character of the Régime. The law of 21 March 1831 authorized communes to elect their councils, and this led to a development of local political life, although the government retained the power to appoint mayors and their deputies. The law of 22 March 1832 would enable the National Guard to choose its officers. But the law of 19 April only slightly reduced the franchise qualification (200 instead of 300 francs), and maintained the existence of a *pays légal* which was not the nation. As a result, political life remained extremely narrow: the deputies were elected by arrondissement colleges which numbered at the most 3,000 persons in Paris, but only 150 in the Hautes-Alpes; the vote was often only the culminating point of countless deals; and it revealed nothing but struggles between notabilities supported or opposed by the Prefect and his administration. At bottom the Revolution rested on a misunderstanding: the *haute bourgeoisie* was not prepared to allow a democratization of the régime, insisted on maintaining its property-owning character, and regarded the crisis as over: 'There has been no revolution, but simply a change in the State personnel.' As for the nation as a whole, it did not regard the Revolution in this light; it expected the Revolution to be followed by a peaceful evolution which would gradually extend the franchise and allow the whole nation to share in public life.

Inside the *pays légal*, these divergent interpretations expressed themselves in the divergent attitudes of the party of resistance and the party of change. However, it would be a mistake to regard the two Orleanist parties as radically different from each other; they in no way represented organized groups with distinct personalities and clear-cut programmes, but simply tendencies of mind and temperament directed in one case towards prudence and in the other towards greater boldness. In fact, the statesmen of the July Monarchy formed a single team linked by a closely woven network of interests, ideas, and sometimes backgrounds.

Stubborn, realistic and thoroughly unscrupulous, Louis-Philippe concealed a passion for power under a good-natured exterior. From the very start of his reign, he set out to achieve the triumph of his policies with men picked by himself. But he knew how to proceed cautiously. He therefore chose a first Ministry which, while it included the two principal leaders of the Orleanist parties, Casimir Périer, and Laffitte, also brought in the organizers of the Revolution. The government took certain measures against the losing side in the July Revolution: the legitimist peers were dismissed, the Council of State was purged, and scholarships at the little seminaries were abolished. But it soon became apparent that, in its divided state, it was incapable of maintaining order: with the worsening of the economic crisis a whole series of strikes had broken out; and among those who had fought on the barricades, Republican societies such as the *Amis du Peuple* were formed, which did not hesitate to draw attention to social problems. The King then decided to discredit the party of change by entrusting it with power. In difficult conditions, Laffitte succeeded in defending against the Parisian mob the lives of the ministers who had signed the Ordinances, and they were sentenced by the Peers to life imprisonment. But the legitimist Mass at Saint-Germain l'Auxerrois in memory of the Duc de Berry, followed by violent anti-clerical riots (14 February 1831), reawakened passionate feelings. Laffitte was accused of having failed to maintain order, and sacrificed Odilon Barrot, the Prefect of the Seine, vainly however. For Louis-Philippe was also unwilling to be associated with Laffitte's foreign policy, which was regarded as a danger to peace; he therefore asked for his resignation (13 March) and retreated towards conservatism.

The method of government practised by Casimir Périer has since been given the name of the 'system of 13 March': it consisted of restoring order in the streets, halting the movement for reform, and maintaining international peace. However, Périer had difficulty in imposing his programme, for the new Chamber elected in July 1831 failed to give him satisfaction: he had to make concessions by abolishing the hereditary character of the Peerage and by cutting down the civil list of the King, whose political interventions, incidentally, he limited to the best of his ability. At least he insisted on respect for the authority of the government: he forbade government officials to join political associations, and he brought legal actions against the press which made attacks on the régime extremely difficult. By raising the land tax and reducing the salaries of government officials, he succeeded in balancing the budget. Although the Lyons insurrection was more social than political in character (see p. 91), he gave orders for brutal repression. When he died, a victim of the cholera (16 March 1832), he had not completed his mission of restoring the authority of the government, but he had given Orleanism the character it was to retain throughout the reign.

True, Orleanism also owed a great deal to Louis-Philippe himself. The King inherited in fact a family tradition which as it were laid down his programme in advance: his father had enthusiastically adopted the cause of the French Revolution; he himself had fought at Valmy and Jemappes, and in July 1830 he found it a useful recommendation to have worn the national colours under fire. After 1815, the quiet, orderly life of the duke and his family, the simplicity of their manners, and the decision to send his sons to school with the children of the bourgeoisie, when the young Duc de Bordeaux followed the princely tradition of having private tutors, all suggested a sympathetic attitude towards his times and a desire to join in

contemporary life, which contrasted sharply with the outdated etiquette and archaic way of life of the elder branch
of the Bourbons. However, there was more in Orleanism
than a family tradition, more even than the régime established in July 1830 by Louis-Philippe: it presented itself
constitutionally as a judicial, contractual and parliamentary
monarchy, in contrast to the legitimate monarchy established by divine right. But in practice it was based on the
myth of a bourgeois king, the symbol and surety of the
supremacy of a single class, identifying the State in its
powers and attributes with the interests of that class. There
can be no doubt in fact that a very large number of
Orleanists belonged to families whose careers had begun
under the Consulate or the Empire, who had betrayed
Napoleon in 1814 or 1815, who had opposed the Ultra-
Royalists, and who had firmly installed themselves in
positions of power after the events of 1830: real
‘Dynasties’, which did not shrink from pluralism, whether
in the great financial and administrative bodies or in the
magistrature and the Academies, and which practised
nepotism to an excessive degree. However, it must be
admitted that these Orleanist circles were extremely varied,
and it would be a mistake to identify Orleanism with the
haute bourgeoisie: there was an Orleanist aristocracy, an
Orleanist magistrature, Orleanist parvenus such as Thiers,
and great university figures, such as Victor Cousin, whom
the régime did not starve of favours and honours. Orleanism
could therefore be defined as the government of the élite,
and the meeting point of all the aristocracies, whether of
birth, wealth or intelligence; it accordingly tended to look
towards England, whose parliamentary and administrative
institutions it admired. Finally, if liberalism was, as we
have seen, the philosophy of the Orleanists, it must be
recognized that liberalism involved a certain distrust, on the
spiritual level, of the dogmatic assurance of Catholicism,
a marked preference for either Protestantism or Jansenism,

and often a hint of anti-clericalism; it had an 'eclectic' view of life which was nothing else than a spiritualistic rationalism.

The premature death of Casimir Périer allowed the opposition to raise their heads. For the legitimists, many of whom refused to take the oath of loyalty as officers, government officials or magistrates, and who, turning their backs on the existing régime, took no part in elections, the chief event of the times was the rebellion led by the Duchesse de Berry. Landing on the coast of Provence, she travelled to the west, but without finding the support on which she had been counting among the peasantry : finally, taking refuge at Nantes, she was forced to give herself up to the police. Thiers, then Minister of the Interior, had her shut up in the fortress of Blaye; the birth of a baby girl obliged her to reveal her secret marriage to an Italian nobleman, and the government, considering that she had fallen into discredit, then set her free. These frivolities and mistakes, however, did not prevent the Legitimist party from remaining a political force to be reckoned with. Still enjoying the support of a large part of the Catholic clergy, and strengthening its grip on the lower classes in the provinces thanks to the partial return of the aristocracy to their estates, the Legitimist party also benefited from the activities of a few politicians of great merit : in the Chamber of Deputies, for example, the Marseilles lawyer Berryer defended the legitimist cause with great skill and brilliance. Finally, it could count on a press which, under the direction of the Abbé Genoude, tried, particularly in *Le Gazette de France* and *La Mode*, to reconcile the elder Bourbons and the people of France : in the face of the bourgeois monarchy, these Neo-Carlists stood as partisans of a popular monarchy; and the writers of *La Gazette du Midi* called for political and social reforms which, in more than one respect, resembled the ideas of the party of change and even of the Republicans. Consequently alliances between the Legitimists and the left were quite frequent, though not without causing a certain uneasiness and dissension in the party, in which some rich members of the nobility preferred to vote Orleanist rather than give their support to democrats.

A more serious threat to the régime, the Republican opposition, took shape only with difficulty, for the authorities brought countless actions against the press and harried the members of the political associations which, like the *Societe 'Aide-toi, le Ciel t'aidera'* and above all the *Société des Amis du peuple*, moved towards an open opposition to the monarchy. The attempt to rouse Paris to rebellion on the occasion of the funeral of General Lamarque (5-6 June 1832) was put down by the military and the National Guard. Republicanism was strengthened, however, first by the adherence of Armand Carrell and his paper, *Le National*, and then by the formation of the *Société des Droits de l'Homme et du Citoyen*, which from 1833 onwards outstripped all the other movements by the scale of its recruitment, both in Paris and the provinces, as well as by the originality of its programme. It had at its head a committee including the more dynamic Republican leaders, with Cavaignac as their president, and, in order to comply with and circumvent Article 281 of the Penal Code, it was divided into sections of between ten and twenty members, bearing significant names: Robespierre, Marat, Babeuf. This was because it presented a programme which set out to be both political and social; it adopted the Declaration of Rights presented by Robespierre to the Convention, and called for universal suffrage, the organization of credit by the State, and the emancipation of the working class, though not without arousing some resistance among the Republicans themselves. The fact remains that the original feature of the new republican movement was the interest it showed in the lower classes; thus the sections of the *Société des Droits de l'Homme*, the members of which read Cabet's paper *Le Populaire*, supported strikers by all the means at their disposal.

It is easy to imagine the growing alarm of the government—now headed by Marshal Soult, with Thiers, Guizot and the Duc de Broglie in his Ministry—at the revolutionary and democratic character of this political and social opposition. When it became apparent that incarceration in the prison of Sainte-Pélagie was not succeeding in halting Republican activity, the government tried to deal it a mortal blow by means of a law forbidding associations with more than 20 members. This provoked a positive insurrection, which began after the Lyons trial with heavy fighting in that city, and ended in Paris with the massacre in the Rue Transnonain, carried out by General Bugeaud's soldiers (April 1834). There followed a huge trial in the Chamber of Peers, in the course of which the government made use of the differences which appeared between *Girondins* and *Montagnards*, as well as of the country's weariness at the unending succession of riots. The coup de grâce was given to the Republican party by Fieschi's attempt on the King's life (July 1835): the Press Law of September 1835, by increasing the required caution-money and ordering prosecution for attacks on the form of the régime, forced the Republican press to cease its activities. This was the time when, among other papers, Cabet's *Le Populaire* and Raspail's *Le Réformateur* disappeared.

At the end of 1835, the régime was therefore firmly established, with all the characteristics which it was to retain until its fall in 1848. This was the period when France, despite the narrowness of the *pays légal* and the absence of any sort of popular democracy, would none the less have its longest experience of parliamentary monarchy. From oratorical duels which were often extremely brilliant, between men who were frequently of high intellectual calibre, rules of parliamentary life were gradually evolved, which were largely consecrated by the regulations of 1839: Duvergier de Hauranne, the Duc de Broglie, and many others who survived the Second Republic and the Second Empire, would hand on to the Constituent Assembly of 1875 the lessons of the July Monarchy. It would be impossible to say that the France of Louis-Philippe had a parliamentary system as pure as that evolving in England at that time. The blame for this lay partly with the Orleanist bourgeoisie itself. All too often, in fact, the deputies put private interests before the national interest, as when, against the advice of the liberal economists and despite certain government measures, they retained the harmful protectionist laws passed under the Restoration, or when, under pressure from the settlers in the West Indies, they taxed sugar-beet at a rate which made it impossible to grow and refine. But above all, as the result of an electoral system which separated the deputies from the real nation, they utterly rejected party discipline, and they showed extreme reluctance to keep to a definite political line. Consequently the July Monarchy was characterized by considerable ministerial instability (17 ministries in 18 years), partly offset, it is true, by the continuance of certain ministers in key posts: for the 154 Ministerial portfolios distributed under Louis-Philippe, there were only 60 ministers. As regards the somewhat artificial personal rivalries which brought into conflict the ten or twelve people who, under the July Monarchy, really governed the country, those rivalries were systematically stirred up and even provoked by the King himself, for in the last analysis it was the King's personal influence which more than anything else helped to damage the parliamentary system. There can be no doubt that Louis-Philippe suffered throughout his reign from a complex about his non-legitimacy and usurpation; he had only one ambition: to shed his condition of royal upstart—with which the formidable cartoonist Philipon mocked him in *Le Charivari*—and to take his place among the great royal families. He did not simply want to reign, but also to govern; but as he knew the admiration of the *pays légal* for the English system, he resorted to underhand methods to achieve his purpose, weaving countless parliamentary plots, and not hesitating to use the right of dissolution, so that in the end he succeeded in forming a 'Crown party' which he filled out by favouring the election to the Chambers of government officials open to ministerial pressure. Playing a vital part in the choice of his ministers, who rarely met except in his presence, he reduced to the minimum the powers of the Council, when there was one. While ostensibly observing the rules of the parliamentary game, the King would end up by seriously distorting them, and like Charles X would cease being the umpire to become himself a party leader.

In point of fact, the régime became increasingly identified with the party of resistance. True there remained a party of change, known as the 'dynastic left', which, cautiously led by Odilon Barrot, advocated decentralization and the extension of the franchise at home and a firmer attitude abroad, skilfully defending these ideas in the newspaper *Le Siècle*. But most of the deputies and statesmen belonged to the party of resistance, whether they were liberal noblemen, like Victor de Broglie or the Comte Molé, *grands bourgeois* like André Dupin or the Minister of Finance Humann, university professors like Guizot or Cousin, or self-made petty bourgeois like Thiers. All of them upheld what would serve for some fifty years as the Orleanist ideology, skilfully expressed during Louis-Philippe's reign by the writers of *Le Journal des Débats*. However, among these men of the party of resistance, it is essential to note certain differences: some, like Thiers, were aware of the gap existing between the *pays légal* and the real country, and did not hesitate on certain occasions to join their voices with those of the Orleanist left: they formed the left centre, whose organ was *Le Constitutionnel*, the systematic opponent of the personal power of the King. Guizot's friends formed the right centre, shunning every opening on the left and agreeing to leave the King an important role in political life. As for Dupin's third party, it made no secret of the fact that its only ambition was to make the most of its position as an arbitrator, and thus enable its members to obtain portfolios or lesser administrative favours.

Consequently the political history of the July Monarchy was characterized by a series of sudden changes. As early as 1834, the King got Roederer to write a pamphlet stating that 'administration is the function of the King with one or more of his ministers'. If he failed to obtain acceptance of a personal régime straight away, Louis-Philippe was able to exploit personal rivalries and ambitions and set the members of the conservative party at loggerheads: in February 1836, appointing Thiers president of the Council, he persuaded him to abandon his political friends. Thiers' usefulness was rapidly exhausted, and in September the King formed a Ministry which suited him, under the Comte Molé. Taking advantage of the general recovery of business, as well as of Prince Louis-Napoleon Bonaparte's failure to rouse the Strasbourg garrison in revolt (October 1836), Molé managed to maintain himself in power for three years. This was not, of course, without arousing lively animosities: Guizot, Thiers, and Dupin, in the name of the parliamentary system, which Duvergier de Hauranne had just defended in his articles in *La Revue française*, formed a 'coalition', and Molé, after dissolving the Chamber, resigned (March 1839). But the impossibility of securing agreement between the leaders of the coalition enabled the King to resume his undermining activity. In March 1840, he once again appealed to Thiers, who ordered the return of Napoleon's ashes and crushed a Bonapartist attack on Boulogne, but whose position was endangered by his attitude in the crisis caused by the Eastern Question (see p. 239). In October, the King formed a Ministry to his taste, with Soult as President of the Council and Guizot as Minister of Foreign Affairs. In point of fact, a community of ideas had rapidly been established between Louis-Philippe, who became increasingly attached to personal power as he grew older, and Guizot, who thought that the Charter was enough to 'padlock' the political development of the country. The King was grateful to his Minister for not leaving him an 'empty chair', and yet Guizot governed in a strictly parliamentary fashion, with a Ministry responsible to the Chamber. And it was this compromise between the personal system and the parliamentary régime which gave the last years of the July Monarchy a certain political stability.

In reality, this stability was obtained only at the price of corruption, first on the electoral level and then on the parliamentary level, by promises of promotion to deputies who were also government officials and by the granting of substantial favours to businessmen. Guizot was convinced that the country's economic progress—this was the great period of railway construction (see pp. 29-30)—would be enough to rally public opinion to the dynasty, through the bonds of material interest. With the formula 'Get rich' he thought that he could satisfy all the nation's aspirations. Was he correct in this belief? Apart from the fact that on the question of freedom of education a Catholic party had been formed which had to be reckoned with in future (see p. 199), the Republican opposition, after keeping silent for a long time, was becoming more vocal every day. True, it had been compromised by the attempted rising of the *Société des Saisons*, with its Blanquist leanings (May 1839), and had since become 'law-abiding'; and there were only a few Republican deputies in the Chamber, such as the elder Garnier-Pagès and later Ledru-Rollin, the deputy for Le Mans. But they had some remarkable news-papers at their disposal, like *Le National* edited by Auguste Marrast and *La Reforme* edited by Cavaignac and then Flocon: while the first stood for liberal economics, the second advocated reforms of socialist inspiration and pro-claimed the right to work. But both considered, like many socialists for that matter, that there could be no serious social transformation without a previous change in the electoral system. To an increasing extent, a Republican 'climate' was developing in the country. The great revolu-tionary studies, those of Buchez and Roux on the French Revolution, and that of Lamartine on the Girondins (1847), the novels of George Sand and Eugène Sue, Lamennais's *Le Peuple*, and Renouvier's first philosophical treatises all contributed to it. This Republicanism had a spiritual quality; it believed in universal brotherhood; it was more outspokenly pacificist than in the previous generation.

If the 1846 elections were an apparent triumph for Guizot (291 ministerial deputies compared with 168 belonging to the other parties), it was in the *pays légal* that the most serious developments were taking place. By asking the bourgeoisie to consider nothing but material issues, Guizot had in fact alienated his active supporters. When, as from 1846, the food crisis, leading to a decline in business and financial chaos, ruined the prosperity on which the régime had been built, disaffection grew worse. A series of scandals, notably those involving Teste, a former Minister of Public Works, and General Cubières, in connection with a salt-mine concession, and the suicide of the Duc de Choiseul-Praslin, a Peer of France, suggesting a decline in the moral standards of the 'notabilities', tar-nished the régime; and de Tocqueville was not mistaken when he wrote that public morality—and finally the mon-archy itself—were endangered by the character of a 'private industry', run for the benefit of a few privileged persons, which Guizot's government was increasingly assuming. Its opponents had this in common that they felt a vague distaste for the narrow egoism of the people in power. The opposition clamoured more vociferously than ever before for parliamentary reform (a ban on government officials becoming deputies) and electoral reform (a reduction of the property qualification and the enrolment of talent). But the proposals put forward by Rémusat and Duvergier de Hauranne (1847) were rejected by the Chamber, at the request of the Minister of the Interior Duchâtel. It was then in July, that the 'banquet campaign' was opened, a tactical scheme which was devised by the dynastic left (Odilon Barrot), the left centre (Thiers and Rémusat), and the Radicals (the former Republicans), and which quickly spread from Paris to the provinces. Extremist elements rapidly took control of this campaign, and the royal policies soon became the target for fierce criticism. At Mâcon, Lamartine prophesied a 'revolution of contempt', and at Lille Ledru-Rollin extolled universal suffrage. Really public opinion did not as yet want a change of régime, but simply institutional reforms. But these Louis-Philippe did not seem ready to grant: the speech from the throne at the end of 1847 was particularly aggressive. It was the King's intellectual rigidity which led to the collapse of a régime which nobody had thought of overthrowing, but which had lost all real support in the nation.

For eighteen years the *grande bourgeoisie* in power had shirked its promises and had disappointed, one after another, all the hopes which its allies of 1830 had placed in it. By refusing to enrol the nation's talent or to promote electoral and parliamentary reform, the régime had finally alienated the social groups which could have been its most loyal supporters. The middle classes had accumulated a store of rancour and hatred. The July Monarchy had dug its grave with its own hands.

II. *The Operation of the Parliamentary System in England*

Nothing could be further from the truth than the descriptions of the English constitution given to the French by Montesquieu and Voltaire and still credited by the political theorists of the early nineteenth century. What in fact foreigners most admired about England was her government, and what they envied most of all was the liberalism of her institutions. But in point of fact the English consitution was simply an agglomeration of disparate texts, such as the Test Act of 1673, the Habeas Corpus Act of 1670, the Bill of Rights of 1689, and the Act of Settlement of 1701, defining the liberties of the English people as well as the Protestant character of the State. It was not the letter of these laws but custom which had established a number of parliamentary forms and institutions, consisting after 1688 in the marriage between Crown and Parliament. But as a result of the madness of George III, who was replaced after 1811 by his son the Prince Regent, this association tended to become one in which the Crown was subordinate to Parliament. The Palace of Westminster, rather than the Court of St. James, had become the centre of political life.

In law the monarch was 'King in his Parliament', the supreme legislative power, and 'King in his Council', the supreme judicial and executive power. But the royal prerogative, though not inconsiderable, consisted only of the following powers: the right to grant pardon, to coin money, to confer nobility, to appoint to public office, to command the armed forces, to call Parliament and to dissolve the Commons. The King was provided with a civil list; his subsidies were voted annually; he could have a subject arrested without a magistrate's warrant. The King was assisted by a Privy Council, and from this Council a

Government of some twenty members was formed at the King's request by the leader of the Parliamentary majority. This was the origin of the loyalty shown by the Ministers to the Prime Minister, a title with no official sanction but a *de facto* existence. Proceeding to a further choice, the Prime Minister gathered together in a smaller committee his closest colleagues, who formed the Cabinet, a body which had no legal existence but was in fact the real government. This system did not involve a schematic separation of powers, since the Cabinet was at one and the same time an offshoot of the legislative majority and a Privy Council Committee representing the Crown. The present-day Parliamentary system, which assumes that the government resigns in the event of a vote of no confidence, was still a long way from being firmly established, since in 1834 a government was dismissed simply at the King's wish, and the personal intrigues of the Court constantly bedevilled the political game; similarly, some ministers occasionally broke the rules of collective responsibility. The fact remains that it was towards this regulation of the parliamentary system that England was moving at the beginning of the nineteenth century.

Parliament consisted of two Houses, both sitting at Westminster. The House of Lords was an assembly of between 300 and 400 peers, including a number of representatives of the Church of England and 16 representative peers from Scotland; the rest formed a hereditary peerage which could be increased by the King without limit of numbers. This House could reject bills already passed by the Commons; it also enjoyed supreme judicial power. As for the Commons, they theoretically represented the nation, but the electoral system made them an oligarchical, aristocratic body: in 1815, nearly all the members of Parliament were great landed proprietors. The right to vote was in fact regarded as a privilege, a franchise, which was granted in the country to landed proprietors with an income of forty shillings (2 members per county), and in the boroughs to a given number of freemen, members of certain corporations and in some cases to tax-payers paying the poor-rate. The electoral map had not been revised since the Middle Ages, whence the existence of a great many 'rotten boroughs', the advantage given to the country over the big towns (London had only 4 members of Parliament while Cornwall had 44), and the practice of electoral corruption, which enabled certain peers to give their 'patronage' to ten or twelve members of Parliament. Political life accordingly remained the privilege of an antiquated aristocracy. The defects of the electoral system were further aggravated by certain practices, such as that of voting for candidates by a show of hands, or again that of requiring the voter to write his candidate's name opposite his own: in these conditions electoral pressures could be exerted in shameless fashion.

This high society which held power in Parliament was divided into two political parties: the Tory party which declared its respect for the rights of the Crown and the Church of England, and consequently defended the royal prerogative against Parliament. Having led the fight against the French Revolution and Napoleon, it was regarded as a bulwark of political and social conservatism in the face of the Jacobin peril. As a result, it had gained a preponderant position among the English electorate which it would retain for a long time; it drew most of its support from the country gentry, but many middle-class families had already joined its ranks out of self-interest. As for the Whig party, it appeared in 1815 as a coalition of political and religious interests which stood for the individual and Parliamentary 'liberties'. It was fond of invoking the Calvinist tradition and the 1688 Revolution, and drew its support from the Non-conformist sects, but it would be a mistake to regard it as a democratic movement: the Whig tradition was represented by great families of lords and dukes.

What were the forces of rejuvenation in an England that still in so many ways belonged to the Ancien Régime? Economic changes, the extent of which has already been indicated (see p. 23), had started a movement in the capitalist class, the manufacturing bourgeoisie, which was beginning to counterbalance the gentry, while the working class was already caught up in wild, tumultuous movements, and engaged in sporadic but disturbing riots. If the divided Whigs, without a leader and without a programme, confined themselves to criticising ministerial policy, two groups, the agrarian communists inspired by Spence's doctrines and above all the Radicals, distinguished themselves by the violence of their attacks. Jeremy Bentham, who had published his famous *Treatise on Offences and Penalties* in 1811, settled at Ford Abbey in 1817 and exercised the charm of his genius through correspondence, speech and the press. In the House of Commons, Ricardo defended the liberal principles of the Benthamite group, but whatever the intellectual merit of these two leading theorists and their secretary James Mill, the principal role in these troubled years was played by the propagandists and the men of action. Old Major Cartwright, who had previously called for universal suffrage and annual Parliaments, founded an increasing number of clubs. Cobbett, the first Tory to go over to the democrats, a vulgar, violent orator, but powerful and straightforward, decided to found, in opposition to a press which was making rapid progress but was so far intended solely for the rich, a penny paper, the *Weekly Register*, which enjoyed amazing success. Yet the most important figure in the movement was possibly Place, whose house was the headquarters of the reform party, acting as a link between the workers' leaders and the bourgeois élite, whose influence secured the election of a second Radical, Hobhouse, in 1820.

The Radicals used the crisis of 1815 to launch a large-scale offensive. The government headed by the Earl of Liverpool, which, with a few changes, lasted fourteen years (1812-1827), was the very incarnation of intransigent Toryism. While the Corn Laws, prohibitive customs tariffs imposed in 1815, kept the price of bread extremely high, English industry, to which the Continent had partly closed its doors, was suffering from over-production and unemployment; as a result of monetary deflation, credit was restricted, paralyzing business activity. The Treasury was obliged to retain the income tax, although this measure had been introduced simply for the duration of hostilities. The idea of the reformers, in these conditions of general discontent, was to organize a sort of general plebiscite which would show the absurdity of the electoral system. They called public meetings at which orators such as Hunt denounced the existing abuses from the platform, and obtained cheers for reformers: this marked the introduction of American methods into Britain. It was one of these meetings at Spa Fields in London, which towards the end of 1816 sent a petition for electoral reform to the Regent. The Radicals, and Cobbett in particular, were careful to repudiate violence, but in vain; disorderly elements from circles inflamed by Luddism inevitably introduced themselves into the movement. There was talk of attacks on the Tower of London or the Bank of England, and a march on the Commons was proposed. Attacked by Tories of the extreme right who, like Eldon and Sidmouth, conjured up the horrors of Jacobinism, the Cabinet was persuaded to take a whole series of repressive measures and to initiate a sort of White Terror: the Habeas Corpus act was suspended and wide powers were given to magistrates. After a worsening of the industrial crisis in 1819, a clash occurred between the masses summoned by Hunt to St. Peter's fields near Manchester and the armed yeomanry. The massacre which resulted, to which legend lent epic proportions (by analogy with Waterloo it was referred to as the Battle of Peterloo), enabled the government to put through the Six Acts, which contained martial law provisions and which, leading as they did to the imprisonment or deportation of the principal leaders, dealt a mortal blow to the Radicals. Certain elements, however, refused to give in; in 1820 there occurred the Cato Street conspiracy to seize and assassinate the Tory ministers; after George III's death, there came the stupid divorce action which George IV brought against his wife Caroline of Brunswick, and which, for a while, seemed bound to rouse the indignant capital to revolution. But in the event, the agitation died down. The resumption of economic activity in its turn altered the political climate.

By bringing Robert Peel into his Cabinet as Home Secretary (1822), Huskisson as President of the Board of Trade, and Robinson as Chancellor of the Exchequer, Lord Liverpool directed his government in the direction of a constructive and reformist Toryism: a tendency which became more marked after Castlereagh's suicide (see p. 221), under his successor at the Foreign Office, Canning. These men, often referred to as the Canningites, had this in common that they did not belong to the old aristocracy: their horizon was not limited by the sole consideration of landed interests. Peel was the son of a leading manufacturer, and Canning and Huskisson represented Liverpool; they had received a broad education and were in touch with the advanced elements in the country: Huskisson was imbued with Ricardo's ideas and sometimes found himself in agreement with the Radical Joseph Hume. The movement towards reform grew more pronounced when Canning, who had become Prime Minister after Lord Liverpool's death, brought some Whigs into his cabinet. Although Canning, who died in August 1827, was followed by the Tory Wellington, who was accused of reactionary views, the Canningites remained in the government until 1830.

Drawing his inspiration from the proposals of the Whig jurist Mackintosh, Robert Peel, as Home Secretary, reformed the criminal code by abolishing the death penalty in certain cases, humanized the prison system, and modernized the organization of the police. But it was on the economic and social level that the government was most active: Huskisson abolished the outdated parts of the Navigation Acts, reduced the customs tariffs, and, by means of a sliding scale (1827), allowed the free entry of foreign corn in certain circumstances. Impelled by economic problems to make a study of social questions, Huskisson was led, in accordance with the plans of Bentham and Place, to put through Parliament a law allowing the workers to organize (1824), a law whose scope, as a result of repeated strikes, was limited the following year.

The most serious question which faced the government at that time was the problem of Catholic Emancipation. Canning was personally in favour of removing the remaining disabilities on Catholics, but he was thwarted by the opposition of George IV, the Church of England and the House of Lords: in London, the question of emancipation was regarded as an Irish issue, and while the Irish Catholics had been electors since the Act of Union, they could not be represented at Westminster except by Protestants; many people were terrified of seeing a Parliament invaded by Catholic members. However, a campaign for emancipation was organized by Daniel O'Connell, a formidable orator who managed to unite the three noble causes of religion, freedom and patriotism. In 1823 he founded a Catholic Association whose strength was revealed in two parliamentary elections, one in 1826 at Waterford, where a great Anglican family was routed, and the other in 1828 in County Clare, where O'Connell, though ineligible, defeated his opponent, a liberal Protestant. After a bill passed under the influence of the Whig Lord John Russell had abolished the legal disabilities on nonconformist Protestants (1828), it seemed impossible to refuse equal rights to Catholics alone. Faced with the formation in Ireland of Protestant Brunswick Clubs, which brought the country to the verge of civil war, the realistic Peel came round to the idea of emancipation which he had hitherto opposed, and succeeded in convincing the King. The Catholic Emancipation Act of 13 April 1829 opened all offices to Catholics, except those of Lord Chancellor and Viceroy of Ireland. However, by initiating vexatious proceedings against O'Connell and depriving the small Irish freeholders of the franchise (the number of Irish voters fell from 200,000 to 26,000), the government cancelled a great part of the effect of the reform it had just conceded.

On the other hand, it raised the question of electoral reform, which would dominate English political life until 1832. Many Whig leaders had already spoken in favour of Parliamentary reform, which, by striking at the rotten boroughs, was expected to enable them to recover the power of which they had been deprived for so long; but two men, Russell and Grey, were too deeply conservative to wish to reduce the authority or the prestige of their caste. It was in Radical circles, notably the Birmingham Political Union and the London Mechanics' Institute, that advanced technical school founded by the Benthamites, that the desire for far-reaching electoral reform was expressed most strongly. The 1830 Revolution in Paris, coinciding with the General Election caused by the accession of William IV (July 1830), altered the political situation: the Tories lost a few seats, and in the face of attacks by the Whig leader, Lord Grey, Wellington was obliged to resign. The new Grey Cabinet, consisting of Whigs, Canningites and Radicals, introduced a Reform Bill in March 1831, which immediately met opposition from the majority in the

Commons, whose leaders pointed out that the rotten boroughs, which it was now proposed to reduce in number, had provided Parliament with some of its greatest names. Grey accordingly called new elections in April, which— for the first time since 1783—gave the Whigs a substantial majority: the Bill was passed in September. There remained the House of Lords: its rejection of the Bill aroused bitter anger in the country, which the liberal middle class turned to good account, supported by the working classes which were seriously affected by the economic crisis. The bishops who had voted against the Bill, like the militant Tory leaders, were attacked in their persons and their property: the Bishop's palace in Bristol was set on fire and the rioters were in control of the city for several days. Alarmed by this wave of violence, the Cabinet would have been glad to come to an arrangement with the opposition, but the terms offered by the Tories ruled out any possibility of agreement. In the face of the King's refusal to create enough new peers to pass the bill, the Cabinet resigned (May 1832), but Wellington was unable to form a government. When Grey was recalled, the Lords bowed to the inevitable. In point of fact, the Reform Bill, which it is no exaggeration to describe as a turning point in British history, was a partial answer to the problem, a compromise solution. It retained from the past the property qualification for the franchise, and a House elected every seven years by public vote, and merely abolished a few flagrant abuses. In the country, the right to vote was given to any owner of property yielding an annual income of ten pounds: what was new was the granting of the franchise to tenants as well as property-owners. Finally, 56 rotten boroughs were abolished, and 30 were reduced to a single seat. The right to vote, though still restricted, was extended from 430,000 to 800,000. This was still a long way from being a clear, rational system: no fixed connection was established between population and representation. The Reform Bill of 1832, which in no way satisfied the hopes of the Radicals, was unacceptable to the vast majority of the nation. The fact remains that the middle class could henceforth sit in Parliament beside the landed aristocracy; the privilege of wealth had become equal to that of land. No doubt the political changes born of the new law would make themselves felt only slowly; but 1832 was none the less regarded as marking the death of the old political system in England.

New conditions began to appear after 1832 in English political life: the disappearance of press trials, increased publicity for parliamentary debates, and above all a transformation of the parties and constitutional practice. The Whigs and Tories were followed by Liberals and Conservatives, whose supporters admittedly remained the same, but who, in the absence of a precise programme, were no longer sharply divided: it was easy to pass from one party to the other, especially as each party had a conservative right wing and a progressive left wing. Among the Tories, Lord George Bentinck and the Earl of Derby championed agricultural interests, while Peel was converted to the idea of industrial reform; among the Whigs, Palmerston was regarded as a rigid reactionary Liberal, while Lord John Russell enjoyed the support of the reforming Radicals. Thus, after 1832, the two parties came into equilibrium, and the balance of powers (Crown, Lords, Commons) was replaced by a balance of parties, whose alternation at the head of affairs seemed to become a classic system: henceforth there were to be two ministerial teams, one in office, the other ready to take office, and the royal prerogative was reduced to calling to power the leader of the majority in the Commons. The two parties influenced public opinion through high-quality newspapers which succeeded in retaining their independence: *The Times* and *The Morning Post* for the Conservatives, *The Morning*

Chronicle and *The Examiner* for the Liberals. However, until the end of the first half of the century, the lead was held by the Whigs who were responsible for the new political situation. Grey, then Melbourne, governed from 1830 to 1834, Melbourne from 1835 to 1841, and Russell from 1846 to 1852. Although a sceptic and a dilettante, Melbourne was to guide the first steps of Queen Victoria, who came to the throne in 1837 and married one of her first cousins, Albert of Saxe-Coburg-Gotha, who proved a valuable and discreet adviser. Without leading to any increase in the royal prerogative, the dignity of the royal couple's life would restore the Crown to a popularity and a moral authority which had long since disappeared; the result would be an undeniable reawakening of loyalist feeling to England.

In home affairs, the Whigs pursued a policy of democratic reforms which resulted in the creation of a modern civil service. As early as 1829, Peel had created for the London boroughs a centralized metropolitan police force. In 1834 Unions of parishes were created, with boards intended to administer poor relief in the workhouses; these boards were elected by all the ratepayers and given wide powers, thus reducing the authority of the magistrates. In 1835 the Municipal Corporations Act abolished the privileged hereditary bodies in the old boroughs and replaced them with elected aldermen. Finally, in 1833 and 1839, the first grants were made in aid of public education. Admittedly, the Whig ministers had no intention of abolishing the old institutions, but simply of gradually adapting England to the needs of modern life.

The major problem remained that of protection and Free Trade, a problem to which the legislation of the Canningites had provided only an empirical solution, widely regarded as inadequate. British industry wanted to conquer foreign markets by means of massive sales of cheaply produced goods; it therefore wanted the abolition of the prohibitive import tariffs which were imposed on raw materials and foodstuffs. A fresh crisis, in 1836, accompanied by distress which provoked a renewal of Chartist agitation (see p. 89), alarmed the manufacturers, especially in the cotton industry.

The result was the founding of the Anti-Corn Law League, which was led by a Lancashire employer, the ardent Quaker John Bright, and a former commercial traveller, Richard Cobden, a fiery orator and an excellent propagandist. The Manchester movement erected its own building, the Free Trade Hall, published its own papers and pamphlets, such as the *Free Trade Catechism*, and used meetings, petitions and songs to put over its point of view: it struck the imagination of a religious people with the aid of mottoes such as *Give us our daily bread*, and represented Free Trade to Parliament as a panacea capable of overcoming economic crisis, turning the country's technical progress to good advantage and offering the best antidote to social subversion. The League also condemned commercial exploitation of the Colonies and gave its approval to the experiment in self-government in Canada, provided that the autonomous colonies continued to trade with the mother country; but the theme which it stressed most of all was that of cheap bread, especially as corn had to be imported and had risen steadily in price since 1835. If Cobden refused to support the Chartists, who for their part accused him of putting the working class to sleep with promises of cheaper food, he was equally unwilling to give his allegiance to either of the two great traditional parties; while the latter were reluctant to abandon the sliding scale, which represented the last ditch for the gentry.

However, when the elections of July 1841 brought the Conservatives back to power, Peel showed his independence of mind and broadness of outlook by breaking away, for practical rather than theoretical reasons, from agrarian Toryism, even though his gradual personal conversion to

1834), he gave way, and this cost him his popularity. Arrested by the English authorities and convicted, he appealed to the House of Lords against his sentence, and this completely discredited him. For his part, Peel had realized that concessions were necessary: as Catholics were not allowed to study at Trinity College, Dublin, he had founded three undenominational State colleges and increased the subsidies to the Catholic College at Maynooth (1845). However, the indignation aroused by the agrarian outrages prevented the continuation of a policy of reform. The Irish problem therefore remained unresolved at the time when, as a result of the potato disease, famine struck the country, producing a terrible toll of victims, and a massive emigration which, in two years, reduced the population of Ireland from 8 to 4 million inhabitants.

Leaving aside the Irish question, which the British government proved incapable of solving, it must be noted, at the end of this study, that, while the political evolution of France and Britain between 1815 and 1848 followed a largely parallel course, it was marked by two revolutions in the case of France, whereas it was peaceful in England. There can be no doubt that revolution was avoided in England because the government gave way in time, making the necessary sacrifices. While in France Polignac secretly prepared to violate the Charter, thus limiting its scope, and thought that he could distract the attention of the French people by the conquest of Algiers, in England the crisis of 1830 resulted in a new ministerial coalition which, by a series of compromises, prepared electoral reforms which succeeded in disarming the Radical movement. It remains to be explained why the British rulers were able to carry out reforms in time and why the French politicians were not. Was it a question of national character? Possibly, but before adopting that fragile and superficial explanation, it should be pointed out that the English governing classes were far closer to the economic life of their country than the corresponding French classes, that they were therefore able to understand the tragic nature of certain circumstances, and that they saw more clearly the nature of the social peril. Instead of politicians who had obtained power by means of bargains and deals, and who represented only local interests, England was governed by statesmen whom the disciplined practice of the parliamentary system had provided with the elements of a true political culture.

Chapter VI

LIBERALISM AND NATIONALISM
IN CENTRAL EUROPE

In a large part of Europe, liberal aspirations were so closely associated with national aspirations that they could not be distinguished. These national aspirations had been aroused in the course of the wars of the Revolution and the Empire, either because territorial simplification had favoured the awakening of national consciousness, or on the contrary because the peoples of Europe had become aware of their solidarity in the struggle against foreign occupation. The supporters of the idea of nationalism, in their desire to make the frontiers of the State coincide with those of the nation, could appeal either to the French concept of nationality, which held that the nation was based on the conscious and voluntary consent of the various elements of the population, determined to live under the same laws, or to the Herder concept, which, adopted by the German Romantic writers, compared nationality to a living organism and held that it was based on an unconscious community of race, language or customs. Finally, it is worthy of note that as a result of the reaction which in 1815 banished the memory of imperial oppression, Napoleon appeared, by a process of idealization, as a supporter and a prophet of the idea of nationalism. Certain declarations in the *Mémorial de Sainte-Hélène*, such as : ' I would have liked to make a single national body out of each of these peoples ', were taken to mean that the Emperor had envisaged the unification of Italy or Germany; in any case, the Napoleonic Legend helped to further the nationalistic cause, and also gave France the reputation of a teacher leading the peoples of Europe towards unity.

In central Europe, the nationalist principle played the part of a consolidating force in the case of Germany and Italy, and of a dissolvent in the case of the Austrian monarchy.

I. *The German Vormärz*

The German patriots were bitterly disappointed by the dishonouring of the promises made in 1813. Their desire to see the German Reich re-established had been disappointed; and despite an embryonic federal military and financial organization, the new German federation of 39 Sovereign States, with a Diet at its head presided over by Austria, could only condemn Germany to impotence. As for the liberal promises embodied in Article 13 of the Federal Act of 1815, they had all been broken: Frederick William III of Prussia would only grant his subjects provincial Diets with limited powers (1823); he went on governing with the help of the bureaucracy and aristocracy of the eastern provinces, which provided the upper echelons of the army and the civil service. Only a few sovereigns in southern Germany granted constitutions, and then generally of a purely advisory character, in order to consolidate territories that had been artificially united after Napoleon had secularized them. If public opinion, which was still particularistic, remained indifferent, the old national party was outraged; and Joseph Görres had to stop publishing his *Rheinische Merkur* in 1816, for having expressed his discontent too loudly.

In spite of everything, the nationalist movement continued in university circles, within the German Societies formed immediately after liberation. A sort of purification of the rowdy student societies took place, and under the influence of a professor at Jena, the historian Luden, the *Burschenschaft* was formed, which adopted the uniform of the Lützow corps, as well as the black, red and gold flag, and in which the spirit of patriotic devotion of the age of reform soon crystallized. It was the *Burschenschaft* associations which, in October 1817, organized the Wartburg Festival, where the anniversary of Luther's theses and the Battle of Leipzig were celebrated in a spirit at once religious and romantic, patriotic and liberal. In this movement there was of course no revolutionary plan. But at the University of Giessen, Karl Follen, a student who advocated a unitary democracy, had formed a group of 'intransigents' known as the 'blacks'; one of his admirers, a certain Karl Sand, thought that he was helping to save his country by murdering the reactionary poet Kotzebue, who was known to be an agent of the Tsar (1819).

This murder, which was aggravated by the attempted assassination of the head of the government of Nassau, Ibell, provoked a violent reaction. After making contact with the King of Prussia at Teplitz, Metternich called together the representatives of nine states at Carlsbad; their decisions were later ratified by the Diet. Inspectors were appointed for the universities, the *Burschenschaft* dissolved, the press muzzled, and a federal commission created at Mainz to study the revolutionary movements. It is true that Metternich the next year at the Congress of Troppau, while strengthening the control exercised by the Diet over the German States, could not obtain the abolition of the constitutions of southern Germany. Reaction had none the less triumphed: Arndt was deprived of his chair at Bonn and Görres was forced to flee to Strasbourg. Particularism and reaction made virtually all political life impossible. Neither the existence of State assemblies (*Stände*) in Hanover and Saxony, nor the constitutional régime in southern Germany could limit the authoritarian government of the sovereigns. Nor was there anything to hope for from the princes in favour of German unity.

The 1830 Revolution acted as a spur to the liberal movement, especially as Prussia and Austria, absorbed by foreign affairs, could scarcely take any interest in the fate of Germany. In Brunswick the sovereign was overthrown; in Hesse-Cassel, Hanover and Saxony, liberal constitutions had to be granted. What was the part played by the nationalist idea in these events? At Karlsruhe the deputy Welcker called for an assembly for the Confederation; later, in May 1832, democrats from all over western Germany gathered together at the castle of Hambach, where the tricolour flag was hoisted and toasts were drunk to the sovereignty of the people and the brotherhood of nations. But there were very few people as yet who had any precise ideas on the formation of the national State. Even fewer were those who, like the Swabian author Pfizer, foresaw the role Prussia might play in German unification—a Prussia which, turning liberal, would promptly merge into a unified Germany. For want of co-ordination, the net result of these movements was fresh progress for reaction. The Six Articles which Metternich persuaded the Diet to pass (1832) aggravated the decisions taken in 1820 and created a federal commission to supervise local assemblies. The unsuccessful *putsch* of a few liberals against the Frankfurt Diet (1833) led to the creation of a commission of inquiry which strengthened the measures against the press and the universities. From then on, the political movement had to take refuge abroad, as in the case of the Paris *Deutscher Volksverein*, affiliated with the *Société française des Droits de l'homme*, or else to go underground, as did the poet George Büchner and Pastor Weidig, the publishers of the *Hessische Landsbote*, who gathered comrades and Hesse peasants round them and gave them revolutionary instructions at a meeting at Badenburg (July 1834). The culminating point of the reaction was reached in 1837 when the Hanover Constitution was revoked and seven professors were dismissed, including the historians Dahlmann and Gervinus, who had ventured to protest in the name of the oath they had taken. The reaction struck just as violently at the purely intellectual movement of Young Germany which, inspired by the writings of Heine and Börne, was trying to rid German patriotism of its anti-French chauvinism, and to spread together with the ideas of liberalism the Saint-Simonian doctrines of international peace and free love. In 1835 the Diet banned the *Deutsche Revue* edited by the playwright Gutzkow.

In these years of political discussion which came to be known as the Vormärz, the only notable event was the creation of the *Zollverein* (see p. 32); this was the foundation on which, after 1840, German national consciousness was built. But the start gained by Prussia in the economic sphere would soon face the Germans with the following problem: was there not a contradiction between the material power which that country enjoyed in Germany and the retrograde character of its institutions? As a reactionary power, was Prussia capable of directing the movement towards unification? Were not national aspirations inconsistent with the demands of liberalism?

The latter were expressed with particular force in the States of southwest Germany, where the *Landtage* remained open to political controversy. All eyes were turned towards the Grand Duchy of Baden, where two professors at the University of Freiburg, Rotteck and Welcker, had been publishing their *Staatslexikon*, the breviary of the liberal bourgeoisie after 1834. Although opposed to popular sovereignty and a democratic republic, and attached to the principle of a moderate property qualification for the franchise, these writers, who retained a certain nostalgia for the liberalism of Joseph II, but who owed most of their political culture to French constitutional thought, wanted to base the separation of powers and the sovereignty of the law on the notion of *Recht*, as defined by the German idealists. Rotteck, it is true, was more individualistic than his colleague, and Welcker more susceptible to the example of Anglo-Saxon institutions and the lessons of history. But both men had fought against the oppressive instruments of absolutism, against bureaucracy and the army, seeking to awaken respect for the dignity of man and the dignity of the citizen; their liberalism had tended to take a pacifist and anti-militarist turn, far removed from the ideal of Hegel's *Machtstaat*. What in fact these men brought to German liberalism was the conviction that above the patriarchical will of the sovereign and the requirements of the State, there was a Right which constituted the essence of the State. Finally, for the first time, liberalism in the southwestern States was tending to take the form of a political party, thus breaking up the ancient organization of the *Stände* and dealing a mortal blow to the system on which Metternich had built the Europe of 1815. It is interesting to note that in fact the idea of political parties was linked with the rise of bourgeois society. The basic role of the parties, as they would develop in the various representative assemblies of the *Vormärz*, would be to serve as intermediaries between society and the State, in other words to 'resocialize' a State which the practice of absolutism had completely diverted from social preoccupations, without those parties abandoning their independence with respect to the central power.

After a long period, during which an autocratic form of government continued in different forms in the southwestern States, the liberal party won a series of resounding victories. In Baden, where half the members of the Second Chamber were government officials converted to liberalism, the suspension of two of them in 1843 led to a vote of no confidence proposed by the deputy Itzstein, and the eventual defeat of the Blittersdorf Ministry:

strengthened by the 1846 election, the liberals, led by Bassermann and Mathy, obtained ministries presided over by Nebenius and later by Beck, a modification of the censorship and the police system, as well as reforms in the administration of justice. At Stuttgart demands for similar reforms were made by the deputy Rohmer. In the parliament of Hesse-Darmstadt, resistance to the reactionaries was powerfully led by Heinrich von Gagern, who had defended the institutions left by the French, particularly civil marriage, and who, on his return to the *Landtag* in 1846, appointed himself the champion of an electoral system and a press worthy of a constitutional State: his liberalism was akin to that of the Rhinelanders, with whom he maintained close relations after the Revolution. Progress was slower in Bavaria, where the fall of the clerical Minister Abel (1847) was connected with the senile passion of King Ludwig I (who had previously encouraged the development of Catholicism in his States) for the Andalusian dancer Lola Montez: when his advisers criticised him for proposing to raise her to the nobility and imposing her on the court, he decided to change his government and to seek the support of the liberals.

While these developments were taking place in the States of southwest Germany, how far had Prussia succeeded in winning the sympathies of the liberals? The prestige which her past conferred upon her, her role in the wars of liberation, the number and reputation of her universities, the sense of duty and the spirit of tolerance which inspired many of her officials, and the place she had just acquired in the German economy, placed her in the first rank of German States. Without her participation, the unification of Germany was inconceivable. But it was generally considered that the conversion to liberalism of the State of Frederick the Great was a necessary condition for Prussian pre-eminence in Germany. Would the accession of Frederick William IV (1840) justify these hopes? The government's first decisions—an amnesty, a slackening of the censorship, publicity for the debates of the provincial Diets, and the creation of a united commission meeting every two years in Berlin—undoubtedly produced a change of atmosphere in political circles. But it was not long before it was seen that these hopes were illusory. Frederick William IV was as much the enemy of liberalism as he was of the Prussianism of the type established by Frederick the Great. The new occupant of the throne was a real Romantic, a disciple of Stahl whom he summoned to the University of Berlin in 1840; he was unaware of the social forces released by the Industrial Revolution, and was devoid of any sense of reality. He believed in the possibility of restoring on patriarchal, German and Christian foundations the old institution of the *Stände*, an antidote, in his opinion, to modern constitutionalism. By giving shape to these plans, he would help to incite the forces of change against those of conservatism and thus prepare the way for revolution.

About 1840, however, the *Zollverein* began to bear fruit: the growth of trade and industry had led to the formation in the more highly developed provinces of Prussia of a bourgeoisie which wanted a more active share in the government of the country. It was the Rhenish bourgeoisie which would be the first to assert the need for Prussia to become a constitutional State and which would conduct a persistent campaign to achieve that object. Ever since 1815, this bourgeoisie had consistently defended against the centralizing tendencies of the Prussian government the institutions bequeathed to the Rhenish province by nearly twenty years of French rule during the Revolution and the Empire: the Civil Code, guaranteeing open and public justice; and the municipal equality of town and country, the very principle of the civil equality of all citizens before the law. In the course of this struggle the province had developed a keen sense of autonomy, which had been sharpened by the government's religious policy and which had turned public opinion against an absolutist, feudal and Lutheran Prussia. In short, hostility to Prussia in the Rhineland was based on the bourgeois structure of society, as well as on the Catholicism of the bulk of the population. It did not prevent certain business circles from wishing to collaborate with Prussia on the basis of material interest : as early as 1830, a rich merchant of Aix-la-Chapelle called Hansemann, the president of the town's commercial court, had sent a memoir to the King advocating Prussian hegemony in Germany, but he had made this conditional on Prussia's transformation into a constitutional State, whose centre of gravity should be the middle class; the military State should give place to the industrial State. He repeated his gesture on the accession of Frederick William IV, maintaining that only a constitution could awaken civic feeling in the nation and save it from the danger of revolution. He tried to show that by its influence on railways, tariffs and trade, parliamentary debate was necessary for the good government of the State. Together with Hansemann, a number of bankers, manufacturers and businessmen—Camphausen and Mevissen at Cologne, Beckerath at Crefeld, and von der Heydt at Eberfeld—had put themselves at the head of the Rhenish liberal movement which they represented in the *Landtag* and had led it in the direction of collaboration with the Prussian authorities, helped by the cooling of tempers after the painful ' Cologne Affair ', which had inflamed public opinion for a time (see p. 203). The nationalist idea tended to prevail over particularist preoccupations; and the Rhenish deputies now expressed the hope that the spirit of *Staatsbürgertum* should henceforth inspire the whole Prussian State. In 1845 in the Rhenish *Landtag*, Camphausen called for the summoning of a single parliament for all the Prussian provinces. It was in this national spirit, and in order to provide a more solid, liberal basis for this State in the Rhenish province that in 1842 the ephemeral *Rheinische Zeitung* was founded, to which Marx contributed for a time, and in which Mevissen hoped to combine 'the speculative spirit of Hegelian philosophy and Rhenish business acumen', followed by the *Kölnische Zeitung* in which it was argued that liberal institutions, following the traditions of the Stein-Hardenberg period, should help to consolidate the royal authority and not serve to inspire suspicion of it. The Rhenish liberals were, after all, not democrats: in 1845 they had persuaded the *Landtag* to pass a law on municipal elections which later served as a model for the Prussian law of 1849 known as the 'law of the three classes'.

All these preoccupations revealed the influence of the historian Friedrich Dahlmann, then a professor at the University of Bonn, who followed the political struggles of the forties with the greatest interest. His great work *Die Politik*, published in 1835, put forward the following ideas: that true freedom consisted in self-government; that representative institutions were intended to support and inform the monarchical power; and that the exercise of civic rights was a moral obligation which nobody could evade. As the desire for national unity manifested itself in Germany, as suspicion grew with regard to France, whose alleged Rhenish ambitions displayed during the international crisis of 1840 had aroused popular feeling against her (witness Nikolaus Becker's *Der deutsche Rhein*), and as the north-German Protestant element gradually prevailed, the liberals tended to adopt Anglo-Saxon ideas, which slowly took the place of the French influence still predominant in Rotteck's teaching. Under the influence of Dahlmann's *Zwei Revolutionen*, it became normal practice to set against the essentially bureaucratic and centralized Napoleonic State the benefits of *Selbstverwaltung*, which was said to have originated among the Anglo-Saxon peoples. What is more, Dahlmann, in this respect following the Romantic ideology, held that the State was not a 'necessary evil', nor an 'insurance company', nor an 'artificial machine' liable to be changed at will by men; it was a moral personality, endowed with its own life, and independent of the individuals who depended upon it. Through Dahlmann Romantic overtones, and even appeals to the old German liberties, entered into the ideas of the liberals. Dahlmann was the foremost representative of that 'liberalism of the professors' which, as expressed by the historians Droysen, Waitz and Häusser, would later set the tone for the deliberations of the Frankfurt Parliament. They showed themselves anxious both to create for the State the instruments of its power and to define it as a *Rechstaat*, a 'judicial person' before which monarchical authority should bow. They wanted no abrupt break with the past, and claimed to be advocates of 'organic' development; they admitted that only a modern parliament was capable of awakening in the nation that sense of civic responsibility without which freedom remained a dead letter.

Such were the prevailing tendencies influencing those of the governing classes which had been converted to liberalism. Incidentally, the converts to liberalism included a portion of the Prussian aristocracy. Remarkably enough, after Cologne, it was Königsberg, which stood for the traditions of Kantian philosophy and of the enlightened reformers in politics, that had become the most active centre of constitutional demands: it was there that the liberal doctor, Jacoby, and old President von Schön recalled that the States General were among the fundamental rights of the nation. In the liberal Junkers of the East Prussian *Landtag*—the Auerswalds or Schwerins—who were admirers of the British aristocracy, historians have rightly pointed to a survival of the 'Whig' spirit. Another anglophile was Freiherr von Vincke, who in the Westphalian Diet in 1845 condemned the delay in summoning the States General. But among these liberals, the Rhinelanders undoubtedly formed the leading wing: they expressed the will of the most highly developed part of the nation to attain its political majority and to assume its responsibilities at last. Under their influence liberalism had ceased to be an abstract ideology; it was seen to be intimately linked with the economic structure of the modern State. Consequently it is not surprising that they placed themselves at the head of the opposition when the united *Landtag* met in 1847.

However, bourgeois liberalism was not the only form of opposition during the *Vormärz*. Contemporaries in fact had some difficulty in distinguishing the liberal opposition from the opposition normally described as ' radical '. While liberalism could be defined as the desire of the bourgeoisie to assume its share of political responsibility, radicalism was above all an ideology which had developed in limited intellectual circles. While the liberals wanted legal participation in government and worked for the reform rather than the destruction of the monarchical State, the radicals, adopting an *a priori* revolutionary attitude, supported the ideas of popular sovereignty, universal suffrage, a single chamber, and even a republic; they did not share the liberals' regard for dynasties and wanted a State which would be one and indivisible. The development of radicalism was connected, in the late thirties, with the breaking-up of the Hegelian school: the orthodox disciples formed a conservative right-wing, but certain elements, known as left-wing Hegelians or young Hegelians, interpreted the master's doctrine as a philosophy of revolutionary action. Treating the dialectic as an instrument of action, and retaining from the Hegelian diptych the formula: 'Everything which is rational is real', they considered that philosophy should serve to determine the rational progress of the world. Their first attacks, inspired by David Friedrich Strauss's *Leben Jesu*, had been directed against the established religions and their orthodox champions; but subsequently the offensive had taken on a political and social character. The chief organ of the group was the *Hallische Jahrbücher*, which the philosopher Arnold Ruge published under various titles, first at Dresden, then in Paris. In no other paper was the idea of Christian monarchy founded on a positive faith and the Germanic tradition so fiercely attacked. After formerly praising Prussia, the State of the common weal, Ruge had turned violently against her, holding her to be unfaithful to the spirit of the Reformation and the *Aufklärung* and tainted with pietism and bigotry. Meanwhile, confident in the power of the mind to change living reality, the young Hegelians fondly imagined that the victorious advance of their ideas could produce a transformation of the world. They lacked the support of a clearly defined social class, and this at a period when the bourgeoisie was moving towards a more constructive liberalism, and when the working class had as yet no ideal of its own. A sort of schism accordingly took place among them. Some of them would move towards a kind of extreme individualism and nihilist anarchy : this was the case with the so-called 'emancipated' Berliners who gathered around the brothers Bruno and Edgar Bauer, and around Stirner, the author of *Der Einzige und sein Eigenthum*, which, rejecting any constraint imposed on the individual by religion, society or the State, held that absolute egoism was the only rational motive for human activity. Others—particularly Feuerbach, Moses Hess, and Karl Marx himself—were to found a new critique of society and prepare the way for communism : their role has already been examined.

In any case, it would be a mistake to exaggerate the importance of this radicalism during the last years of the *Vormärz*: if it can be found in the work of certain progressive poets such as Herwegh, Hoffmann von Follersleben and Freiligrath, its influence was strongest in the numerous sects which developed at that time, either among the

Protestants under the name of *Lichtfreunde* or among the Catholics within the framework of *Deutschkatholizismus*. As a result of the exhibition of the Holy Tunic at Trier in 1844—which the historian Sybel had shown to be a fake—the movement of 'German Catholicism', directed by the Saxon priest Ronge and supported by Gervinus because he saw it as a possible starting-point for a supraconfessional German Church, had 200 communities in 1846 with 80,000 members. In 1848 its leaders often formed the echelons of the democratic party. But these were movements which could exert no effective pressure on government decisions.

On the eve of the Revolution the principal source of discontent lay in the practice of absolutism, the general absence of freedom, the feeling of personal insecurity, and the hatred of the police state and its despotic methods. What most antagonised the country as a whole was the unjustifiable prosecutions brought against liberals and patriots, such as List in Württemberg and Jacoby in Prussia, and the atmosphere of quibbling and constraint which the ostentatious orthodoxy of certain governments imposed on intellectual life. It therefore seems that if these governments had abandoned their policy of arbitrary oppression, the Germans would have been content with a process of gradual reform: in fact, in 1848 a very small number of citizens envisaged playing some part in government; and even when the question of ministerial responsibility was raised in Parliament, it was regarded as a legal responsibility, and not as an essential element of the modern State. The German nation certainly did not want an abrupt break with the dynastic world and monarchical institutions, but simply a compromise with them. It none the less wanted to shake off the old tyrannies, replace them with the *Rechtstaat*, and employ the power of the law to ensure the participation of an élite in public life and the substitution of a legal order for the despotic régime which had lasted so long. It was therefore the oppressive nature of the

German governments which created a desire for change and developed throughout the country a revolutionary attitude.

This attitude was given added emphasis by the economic and social crisis which culminated in 1846, shaking the authority of the States to their foundations and often leaving the smell of insurrection. Many liberals considered that, if the worst were to be avoided, the time had come to obtain substantial reforms from the Crown and to shake off the tutelage imposed upon them by a decaying bureaucracy. The situation took a turn for the worse in Prussia when Frederick William IV, after hesitating for a long time, but now hard pressed by financial problems which an appeal to the Rothschilds had failed to solve, decided, in spite of Metternich's protests, to summon a united *Landtag* consisting of all the deputies in the provincial Diets (February 1847). After delaying for a long time their reply to this royal invitation, which they considered inadequate and inconsistent with the promises previously made to the nation, the liberals let it be known as soon as deliberations opened in Berlin that they would not be satisfied with advisory powers for the *Landtag*, and that they demanded regular meetings. To show that they meant business, they refused to vote a loan required for the building of the Berlin-Königsberg railway. However, they failed to persuade the King, who was attached to the theory of divine right in spite of his liberal tendencies, to grant a constitution or even to agree to regular meetings of the *Landtag*. He had been encouraged in his resistance by the aristocracy, and in particular by Otto von Bismarck, who had envisaged the creation of a Prussian conservative party. If, out of fear of riots, the liberals avoided in spite of everything a complete break with the Crown, there none the less occurred an undoubted radicalization of public opinion, as was shown by the success of Heinzen's republican pamphlets. The democrats held a congress at Offenburg in September

1847, where they called for a national parliament common to all the Germanic countries and elected in a democratic manner. In their desire for a unified Jacobin State, the radicals, with the Baden deputies Hecker and Struve, went much further than the liberals from the various provinces of West or South Germany, who, judging by their declaration at Heppenheim (October 1847), would have been content with the convocation of a customs congress.

It was towards the end of that year that the nationalist movement reached its climax, as was shown by the creation at Heidelberg, under the significant name of *Die Deutsche Zeitung*, of a newspaper which brought together, with the historians Gervinus and Häusser, the entire intellectual élite of the country. However, the nationalist movement no longer confined itself to establishing a form of political union between the German States; henceforth it turned its attention to the German communities under foreign domination. In the Danish duchies of Schleswig and Holstein there existed a demographic problem, since the vast majority of the inhabitants were German-speaking apart from 150,000 souls in northern Schleswig, and a problem of succession, since the tradition of inheritance through the male line brought the claims of the Duke of Augustenburg in conflict with those of Christian von Glücksburg. Faced with the threat made by the King of Denmark, Christian VIII, in his open letter of July 1846, to bind Schleswig to his States by a constitution, the German reaction, led by the professors of the University of Kiel, was immediate: there could be no question of separating the two duchies, which Dahlmann had long since shown to be indissoluble. And a Congress of Germanists which was held in 1847 in nearby Lübeck claimed the duchies for Germany.

However, there can be no doubt that the aspirations of the German nation continued to encounter serious obstacles. These included the persistent particularism of the princes and peoples, the complexity of the Austro-Prussian dualism, and the difficulty of providing a framework for the nation; but the principal obstacle was the need for the German bourgeoisie—incontestably the most highly developed and politically aware force in the country—to wrest its place in the sun from the Ancien Régime, at the same time as it had to defend itself on the left against the pressures of social democracy.

II. The Italian Risorgimento

Regarded for a long time as a specifically Italian phenomenon, the *Risorgimento* is now placed to an increasing extent in its European context by present-day writers on Italian history. If it was preceded by the wave of illuminism which influenced the very different States and mentalities of the Ancien Régime, and if enlightened despotism prepared the ground and the men, the force which broke up the old order, crystallizing and accelerating the Revolution, was the external force of the French Revolution. It was the French Revolution which gave Italy the inspiring concept of the nation as a community of citizens held together by the contractual bond and by civil conscience.

Yet in 1815 the emancipation of Italy met even greater difficulties than those encountered by Germany. The retrograde nature of the economy, the separation of social groups, the mediocre quality of the middle class, the influence of the clergy, and the strength of local feeling account for the almost complete absence of national life in 1815. Consequently at first the struggle against the Holy Alliance could only assume a local character directed against the despotic nature of the political and judicial institutions: while the opposition was the same everywhere, there were no concerted movements. Even more than Germany, the Italy of 1815 seemed a 'geographical formula'.

However, closer examination reveals that until 1820

the Restoration was generally moderate, and, within the framework of the Napoleonic administrative and legal systems, maintained in both letter and spirit, continued the tendency of paternalist reform of the age of enlightened despotism. This was particularly the case with the Parma of Marie-Louise and her second husband, Neipperg; and with Lucca and Tuscany, where Leopold's laws were restored, and which were skilfully governed for twenty years by the sceptical, conciliatory Fossombroni. In Lombardy-Venetia, while the fiscal system was severe, the careful, scrupulous Austrian administration confirmed the sale of *biens nationaux* and did not noticeably depart from the legislative tendency initiated by the Kingdom of Italy. In Naples, while the feudal system was partially restored and the *émigrés* indemnified, the Minister Luigi de Medici pursued a policy of 'amalgamation' which aimed at retaining the best men and institutions of the French régime. The picture was darker in Modena and above all in the Papal States, where, in spite of Consalvi's efforts, the government relapsed into inertia and impotence. In Piedmont, which was less affected than the rest of Italy by the 'enlightenment', where the old privileged classes, influenced by the writings of Joseph de Maistre, had not yielded an inch, and where the monarchy remained despotic and militaristic, haunted by old dynastic dreams of territorial aggrandisement, the reaction, more conservative and clerical than anywhere else, seemed unbearable to a Jansenistic, 'Jacobin' bourgeoisie, which in 1796 had given its support to the ideal of the Great Nation. Hence the opposition to Piedmontese tutelage shown by the merchants and shipbuilders of Genoa, and their nostalgia for their old Republican constitution.

Was the *Risorgimento* an ethical phenomenon, in which the concepts of an élite took precedence over the action of the masses and of economic problems? Or are the common people to be credited with a considerable influence on events? What is certain is that the *Risorgimento* was above all the work of a bourgeoisie whose political ideals and material interests coincided in the demand for a new order. Except in certain northern sectors, the rural masses, which formed the bulk of the working population, were too much preoccupied with the everyday problems of their material life to aspire to civic awareness or even to an elementary understanding of events. In the Sardinian States, the cradle of independence, 64 per cent of the men were illiterate, and 77 per cent of the women; and fifty years later, the percentage of illiteracy was still 54 in the north and 86 in the south. The strength of the masses was exerted in violent, contradictory movements, but never constituted a dominant motive force. On the other hand, in educated circles a positive eruption of ideas took place in which political theories and aesthetic preoccupations were mingled. In Milan, Confalonieri, Berchet and Pellico published the *Conciliatore*, which called for the cultural and economic awakening of Lombardy, while in Florence, the bookseller Vieusseux founded the eclectic *Antologia* and, with the Dalmatian philologist Tommaseo and the Tuscan historian Capponi, spread the ideas of moderate liberalism. These authors were the intellectual leaders of the governmental élite of the great years of the Unification. Their works helped the Italians to form an ideal which was no longer merely local but national. As everywhere else in this Europe inspired by the idea of nationalism, history was one of the favourite instruments of the intellectual *Risorgimento*: apart from the works of the professional historians Cantù and Troya, the historical novels of Guerrazzi and Massimo d'Azeglio revealed the glories of Italian history. But it was Romanticism above all which tried to bring together the forces of intelligence, tradition and popular aspirations, and to use literary feeling for the political education of the nation: while Leopardi's proud, lonely pessimism refused to commit itself and Manzoni's religiosity was tinged with a certain conservatism in his *I Promessi sposi*, a whole series of works appeared which throbbed with patriotic fervour, from Berchet's poems to the moving testimony of Silvio Pellico, the prisoner in the Spielberg, and Giusti's vengeful satires.

However, the liberal bourgeoisie could offer no legal opposition to the absolutist governments. It resorted instead to underground activities in which the Romantic mentality drew its strength from the myths of the hero and the conspirator. Italy was the promised land of secret societies. On the ruins of Freemasonry the Carbonari had sprung up, with their Lombard and Piedmontese variations of the Guelfi and the Adelfi, whose secret organisations were perhaps modelled on the trade-guilds of the foresters and charcoal-burners of Franche-Comté. The localization of the Carbonari, divided into *ventes* and provided with a secret vocabulary, was particularly noticeable in the absolutist States such as the Kingdom of Naples, the Papal States and Piedmont. The society was recruited from the middle class, and also from the army, for in the enclosed world of provincial garrisons, the Napoleonic Legend was strengthened by a certain nostalgia for a life of action, and by the liberal aspirations excited by the experience of the revolutionary years. Without any links with the masses, and without any constructive programme, the Carbonari were inspired by a desire for a powerful, democratic State. But their activity was doomed to take the form of isolated, sporadic outbursts of sedition, sparked off by the news of events abroad. Fighting in isolated pockets, they invited defeat. That was what happened in 1820, and again in 1830.

The first revolutionary outbreaks occurred in Naples, where General Pepe tried to take advantage of the events in Spain to rouse the garrisons to revolt. King Ferdinand IV gave way at first to the revolution and promised to establish a constitution, based on the one the Cortes had given themselves in 1812; but after the Congresses of Troppau and Laibach, to which he had been summoned, the Neapolitan liberals, already weakened by the dissidence of an autonomist Sicily, were wiped out by the Austrian army at Rieti (1821).

The Piedmontese Revolution followed a more complex course. Led by veterans of the Napoleonic armies, such as Santorre di Santa Rosa, the liberals counted on the support of Charles Albert, Prince de Carignan, who had spent some of his solitary formative years in France, and who in the eyes of a reactionary court seemed to personify the evil genius of Jacobinism. His brother Charles Felix, outstripped by events, appointed him Regent. But Charles Albert, whose complex personality was made up of contrasts and darkened by Romantic melancholy, played a double game and, it seems, made contact with the counter-revolutionaries. The Austrians accordingly found it easy to restore the old order (1821). But the liberals, subjected to repressive measures, reproached their king with his defection; and this led him to a systematic withdrawal into himself and to a despotic authoritarianism, shot with remorseful contradictions, which gave rise to the legend of the 'Italian Hamlet'.

Ten years later came the July Revolution in France, which aroused tremendous hopes. From Paris, the Committee for Italian Emancipation had conducted a powerful propaganda campaign, leading the liberals to suppose that they could count on Francis IV; but, cruelly disappointed, they rose in revolt. The insurrection spread to Bologna, where the Pope's authority was overthrown and the United Provinces of Central Italy were proclaimed (February 1831), as also in Parma, from which Marie Louise was forced to flee. The movement was therefore more extensive this time. But the lack of agreement between the rebels and the indifference of the masses condemned this insurrection to failure; and the inhabitants of the Romagna disarmed the troops of the two neighbouring duchies when they retreated on to their territory. The Austrians had no difficulty in restoring order. But at least this rebellion had raised the Italian question to the level of international affairs: in opposition to Austrian intervention, Louis-Philippe had sent a regiment to Ancona, a spectacular gesture in defence of French interests, although it was of no help to the rebels.

The failure of the revolutions of 1821 and 1831 revealed the ineffectiveness of the Carbonari and pronounced sentence of death on the society. Its place was taken by a new movement which endeavoured to put forward essentially Italian solutions. Political emigration was the hard school in which the political philosophy of Italian unification was gradually evolved. In contact with people of other countries, the restricted limited culture of the former Carbonari, which had been confined to nostalgia for Napoleonic Italy and hatred for Metternich's system, was enriched by a European content. No doubt it would be incorrect to depict these *Fuorusciti*, so different in origins and wealth, as a coherent force; divided by personal rivalries and controversies, soured by the uncertainty of exile, and spied upon by the various police forces of Europe, the refugees wandered across the Continent, often lending just causes their armed assistance. The fact remains that the centres where they were led to settle contributed to the formation of a coherent political philosophy. After Geneva, Paris became in 1830 one of the great centres of Italian emigration: there the economist Pellegrino Rossi succeeded Say in his chair at the Collège de France, later becoming a Peer of France, while Carlo Botta was Rector of Rouen Academy and Libri a professor at the Sorbonne. In these intellectual circles, Victor Cousin's influence was predominant and attracted to the 'happy mean' those who wished to escape both the tutelage of the Church and the excesses of democracy. In Brussels, the Marquis Arconati-Visconti presided over a brilliant circle which included

Berchet, Pepe, and after 1834 the liberal priest Vincenzo Gioberti. In London, around Antonio Panizzi, Mérimée's friend and the reorganizing genius of the British Museum, there gathered a host of friends who drew their strength from the spirit of political and economic liberalism reigning in England.

It would fall to Giuseppe Mazzini to endow the revolutionary movement with a spiritual quality. This Genoese, after arousing the wrath of the Piedmontese government by his contributions to advanced papers, had fled in 1831 to Marseilles, where he founded 'Young Italy'. In 1834 he extended his activities by the creation in Berne of 'Young Europe'. In 1836 he was forced to leave for London. But already, by his disinterestedness and his austerity, he had exerted a positive fascination on his contemporaries everywhere. He reproached the Romantics for not believing sufficiently in Italy's political mission, and the Carbonari for staging local risings without any overall plan. As for himself, he claimed to offer his fellow citizens a lofty ideal, that of nationalism, which he defined as the use of all individual forces for a common end, faith in the fatherland. But in his opinion each people had a duty to mankind, for it was the instrument which God used to fulfil his plan on earth. Nationalism, he wrote, 'is the share which God grants a people in the work of mankind; it is that people's mission, the task it must perform on earth so that God's purpose may be fulfilled, the achievement which gives it the freedom of the city of mankind, the baptism which endows it with its character and assigns it a place among the peoples, its brothers.' It would therefore be a crime for Italy to abandon her mission; the third Rome, heir to the Rome of the Caesars and the Rome of the Popes, must be the inspiration of a reformed humanity. To be equal to her task, Italy had to become 'independent, united, free': rejecting the possible support of the sovereigns and any concept of federation, Mazzini wanted a united Italian

Republic. He counted on purely moral forces to attain his ends. 'God, the People, Mankind': such was the trilogy he placed at the head of his doctrine. Not that he had any faith in the Catholic Church, which he held responsible for the fragmentation of Italy; but, a Jansenist by breeding, he wished to win over the lower clergy, whose interests he defended against the hierarchy. This vision of the future Italy, through the disinterested enthusiasm it aroused and the appeal it made to the whole nation without any division of class, forged a certain concept of Italy from which it has been impossible for any Italian to free himself since Mazzini.

Unfortunately this great patriot, who had no political genius and little knowledge of human nature, did nothing in practice but copy the methods of the Carbonari, resorting like them to secret societies and conspiracies. As early as 1833, the discovery of a plot organized by his friend Ruffini obliged the latter to commit suicide in order to avoid execution. The following year, the Savoy *putsch* forced Garibaldi to flee to America from Genoa; at the same time the Rossaroll brothers failed at Naples in their attack on Ferdinand II. A similar setback was suffered in 1837 in Sicily, where the King suppressed what municipal autonomy remained; in 1841 at Aquila, where the insurrection enabled the Neapolitan police to discover the links between Mazzini's supporters and the revolutionaries of the south of France; and in 1843-44 in Calabria, where, after an initial period of repression, the Bandiera brothers, with a band of exiles, died crying: 'Long live Italy!' In his abstract theory of the revolution of the masses, Mazzini had failed to take into account the real condition of Italian society in which the peasantry, inert and illiterate, would remain deaf to incitements to revolt, when it did not help the forces of order to crush the rebels.

The failure of these various revolts resulted in a certain discouragement. But if fate frowned on the eternal con-

spirator, another movement sprang up—the *Risorgimento*—
which far surpassed the previous movement in scope. It
was in fact partly a product of the growing development
of the Italian economy, of the building of the first railways,
and of the scientific congresses which were held regularly
after 1839 in the various Italian capitals and which helped
to destroy parochialism by bringing national questions to
the fore. These seemed to be inseparable from the organization of customs tariffs in Italy on the pattern of the
Zollverein. From the economic point of view, the Milanese
periodicals had considerable importance as a formative influence. Finally an Agricultural Association founded in
Turin enabled the various economic circles in northern
Italy to make contact with one another.

It was in the form of Neo-Guelfism[1] that this extension
of political thought expressed itself. Catholic opinion had
been guided in a liberal direction by Menaisian propaganda
and the influence of the Abbé Rosmini, a clear-sighted
observer of the enslavement of the Church in an absolutist
Italy. A whole school of historians had endeavoured to reawaken respect for the traditions of medieval Guelfism:
the Neapolitan Troya pointed to the struggles waged by
the Lombard communes against the Emperor as a pledge of
confidence and hope. It was the Dalmatian writer Tommaseo who in 1835, having settled in Paris, launched the
idea of a reforming Pope leading the regeneration of the
country. Thus public opinion, moulded by Romanticism,
found itself ready to understand the appeal made by the
Piedmontese priest Gioberti (1843). Trusting in the
' primacy' of Italy, the mother nation of the human race,
Gioberti called for the union of all Italians, which pre-
supposed the union of the civil nation around the Papacy.
Hence, in his opinion, the need for a confederation of the

---

[1] In the struggles of medieval and Renaissance Italy the partisans
of the Pope were styled Guelfs and those of the Emperor
Ghibellines.

Italian princes under the leadership of the Pope, with the House of Savoy entrusted with the task of defending its material and political interests. Neo-Guelfism was adopted by a large section of the middle class and the nobility, which thought in national terms, but which dreaded any sort of revolutionary upheaval and saw the Papacy as a guarantee of the stability of political and social institutions.

Public opinion was also influenced by the evolution of the Piedmontese monarchy. Charles Albert (1831-1849) admittedly had nothing of a liberal about him; however, jealous of his authority, he wished to avoid falling under exclusive influences. His Minister, Solaro della Margherita, although a conservative, was induced to follow a progressive policy, abolishing feudalism in Sardinia, publishing the Albertine codes, and pursuing the economic development of the country on free trade lines. Gioberti's *Primato* helped, incidentally, to reinforce these tendencies of Piedmont's policy, and, what is more, gave it a national, anti-Austrian direction : Charles Albert loathed Metternich, who had tried to prevent him from taking possession of his throne. Piedmontese diplomacy found itself in conflict with Austria on the question of railways (was Genoa or Trieste to be the terminus of the transcontinental lines?), on the supplying of the Ticino with salt, and finally on the import of Piedmontese wines burdened with heavy tariffs by Austria. However ambiguous the royal policy might be, and however reactionary the State of Sardinia remained, Piedmont was destined to draw Italian sympathies towards herself.

In 1844 in *Speranze d'Italia*, Balbo had shown that unity, which he declared to be more important than liberty, depended on the exclusion of the Austrians, for whom, however, some compensation would have to be found in the Near East; according to him, Italian federation would be achieved by the King of Piedmont. In 1846, after the revolt of the Papal States, Massimo d'Azeglio, an artist, novelist and politician, published his book *I Casi di*

Romagna, in which, after criticizing the Roman Government, he asked his fellow countrymen to give up local insurrections and to put their trust in Charles Albert. Among the Piedmontese nobility, who controlled the administration and the economy of the country, these ideas henceforth found a powerful echo: young Count Cavour, after completing his economic and political education in France and England with men such as Rossi, de Tocqueville, Senior and Cobden, had come home to farm his estate at Leri; instead, he took up a position in the Press on the great problems of his times, in favour of free trade, the railways and a nationalist policy, and by founding the *Risorgimento* (1847), he would give the 'Albertist' party an organ. As for Gioberti, he himself was led to revise his opinions: in his *Prolegomena* (1845), he held up the reactionary princes to the execration of the patriots, and in his *Gesuita Moderno* (1846) the hated Society of Jesus which was the principal support of the temporal power of the Popes, a power which writers such as Durando and Torielli prophesied would disappear, with the consequent advantage of simplifying the Italian political map. However, Piedmont was still a long way from commanding unanimous support. Mazzini remained the implacable opponent of the Sardinian monarchy; while the Lombards Cattaneo and Ferrari were democrats and federalists, the former extending his programme to a regenerated Europe, the latter criticizing Charles Albert's *Farà da sè* and counting on French aid to expel the Austrians.

However, of the three tendencies dominating Italian politics—Mazzinian unitarianism, Gioberti's Neo-Guelfism, and the movements in support of Piedmont—it was the second which, on the eve of the events of 1848, seemed destined to win the day. It was in fact the election of Pope Pius IX in 1846 which gave concrete form to national and liberal aspirations. Although Cardinal Mastaï was a long way from being a liberal, the spirit of simple Christianity in which he approached Roman problems, the amnesty declared immediately after his accession, and his first measures of reform promptly won him enormous popularity. Moreover, the occupation of Ferrara on Metternich's orders, against which he protested, set him up against his will as a champion of Italian unity and brought him a pathetic letter from Mazzini. Henceforth, to meet the Romans' expectations, he was obliged to go beyond his original intentions : hence the *Motu proprio* of October 1847 creating a State Council, and that of December 1847 providing for the admission of laymen to the government, although these reforms, which were incoherent and doled out in driblets, failed to satisfy an increasingly excited and stormy public opinion. However, the original impetus had been given from May to October 1847, in Turin and Florence alike, liberal reforms followed one after another, and Charles Albert replaced Solaro della Margherita with a more advanced cabinet. Was it possible to combine the policies of the different States? Negotiations which were opened towards the end of 1847 between Rome, Turin and Florence, on the subject of a future customs union, seemed to mark an important stage on the road to unification.

III. *Struggle of Nationalism under the Austrian Monarchy*

While in Germany and Italy centripetal forces were at work, in the Austrian Empire the nationalist principle set in motion centrifugal forces which, if they represented no threat as yet to the existence of the State, already clearly demonstrated the difficulties which people of different languages and races experienced in living together.

The Austrian State had not developed to any noticeable degree since the reforms carried out in the late eighteenth century under the aegis of enlightened despotism. It was based on the strength of dynastic sentiment, the authority of the aristocracy and the great institutions of the State: the bureaucracy, the army, the Catholic Church. The government remained an absolutist government, assisted by several institutions with ill defined functions: chancelleries occupied with particular regions, ministries entrusted sometimes to a college or sometimes to an individual, an advisory State Council, and a State Conference taking government decisions. There was no participation by the nation in the government of the State: the *Landtage* of the various *Länder* had a purely advisory capacity; only in Hungary, where the historic constitution had been preserved, were the laws passed by a Diet consisting of two chambers. In these assemblies the only effective role was played by the nobility: in Hungary it was the nobility which directed the work of the *Comitatus*, and throughout the Monarchy it retained a dominant social position, collecting the feudal dues, in money in the German countries, in work (*robot*) in the Slav countries. Finally it was the nobility, especially the German nobility, which provided the high officials, officers and prelates, whom the Josephine laws kept under the strict control of the State.

Within the monarchy, Metternich's system aimed at preserving in their entirety the Austrian traditions of government, and consequently at preventing any supervision of public life by the nation. It would be a mistake to see the Chancellor as a systematic opponent of the nationalist principle, and in this respect he never ceased to set against the Emperor's narrow ideas the concept of a dynamic and spiritual unity, maintaining a balance between large bodies endowed with administrative autonomy, and cultivating within each of these bodies the useful aspects of their temperaments and special traditions. In short, Metternich's intention was not to impose a centralist uniformity on the various States under Habsburg rule; in his opinion, each nation should follow its own cultural bent, and in his eyes federation represented the political personality of Austria as well as providing a solid basis for the concert of Europe. But his hatred for constitutions prevented him from giving any real impetus to modern representative institutions.

As long as Francis I was alive, namely till 1835, Metternich retained complete control of affairs, provided that he spared the feelings of the old monarch, who wanted to give the impression of exercising a personal power of which he was no longer capable. Things changed when young Ferdinand I (1835-49) came to the throne. He was a mental and physical defective who was incapable of reigning, but Metternich, out of respect for the hereditary principle, had insisted on his succession in spite of everything. Power passed into the hands of the Council of State, consisting of three people: Archduke Louis, the late Emperor's brother, Metternich and Graf Kolowrat. Now the latter, a great nobleman from Bohemia, who had been Minister of the Interior since 1826, had made himself indispensable by his financial ability; and to win personal popularity he made a show of liberal tendencies. Probably out of indolence, Metternich made no attempt to get his rival dismissed; but soon the struggle for influence between the two men took the form of complicated intrigues which Archduke Louis witnessed with a certain satisfaction. It was to please the court, which had become very bigoted, that towards the end of his life Metternich adopted a favourable attitude towards the Church. Abandoning the Josephine principles to which he had been attached for a long time, he opened the way to the influence of Rome and showed increased intolerance towards non-Catholic elements.

Power was left to an underpaid bureaucracy of poor quality and little prestige. Its only remarkable element was the police force organized by Sedlnitzky. Among the higher officials there were, it is true, some men of ability, but they received little support from the government. One of the most noteworthy bureaucrats of this period, Kübeck, devoted his activity to developing the economic resources of the country; and in certain spheres, such as the railways, he succeeded, thanks notably to the support of Solomon Rothschild, the friend of Gentz and Metternich, who in 1841 obtained the title of 'honorary citizen' of the city of Vienna. But the government, which did not dare to increase taxation for fear of stirring up discontent, and which raised the funds it needed by means of loans, could never manage to balance the budget, lower customs tariffs, or secure Austria's entry into the German *Zollverein*.

The foreigner who visited Vienna during this period was struck by the quiet romantic charm of the *Biedermeier* style, by the rapturous applause to which the satirical plays of Raimund and Nestroy were performed, by the way in which Schubert's *Lieder* reflected Viennese feeling and taste, above all by a passion for dancing nourished by the waltzes of Lanner and Strauss. Vienna kept its character of a cultural Sybaris, a town that smiled, that enjoyed itself; a town where a sense of religion was not the less genuine for allowing aristocrats to sow their wild oats and ordinary people to have fun. In reality the censorship and the police between them had all but extinguished any sort of public life. Among the principal victims of reaction was the theologian Bernard Bolzano, professor at the German university of Prague, who based his apologetics on the dictates of reason and morality rather than on revelation. The intellectual life of Austria wilted under a régime that had no respect for privacy and whose absolutism was only qualified, as a Viennese wit put it, 'by the nonchalance of the authorities'. On the other hand nothing would be more misleading than to believe that the mind of the nation had frozen into immobility. The liberal tradition of Joseph II was still far too strong for a passive acceptance of total reaction. Athanasius Grün (Graf von Auersperg) suggested in his *Spaziergänge eines Wiener Poeten* (1831) that only the granting of public liberty could resolve the disturbing conflict between the various nationalities. The most moving testimony was that of Grillparzer, for he could not be suspected of indifference towards the Habsburg dynasty, which he had glorified in his famous play *König Ottokars Glück und Ende*, and in which he saw the symbol of a great, powerful and prosperous Austria. Nor could he be regarded as a democrat, since he held that personal loyalty to the sovereign and instinctive obedience were the mainstays of the State. Yet he bitterly denounced Metternich, that 'Don Quixote of legitimacy', stigmatizing his frivolity, his lack of principles and his taste for intrigue, which led him to misread all the unmistakable signs of the times. And his thoughts turned towards Joseph II, the great reforming Emperor, who had at least tried to create for his peoples a great German fatherland. In the years preceeding the Revolution, opposition to the régime became more vocal. In 1842 a pamphlet by a Tyrolean aristocrat, Baron Andrian, on Austria and her future, pointed to a decline in Austrian national feeling and expressed the hope that in order to combat this lethargy, the provincial Diets might be given increased autonomy and that a national *Reichstag* might be created with legislative powers. Echoing such suggestions as these, the Diet of Lower Austria, which had spontaneously opened its doors to deputies from the bourgeoisie, called in 1847 for publication of the Treasury accounts. In short, enlightened public opinion, well aware of the weaknesses of the 'system' had the impression that the machinery of government was operating to no purpose, for want of direction and control from above. The government had ended up by creating an administrative tyranny conceived not as a means of action but as an end. 'I have sometimes held Europe in my hands,' Metternich admitted, 'but never Austria.'

However, the only serious threat to the multinational

Empire consisted in the unrest among the various nation-alities.

Hungary was the only one of the Habsburg States which constituted a distinct kingdom, with its own Diet and its autonomous administration divided into fifty-five *Comitatus*. In spite of the absence of a middle class, political traditions in the country were of long standing and public opinion highly developed. Everywhere the nobility played a domin-ant role, but there was considerable rivalry between the few hundred grandees who possessed vast estates and a poverty-stricken, unruly aristocratic plebs. The Diet, after a long period of eclipse, was summoned in 1825 and promptly protested against Viennese absolutism: it asked at once for Hungarian to take the place of Latin in its deliberations and subsequently obtained a whole series of concessions of a linguistic nature. However, the opposition remained divided for a long time. Count Széchenyi, a great landed proprietor, and an admirer of the British aristocracy, hoped for social reforms which would improve the status of the peasantry, whose condition was steadily deteriorating, and would permit the substitution of paid work for serf-dom; he believed that feudalism had to give place to a commercial and capitalist system. He also claimed to be making an active contribution to the economic revival of the country by the development of steam navigation on the Tisza and the Danube and the canalization of those rivers (it was he who built the suspension bridge between Buda and Pest); and in order to promote the intellectual emanci-pation of Hungary as well as the purification of the Magyar tongue, he founded the Budapest Academy. On the other hand, this grandee, whose actions were the subject of heated discussion among his fellows, considered that political demands should be temporarily shelved, to avoid annoying Vienna. As for Count Eötvös, an admirer of the French doctrinaires, he advocated a centralized liberal government. These men were opposed by the mass of minor aristocrats, who were hostile to any social reform which might reduce their income. It was to this latter group that the lawyer Kossuth belonged; but under the influence of western ideas he adopted an increasingly democratic programme and ended up by demanding in his paper *Pesti Hirlap*, the first great Hungarian journal, the formation of a Magyar Ministry and an autonomous customs system. He also came out in favour of emancipation of the serfs in return for compensation largely paid by the State, in which policy he was supported and indeed outstripped by certain intellectuals, such as the schoolmaster Tancsics, the author of the *Book of the People*, and the poet Petöfi. The variety of these opinions was not calculated to displease Metternich, who took advantage of it to make no concessions at all, except in the matter of language. But when, reinforcing his centralizing policy, he tried to tackle the institution of the *Comitatus* by dispatching 'administrators' appointed by the Crown, he came up against formidable opposition in the Diet of 1847, led in a masterly manner by Kossuth. Not that this prevented the latter from advocating coercive measures against the minorities under Hungarian rule.

In the Slav countries, where the nation had often lost all awareness of its personality and tradition had taken refuge only among the rural classes, philologists, historians and men of letters devoted themselves to a patient labour of exhumation and reconstruction. They drew their inspiration either from Herder's ideas on the primitive origins of the Slav peoples, which his pupil Meinert had expounded at the University of Prague, or from the contemporary Romantic concepts of the formation of nations; and finally they acted under the influence of the French Revolution, a great source of patriotic fervour. Here, therefore, the work of scholars and men of letters prepared an intellectual revival which would lead to a political revival.

In Bohemia, the precursor of Slavonic studies was the Abbé Dobrovsky, who, starting with linguistics, demonstrated the close affinity of the Slav peoples. In the following generation, Romanticism introduced the cult of nationality, a term which Jungmann made the rallying-cry of the subsequent struggles for the rights of the Czech language and nation. In 1818 the National Museum was founded in Prague, whose *Bulletin*, written in Czech, became the focal point of national scholarship; its first librarian, Hanka, although he published several apocryphal poems, popularized Slavonic studies. The greatest Slavonic scholar of the Romantic era was P. J. Safarik, a Slovak Protestant, who depicted the Slav nation as pious, peace-loving and hard-working. In *The Daughter of Slava*, another Slovak Protestant, the poet Kollar, described the calvary of his fellow Slavs, oppressed by the Germans and the Hungarians; and it was on the idea of the reciprocal enrichment of the various Slav languages that he based his theory of literary reciprocity, a manifesto of intellectual Panslavism. As for the historian Palacky, he demonstrated that the history of his nation was founded on the conflict between Czechs and Germans; he was the first to define the historic rights of the Kingdom of Bohemia. However, on the eve of the 1848 Revolution, Kollar's Panslavism was opposed by the journalist Havliček, who was suspicious of Romanticism; a declared opponent of Tsarist Russia and an advocate of specific democratic reforms for the benefit of the Czechs, he outlined the programme of these reforms in the *Prague Gazette*. However, none of these writers went so far as to call for independence. How, then, was political opposition demonstrated in Bohemia? In the Diet it was led by the aristocracy, whether German or Czech, which ever since the reign of Joseph II had been resentful of Viennese absolutism: in 1847 a delegation from the Diet laid the States' demands before Ferdinand. But in Prague the bourgeoisie, grouped together in the

Besedas, had become the predominant element: already a liberal element and a radical element could be distinguished within it.

The educated Czechs and Slovaks used the same literary language. However, in 1845 the Slovak Stur, wishing to defend his people against the threat of Magyarization, brought Catholics and Protestants together and urged them to adopt as their written language the popular dialect of central Slovakia, thus creating a linguistic schism. But the Slovak demands found no echo in Hungary: in 1847 the Magyar tongue was imposed on the Slovaks as their official language.

As for the Slavs of the south, divided between the Catholic and Orthodox faiths, and without an educated governing class, their spiritual emancipation made slower progress. However, the idea of a community of language and tradition, favoured by the existence of an independent Serbia and the provisional formation of an Illyrian State, revealed by the Slovene Kopitar and the frontier Serb Vuk Karadjitch, found its most active representative in the person of Ljudevit Gaj, a former student at various German universities and a disciple and rival of Kollar. At Zagreb, where he settled down, helped by Count Draskovitch, he adopted as the 'Illyrian' language the dialect of Ragusa, Stokavian; and then, in his *Illyrian National Gazette* and his *Danica*, he preached the doctrine of Illyrism, in other words the union of the Slavs of the South. However, he failed to convince all his fellow Slavs; and Karadjitch himself, as a Serbian patriot, did not want the formation of a single nation. In Croatia itself, the movement quickly assumed an anti-Magyar character: in the Zagreb Diet, the Croats called for the use of their national language. After initially supporting Illyrism, the Vienna government, under Hungarian pressure, was obliged to prohibit the Illyrian language and emblems. It should be added that among the nobles at Zagreb there existed a Magyar party which regarded good relations with Pest as a surety of a peaceful future for Croatia.

Certainly in the long run nothing could be more dangerous for the unity of the Empire than these national movements, in which the various peoples of the Monarchy turned against one another: Magyars and Czechs against Germans; Serbs, Croats and Rumanians against Magyars. What attitude did the Vienna government adopt towards this tendency to autonomy? Metternich took pleasure in favouring the literary revival, and he thought it fitting to allow the different peoples to use their own language. In 1817 he drew up a memoir in which he criticized the exaggerated centralization of institutions; but this criticism was not followed up, and until 1848 there was no overall policy regarding the question of nationalities. Not that Metternich worried very much about this, for there were sufficient sources of division between the nationalities for him to be able to impose his decisions: thus in the 'republic' of Galicia, which was annexed in 1846, Vienna used the Ruthenian peasantry against the nobility which wanted to reconstruct an independent Poland. Finally confidence in Austria's multinational vocation was not yet shaken; it was considered that the subject nationalities, and particularly the Slav peoples, could best attain maturity within the framework of the Monarchy; and that was the opinion not only of the Germans concerned with the question of *Mitteleuropa*, such as Andrian, Werburg and Schuselka, but also of the intellectual élite of the Slav world which favoured 'Austro-Slavism'. Some indeed went further and, like Karl Moering in his *Sybillinische Bücher aus Oesterreich* (1848), set out to make Austria the spearhead of German culture and the starting-point of a new wave of colonization in the Balkans: ideas inherited from List and developed in the *Augsburger Allgemeine Zeitung* by the

Stuttgart bookseller J. G. Cotta. The memory of the part
played by Austria in the defence of Christendom, the feeling that she represented a bulwark against the threat of
Pan-Slavism, in short the current concept of her ' mission '
—all this was still too much alive for anyone to doubt her
survival.

Chapter VII

TSARIST RUSSIA

In a Europe which was in the process of changing, Russia remained the most stable element, the State in which the Ancien Régime had been most fully maintained. Although the economic and social status of Russia was altering as a result of the collapse of the feudal system, the political system had remained unchanged. The empire of the Tsars continued to be based on the same principles: a national tradition, which gave Russia the mission of protecting the Slav peoples still under foreign rule; a religious tradition, which presented the Tsar as the heir to the empire of Byzantium and the defender of Orthodoxy; and an autocratic tradition, which held that the imperial ukases were the only form of the law.

Somewhat mismanaged by Alexander I, the régime reached its zenith under Nicholas I (1825-55). In 1848 Russia seemed to be the principal bulwark of the society of the old order.

At the end of the Napoleonic wars, Alexander I went through a phase of mysticism: under the influence of Prince Galitzin and Madame de Krüdener, who inspired him with the idea of the Holy Alliance, he adopted a sort of interdenominational Christianity. Not that he had abandoned his liberal ideas: he still looked forward to the emancipation of the serfs, an idea which, under Adam Smith's influence, was winning increasing support in Russian society, and he introduced the reform into the Baltic provinces; in 1818 he opened the first Diet of the Kingdom of Poland and referred to the possibility of extending the constitutional régime to the whole Empire, a plan for which Novosiltsov was instructed to make preparations. But these were only isolated whims. Arakcheiev, the instrument of the Tsar's will and the brutal organizer of the Russian military colonies, imposed a police régime to which Galitzin, the Minister of Education, subjected the censorship and the universities. After the revolt of the Guard at Petersburg (1820), which he got wind of at the Congress of Troppau, Alexander was won over to reaction. Arakcheiev's fortunes reached their highest point in 1824 when he succeeded in having Galitzin exiled for suspected heresy.

However, the reaction did not succeed in preventing the development of liberal ideas among the better elements of the noble intelligentsia, brought up in the spirit of the French bourgeois revolution and Radishchev's works, and impressed by the spectacle of constitutional monarchy as they had seen it working in the great western States. Secret societies were founded at an early date in Russia, against which the Tsar, conscious of having previously favoured the errors of liberalism, took only feeble measures. The more advanced of these liberal aristocrats soon passed from disapproval of serfdom to the idea that the abolition of Tsarism and the revolutionary transformation of Russia had become a necessity. When in 1821 the Union of the Public Good pronounced its own dissolution, two secret societies were formed: the Society of the North, which was based in St. Petersburg, and the Society of the South, which had its headquarters at Tulczyn, an important garrison town in the Ukraine. The former, led by Nikita Muraviev, aimed at the establishment in Russia of a constitutional monarchy of the parliamentary type, with two assemblies and a sovereign who should reign without ruling; its programme included the abolition of serfdom, equality before the law, and the granting of the principal liberties, but, conservative in social matters, it envisaged only the granting of a small plot of land to each peasant household.

The second society, which Colonel Pestel had provided with its doctrine in his *Russian Reality*, proposed not only the abolition of serfdom, but also the division of all land under cultivation into two categories, the one to be handed over to the State and the other to be divided between the workers. A convinced enemy of the monarchy, he dreamt of a vast Russian republic which an elected assembly would endow with a constitution and which would be based on a broad administrative autonomy of the various regions. According to him, an independent Poland should be joined to the Russian State by a simple federal link: consequently, by virtue of his nationalist ideas, he succeeded in attracting the Society of the United Slavs, founded by the Barisov brothers and very influential in Poland, whose aim was to bring all Slavs together in a vast federal system. Whatever the differences between these various groups, the so-called 'Decembrists' formed a huge organization in 1825, many of whose members belonged to the highest ranks of the army and navy—representatives of the most aristocratic families in Russia and the richest landed proprietors in the Empire, but who now wished to give up, in the name of justice, their status as a ruling caste which a system based on autocracy and serfdom had afforded them. The Decembrists were well aware of the sacrifice they were making: in one of his poems in praise of liberty and civic feeling, the poet Ryleiev wrote: 'We know that death awaits those who are the first to rebel against the oppressors of the people.' The Decembrists were inspired by an undeniable idealism. Their weakness lay in the fact that, with a very few exceptions, they made no attempt to make contact with the masses: they were aristocratic revolutionaries. They wished to bring about the revolution by means of a military *coup d'état*, the tradition of which was still strong in Russia: for a whole century, the Guard had done nothing but raise tsars and empresses to the throne, so now why could it not bring about the downfall of tsarism with the help of those regiments which always obeyed a strong hand? Moreover, the Decembrists were not entirely mistaken in thinking that they would find no effective support among either the peasants or the bourgeoisie.

The sudden death of Alexander I (December 1825) and the confusion in government circles after the renunciation of the crown by the heir to the throne, the dead Tsar's brother Constantine, obliged the conspirators to come out into the open. The members of the Society of the North started the revolt in Petersburg on the day the new Tsar, Nicholas I, took the oath. At the summons of the rebel officers, over three thousand soldiers came out into Senate Square: after a heroic resistance, they were dispersed by artillery fire. A few days later, a rising led by the Society of the South was crushed in the Ukraine by government troops. After a mockery of a trial, five Decembrists, including Pestel and Ryleiev, were hanged in July 1826; others were imprisoned or sent to Siberia; many of the soldiers who had taken part in the revolt were flogged, while the officers were posted to disciplinary regiments in the Caucasus.

Realistic, punctilious, and not lacking in political understanding, Nicholas I held uncompromising convictions. Absolutism was a dogma for him; it was his duty to preserve the traditional forms of the régime and to train his subjects in ' good principles '. ' Revolution is at the gates of Russia,' he said; ' but I swear that it shall not enter as long as I have a breath of life left within me.' From the Decembrist revolt he retained a persistent mistrust of the aristocracy, which he intended to turn into a caste of State servants. Changing his political personnel, he placed his trust in General Benckendorff, the chief of the police; and he created a third section of the Chancellery, assisted by a police force, which was charged with the security of the State and the surveillance of public opinion.

The insurrection of the Kingdom of Poland in November 1830 was to make the Russian tyranny still harsher and more suspicious. Not that Poland, with its autonomous status, had any reason to complain of her government: Lubecki, the Minister of Finance, had put into effect a remarkable economic policy. But opposition had arisen in the liberal sphere (a demand for an extension of the Diet's rights) and in the national sphere (a claim to Lithuania and the Ukraine). It was more or less anti-Russian, among both the 'Reds' and the 'Whites'. Planned by the Military Academy in Warsaw, and sparked off by news of the intervention of Russian troops in Belgium, the insurrection forced the viceroy Constantine to leave Warsaw. If the administrative council, which took up the reigns of government and gave General Chlopicki dictatorial powers, did not want to break with Nicholas, the same was not true of the Diet, which proclaimed the deposition of the Romanovs and formed a national government including Prince Adam Czartoryski and the Republican Lelewel. But the Diet failed to win the support of the peasant masses by means of suitable reforms, and Europe did not budge. After some indecisive fighting, Warsaw fell (September 1831). A constitution was then granted, which admittedly left Poland her legal code, her language and her communal administration, but its liberal provisions were repeatedly violated; General Paskievitch subjected the country to a reign of terror and enforced Russianization. Henceforth it would be in foreign lands that the Polish spirit would be kept alive. In his *Book of the Polish Pilgrims*, the poet Adam Mickiewicz would endow the martyrdom of his people with a messianic character, although it proved impossible to resolve the conflict between the 'moderates', who, led by Czartoryski, established in the Hôtel Lambert in Paris, fostered the idea of a renewal of hostilities, and the members of the Democratic Society, admirers of

Lelewel, who maintained that the Poles should rely only on themselves, give the peasants freedom and land, and entrust the conduct of the insurrection to a dictator.

The autocratic character of the Russian régime became more pronounced. It was expressed for example in the corpus of Russian laws, a record of previous legislation drawn up by Speranski which established absolutism as a legal system. The development of the Private Chancellery, which took over the functions of the Empire Council and the Ministries, only complicated the workings of Russian officialdom: bureaucracy maintained a stifling hold on the country, and as the central power lost its control over the provincial authorities, jobbery, corruption, and despotism became rampant. The bureaucrat set himself up between the population and the government, and officialdom lost touch with reality to an increasing extent. As for the nobility, although it was granted a great many privileges, the Tsar found it impossible to persuade it to take a more active share in local government. In the religious sphere, autocracy implied orthodoxy: in Poland the Catholic Church was subjected to countless restrictions, and in Lithuania the Uniate Church was incorporated in the Orthodox communion. The régime extended its strict control to intellectual life. Uvarov, the Minister of Education, who was responsible for the formula 'Orthodoxy, Autocracy, Nationalism', wished to restrict admission to the universities as far as possible to the nobility, to limit their autonomy, and to exclude from the curriculum any subjects which were considered dangerous.

However, this policy, which went against the tendencies of the age, could not prevent an increase in the number of poor students, or the formation of a body of eminent professors in the University of Moscow. Similarly, the censorship could not stop the publication of the writings of Lermontov and Pushkin, or the development of literary periodicals. Thus new ideas made their appearance in intellectual circles, largely derived from Saint-Simonism and German philosophy (Schelling and Hegel). The latter was the subject of endless discussions in private circles, of which the most famous in Moscow was that of Stankeivitch, which produced a whole school of savants, professors and writers, including Bielinski and Bakunin. This new intelligentsia could be divided into Slavophiles and Westerners. The former (Khomiakov, the Aksakov brothers, Kireievski) harked back to the Russia which had existed before Peter the Great, and which they invested with a romantic, vaguely idealistic aura; in Russia (and in the rest of the Slav world, tainted though it was by Germanic, Latin and Turkish superstitions), they distinguished a 'special national type' whose public and private life was based on faith, while western civilization was linked in their eyes with rationalism, selfish individualism, a utilitarian spirit (the bourgeoisie), or social revolution (the proletariat). The Slavophiles considered that government in Russia was based on a community of interests, harmony between the upper and lower classes, and the sentiment of an inner freedom, as opposed to the constitutionalism of the modern democracies. Against Catholicism and Protestantism, which had exhausted their religious enthusiasm, they set the autochthonous strength of the Orthodox Church, which consisted in loyalty to the authentic Christian traditions and the participation of all its members in ecclesiastical life. In short, rejecting the entire legacy of Peter the Great and the reforms carried out under the aegis of enlightened bureaucracy, the Slavophiles were conservatives, although they advocated a 'socialism' consistent with the 'traditional Russian forms' of agricultural collectivism. The Slavophiles were opposed by the Westerners, who held that Russia should follow the example of the bourgeois countries of western Europe, and who saw their political ideals fulfilled in the parliamentary monarchies of England and France. Among them, the literary critic Bielinski, who was less concerned with strictly aesthetic questions than with ethical and political problems, turned in succession from idealism to Hegelianism, and then to revolutionary individualism. More affected by the religious awakening of his time, Tchaadaiev considered that the required westernization of Russia demanded renunciation on her part of the Orthodox faith: it seemed to him that only the Roman Church could revive the country and link it with European culture. In other words, the terms Slavophilia and Westernism concealed very different tendencies. However, both elements felt a profound desire for change and were agreed on the need to solve the problem of serfdom. Combining the views of both sides, Alexander Herzen suggested that Russia, by virtue of the *mir* system, was predestined to socialism. His ideas, like Bielinski's, exerted considerable influence on Petrachevski's revolutionary circle, formed in St. Petersburg in 1845, and marked by a characteristic mixture of extreme individualism, Utopian collectivism of the Fourier type, and materialistic concepts: an intermediary link between the generation of the Decembrists and that of the Nihilists under Alexander II. Petrachevski's group was to be arrested by the police in 1849: its European reputation is due to the presence in its ranks of the young Dostoevsky, who was reprieved at the last moment, while preparations were already being made for his execution.

The harsh repressive measures taken against the Petrachevski circle may seem completely disproportionate to its importance. Yet it showed that twenty-five years after the suppression of the Decembrist movement, the Empire of the Tsars was not entirely impervious to 'dangerous ideas'. The fact remains that at the time the revolutionary movement of 1848 broke out, the Russia of Nicholas I appeared as the principal bulwark of the monarchical principle in Europe. Until the Crimean War, which would reveal the cracks in the structure, the Russian Empire looked like a threatening colossus, an insurmountable barrier to liberal and democratic ideals. The historian Granovski, one of the leaders of the Western movement, wrote in 1849: 'Even the most stout-hearted give way to despair and contemplate with indifference the sad sight that meets their eyes. The dead are the lucky ones. If only one could wipe out this intolerable state of things.' A whole generation was suffocating under a system of despotism and slavery: 'Russia is nothing but a living pyramid of crimes, frauds and abuses, full of spies, policemen, rascally governors, drunken magistrates and cowardly aristocrats, all united in their desire for theft and pillage and supported by six hundred thousand automata with bayonets.'

Chapter VIII

THE CHURCH AND
THE MODERN WORLD

Faced with the rising forces of liberalism, what was the attitude of the Catholic Church? Would it remain, as Metternich hoped and the vast literature born of political Romanticism suggested, attached to the policy of restoration, a bulwark of absolutism and the throne? Or would it consider it preferable, in order to retain its moral authority, to come to terms with the modern world? Now, except for a very brief period during the pontificate of Pius VII, when Cardinal Consalvi had shown his readiness to take account of the changes which had occurred in minds and institutions since 1789, the Papacy had done nothing in this respect; indeed, during the pontificate of Gregory XVI, it had taken every care not to offend the absolute monarchs. It was therefore outside the Church that an attempt was made by a number of laymen and a section of the clergy, often repudiated by the hierarchy, to adapt the Church to the demands of changing institutions. By the time the revolutionary period of 1848 opened, the Catholics had shown their desire to free themselves from the tutelage of the State; and they had used the magic word of liberty to demand that they should be allowed to do, by means of the press, education and social relief, what Christianity required of its adherents in modern society.

It was in an atmosphere of overwhelming veneration that Pius VII resumed possession of the pontifical throne in Rome. The Papacy's greatest asset in the work of restoration which it was about to understake was the Pope himself, his infinite goodness, his total disinterestedness, and his

190

innate tendency to forgive injuries; he would never forget the services Napoleon had rendered religion, even under persecution, and after 1815 he would be the only one to show pity for the exiled Emperor, to try to ease his lot, to receive the whole Bonaparte family in Rome. The Pope knew how to show absolute intransigence in matters of faith, but he had a conciliatory nature and also knew how to make concessions when necessary. Leaving his Secretary of State Consalvi, a remarkable administrator, the task of reorganising the Papal States, he devoted his own energies to the restoration of the Church. A Benedictine himself, he encouraged devotion to the saints and reorganized monastic life : as early as 1814 the Society of Jesus was re-established. Bent on halting the progress of irreligion, he condemned secret societies in 1820. But this glorification of religious fervour was not accompanied by any tokens of intolerance : the Pope quashed the decrees of the Inquisition against the Jews, as well as against certain heresies.

The restoration of the national churches was the chief objective pursued by Pius VII and Consalvi, with the collaboration of the Congregation of Extraordinary Ecclesiastical Affairs. This was a matter of breaking the Josephine and Gallican traditions, which were still very strong in the European courts, even when the latter protested their loyalty to the alliance between Throne and Altar. If the Neapolitan Concordat of 1818, with the abolition of the *Placet*, gave the Church considerable advantages in Rome, and marked the end of the old Caesaro-Papism, the Pope was forced to admit that in Austria—despite the Emperor, who had come to Rome in 1817, and despite the special sympathies of Metternich, who was inclined to regard the Church as the best bulwark of law and order—the Josephine administration was not prepared to abandon the principle of the State Church : only minor concessions were granted, such as the relinquishment of theological instruction and primary education to the episcopate.

In the case of Germany, where secularization had seriously weakened the Church, Rome made use of the 'Eichstätt Confederates', an influential group of ultramontane ecclesiastics, and later exploited the sympathies of the Bavarian government. In spite of Wessenberg, who, after trying to introduce the maxims of the *Aufklärung* into the bishopric of Constance, advocated the organization of a national German church as independent as possible of Rome, Pius VII won acceptance of the principle of separate concordats with each of the German States. Hence the signing with Bavaria of the Concordat of 1817, which incidentally had to be protected against a counter-attack by the Munich bureaucracy (by publication of the Concordat as part of the 1818 Constitution), and which only obtained its full effect as the result of the Tegernsee Declaration of 1821; hence too the Bull *De Salute animarum* establishing the status of the Prussian church, and the Bull *Provida solersque* (1821) reorganizing the ecclesiastical province of the Upper Rhine: decisions which gave back to the faithful their pastors and their hierarchy, but which did not protect the churches from the threat of Josephinism. Finally, in France it proved impossible to re-establish the *status quo* before the Revolution, as had been planned when in 1817 the Concordat was being negotiated: in the face of Gallican opposition the King did not dare to lay the project before the Chambers, and the 1801 Concordat was retained, with the establishment of eighty dioceses. However imperfect this achievement might have been, there can be no doubt that it fostered the awakening of ultramontane feelings everywhere, and the conviction that the Church alone could successfully oppose the destructive forces of modern thought.

However, Pius VII's political achievements had been condemned in Rome itself by a whole party of cardinals—the *Zelanti*—who were intransigent on the subject of the

Church's rights and inflexible with regard to the claims of governments. They criticized Consalvi for being too conciliatory towards the laity, and adopted a strictly conservative attitude on constitutional matters. Now it was they who secured the election of Leo XII (1823-29), who in the event succeeded in gradually escaping from their influence in the diplomatic sphere, but whose encyclical on religious indifferentism (1824) foreshadowed future condemnations of liberalism. Pius VIII (1829-30) did not have time to give effect to his directives in favour of the absolutist States, which he was powerless to help when they were attacked. But with the election of Gregory XVI (1831-46) there began a fighting pontificate. This Benedictine from Saint-Maur, the author of a work, *Le Triomphe de l'Eglise et du Saint-Siège* (1799) which urged the need to proclaim the dogma of papal infallibility, a pious Pope, not by any means without culture or curiosity about the world, was a man of inflexible and tenacious character, steeped in the ideas of the great medieval Popes, and absolutely opposed to the modern world. On his election he proclaimed that it was necessary, 'in face of the attempts to destroy Christianity, and in face of the attacks and wrongs, perpetrated against The Holy See, for all to work together, night and day, to defend the true faith against the ungodly, to protect Christ's flock against the wolves.' Advised by Secretary of State Bernetti, then by Lambruschini, he revealed himself a stern critic of theological innovations: in 1835 came the condemnation of the Bonn theologian Hermes, who had taken doubt as the basis of theological inquiry and, using the Kantian dialectic, accepted human reason as a norm for the understanding of supernatural truths; about the same time, he instituted a close watch on the teaching of the Frenchman Bautain, a professor at the University of Strasbourg, who tended to subject human reason too much to faith, but whose sub-

mission saved him from condemnation in Rome. Against
these doctrines, the Pope set traditional theology as taught
at the Roman College and based on scholastic foundations.
He saw the source of the trouble in the activities of the
secret societies, and he got the French writer Crétineau-Joly
to denounce their evil influence. Gregory XVI's chief pre-
occupation seemed to be to maintain good relations with
the absolutist States; thus in 1832 he thought fit to
condemn the Polish insurrection, and it was only ten years
later that he made a solemn protest against the Russian
government's methods. Similarly the Irish Catholics' efforts
to obtain emancipation were made without his approval.
In short, incapable of adapting himself to the evolution of
his age, he displayed in both the doctrinal and political
spheres a dictatorial, conservative attitude which prevented
him from being able to solve the problems facing the
Church at that time. The Church's weaknesses were
bluntly criticized by the Italian priest Rosmini in *Delle
cinque Piaghe della santa Chiesa*, a book written in 1833
but published after Pope Gregory's death in 1848.

In these circumstances, the attempts to reconcile the
Church with modern society were made outside the Papacy,
by laymen and progressive ecclesiastics. 'I shall only become an unbeliever again,' Chateaubriand wrote in a new
edition of his *Essai sur les Révolutions*, 'when it has been
proved to me that Christianity is incompatible with liberty.'
This struggle, waged in different conditions in France, the
German States and England, changed completely the image
of Catholicism in 1848 from that of 1815.

The alliance between Throne and Altar caused lively
reactions in France as early as the 1820s. Lamennais had
entered the lists as the champion of authority in the Church
and society by stigmatizing so-called freedom of opinion;
hence his sensational adhesion to the doctrine of papal infallibility. But after 1825 he underwent a development
which rapidly brought him to an entirely different position:

experience had in fact taught him that the Catholics could no longer count on a monarchy anchored to the traditions of another age but ought to bank boldly on liberalism, whose victory seemed inevitable. In his work *La Religion considérée dans ses rapports avec l'ordre politique et civil*, and subsequently in other pamphlets, he inveighed against a monarchy which oppressed religion with the collusion of the national episcopate. His great aversion was the so-called 'Gallican liberties' which made it possible to keep the Church in subjection. Noting on the other hand that there were a great many liberals who were prepared to give the Church the freedom it wanted, on condition that it declared unequivocally against the forces of the past, he concluded that 'the union of Catholicism and liberalism is the real means of re-establishing society on its true foundations.' Just as he came to these conclusions in the light of circumstances in France, the Belgian Catholics, whose irreproachable religious orthodoxy was guaranteed by their traditional ultramontanism, had no hesitation about concluding a tactical alliance with liberals who were fiercely anticlerical, on the basis of a mutual recognition of liberties and rights. This was the beginning of 'Unionism', in which Lamennais took no part, but to which, using Belgium as a testing-ground, he was to attribute universal value. 'The Belgians,' he wrote at the time, 'are at this moment setting a great example to the world and especially to France.' From then on, Lamennais exerted an irresistible influence on the young clergy.

The 1830 Revolution confirmed Lamennais's fear that the victory of an exasperated liberalism over the stubborn determination of 'those well-bred fools called royalists' would turn it against Catholicism in France, while in Belgium, Poland and Ireland the causes of liberty and religion were fusing together. It was in these circumstances that Lamennais, together with a small group of his disciples, the Abbé Gerbet and the Abbé Lacordaire, lay publicists such as de Coux, Baron d'Eckstein and later the Comte de Montalembert, decided to launch *L'Avenir*, a journal bearing the motto 'God and Liberty' and calling for the fundamental freedoms: freedom of religion (the abolition of State support for the Church), freedom of education, freedom of the Press and freedom of association, as well as the rights of revolt for oppressed peoples. Showing no indulgence towards the government born of the 1830 Revolution, *L'Avenir* soon transferred its hopes to the coming of a republic. What is more, by founding an agency for religious freedom, Lamennais and his friends laid the foundation of a vast organisation of French Catholics; and in March 1831 he opened a free, independent school in Paris. This led to a sensational trial for offending the existing laws, in which Montalembert appeared before the Chamber of Peers, and opened new avenues of propaganda.

However, liberal Catholicism was the object of repeated attacks by the French episcopate, the Jesuits and the Vienna government; and it was the growing difficulties placed in the paper's way which induced Lamennais, accompanied by Lacordaire and Montalembert, to travel to Rome. How could he imagine that he would succeed in winning over a pontiff anxious to bar the way to the revolutionary spirit, precisely when it was wreaking havoc at the very court of the Papal State? After all their efforts had come to nothing, the pilgrims left for Munich, where they had many friends, and it was there that they read the encyclical *Mirari vos*, which, without mentioning them by name, condemned 'indifferentism' and all its consequences—including freedom of the press, freedom of conscience and freedom of worship—as well as all those doctrines which tended to shake the loyalty and submission of subjects to their sovereigns. It has been suggested that in so doing, the Pope had acted in a strictly religious context and had simply performed his pastoral duty; in fact, he had responded to urgent pleas from Metternich.

In spite of his apparent submission, Lamennais considered that since the Pope's letter had had no dogmatic character, he could stick to his opinions. He embarked on the writing of *Paroles d'un Croyant* (1834), which earned him an outright condemnation, excluding him from the Church, in the encyclical *Singulari vos*. Henceforth, he would move towards a republican, socialistic ' demotheism ' (see p. 78). But his friends, who submitted, made a notable contribution to the religious revival in France and succeeded in raising a number of questions in the challenging spirit of *L'Avenir*. Each in his own sphere brought to fruition the seeds sown by Lamennais. Now in this work the liberal Catholics had their eyes turned towards the Belgian church, which, thanks to the Constitution of February 1831 and the theoretical separation of Church and State, had obtained immense material advantages, while retaining complete independence with regard to the authorities : a system which, on account of its liberal character, Gregory XVI regarded with insurmountable mistrust (though without condemning it in the encyclical *Mirari vos*). None the less it worked perfectly under the Archbishop of Malines, Mgr. Sterck, supported by the ' Unionist ' Catholics.

To consider the spiritual sphere first : as early as 1835 Lacordaire began the Nôtre-Dame lectures, which enabled him to proclaim some of the ideas dear to the liberal Catholics, and which were continued after 1837 by Father Révignan ; as a result, the educated public ceased to regard the Catholic religion as a tissue of superstitions intended for the ignorant. What is more, religious life itself, thanks to the decline of Gallican traditions, was profoundly changed. The Abbé Guéranger, a disciple of Lamennais, waged a campaign against the multiplicity of liturgies, restored the Benedictine abbey of Solesmes in 1833, and laid the foundations of that liturgical revival which was to be one of the chief features of the contemporary Catholicism. When, in 1841, Lacordaire reconstituted the Dominican order in France, he took care not to ask the government's permission, and he was well aware of the distrust which his action aroused among the Gallican prelates. New devotions, such as that to the Holy Virgin, the fervour of which was shown by the apparitions at La Salette, tended to give the religious sensibility of the age wider scope.

To consider the social sphere next: before 1830 there already existed a social Catholicism, certain Ultras having emphasized the duties of the rich towards the lower classes. Legitimists such as Villeneuve-Bargemont tried to work out a Christian economic policy (see p. 75). Less dogmatic, but endowed with inexhaustible reserves of charity, Armand de Melun founded the Society of Christian Economy in 1846; and in the *Annales de la Charité* which he edited from 1844 onwards, he urged the formation of friendly societies and societies for popular education run by Catholics of both clergy and laity. Instinctively suspicious of this conservative paternalism, the lower classes seem to have been more attracted by the Christian socialism of Buchez and his school. But between the two movements, there were a certain number of liberal Catholics interested in social welfare. The most notable example was the Lyonnais Ozanam, first a student and then a professor at the Sorbonne, who in 1833 laid the foundations of the Society of St. Vincent de Paul; in 1848 it would number 388 branches, 282 of them in France, with between eight and ten thousand active members. This charitable organization, whose work consisted essentially of visits to the poor in their homes, was intended by its founder less as a form of poor relief than as a means for the privileged of acquainting themselves with the causes of poverty and of working out 'the science of charitable reforms'.

Finally, to consider the sphere of freedom of education: it was between 1842 and 1846 that there occurred the most spectacular episodes of a conflict between the champions and opponents of the State monopoly. The State party demanded that the liberal system which the Guizot law of 1833 had established for primary schools should be extended to secondary education. Under an electoral system which entrusted the government of the country to an oligarchy of bourgeois educated in the *lycées*, the power to open independent secondary schools was regarded as an essential weapon by the Catholic clergy and laity, who were waging a great battle for the reconquest of a secularized society. In fact Louis-Philippe's government, which after 1835 was anxious to improve its relations with the Church, allowed considerable infringements of the State monopoly. But the bill presented by the Minister Vuillemin in 1841, though less liberal in character than that prepared by Guizot in 1836, came up against opposition from the anti-clerical deputies and academics: an opposition which provoked violent reactions from the bishops, who in their pastoral letters thundered against the University, 'that sink of iniquity', 'that huge receptacle of all heresies and errors, all sophisms and lies'. Under the pen of writers such as Father Deschamps and Father Combalot, the argument became increasingly violent and personal. Louis Veuillot's paper *L'Univers* made a speciality of virulent attacks. After some members of the Society of Jesus had taken part in this onslaught on the State system, Michelet published his *Jésuites*, which was described as 'a book full of error and blasphemy, attacking not so much the religious party as Religion and Christ himself', and which in any case aroused violent indignation and led the government to ask Rome to close the Society's houses in France. Realizing that violence could only hurt the cause of freedom, Montalembert and his friend moved the argument on to the higher ground of the great principles of liberty. During 1845 they set up the 'Committee for the Defence of Religious Freedom', organized petitions, and prepared for the 1846 election, in which 140 deputies were returned who supported their cause. It seemed that a great Catholic party was in the making, and Montalembert, adopting the tone of the old *Avenir*, forecast imminent victory for it. In fact, he was very wide of the mark: Gregory XVI was not prepared to sacrifice his good relations with Louis-Philippe's government for the sake of these 'fanatics'. As for the bill presented by Salvandy, the Minister of Education, in 1847, it was not even discussed. Yet, in spite of everything, the struggle for freedom of education helped Catholic interests to a large measure of self-awareness.

There can be no doubt that, contrary to the forecasts of the freethinkers, Catholicism increased its hold on national life during the July Monarchy. This revival was helped by the government, which, from 1836 onwards, conscious of the assistance it received from religion in its fight against subversive ideas, increased its subsidy to the Church and appointed bishops of real ability, attentive to the administration of their dioceses, careful not to identify the Church with any régime, and often—as in the case of Cardinal de Bonald in Lyons concerning the royal assent, or even of Mgr. Affre, the Archbishop of Paris—showing a determined independence. 'A new clergy is coming into existence,' wrote in 1843 Mgr. Parisis, the Bishop of Langres, who was himself involved in the question of freedom of education, 'foreign to revolutions, accepting without regret, without passing moral judgments, the accomplished facts, possibly understanding more clearly the social situation that actually exists, but also feeling more strongly as a result the need to exercise its ministry in complete freedom.' However, this revival so far involved only a small élite; it was scarcely obvious except to the governing classes. And in the clergy itself, the lively opposition between the bishops and some members of the lower clergy, who were moved about at will by their hierarchical superiors, created a spirit of unrest, as was shown by the writings of the Allignol brothers and the Abbé Clavel.

Matters had advanced further in Germany, where the Catholic Church had laid the foundations of its emancipation from the State.

This was because religious life had been developing fast in Germany since the beginning of the century. Centres of religious fervour had been created at Münster in Westphalia by Princess Galitzin, Fürstenberg and Overberg, at Mainz by Bishops Liebermann and Raess, and at Landshut by Sailer. Through his books, his sermons, and the friendships he managed to create around him, Sailer in particular —who was nicknamed the German St. François de Sales— succeeded in banishing the dried-up religion of the past, bled white by a half-sceptical theology. 'Away,' he wrote, 'with those reformers who expect the salvation of the world when they have turned the priests into tutors in virtue, the sermon into a discourse on ethics, the church into a lecture-room, and the catechism into a register of virtues.' It is true that Sailer has been criticized for placing too much emphasis in his teaching on the heart, and for inspiring a dangerous, fanatical mysticism in his disciples, something which earned him the suspicions of Rome and long delayed his elevation to the episcopate. It must be admitted, however, that he succeeded in breathing a new spirit into the Bavarian Church. It was he who, using his influence with King Ludwig I of Bavaria, helped to have the Bavarian University transferred from Landshut to Munich. Under the aegis of Rector Ringseis, the King's physician, this University became one of the great centres of Catholic culture, thanks to the collaboration of eminent professors: Görres, who taught history and mysticism 'in titanic fashion', Baader, whose philosophy was directed towards a theosophical interpretation of the universe and supported by a vast esoteric culture; and the young Döllinger, then embarking on the study of the Fathers, whose militant ultramontanism gave no hint as yet of the audacities of his maturity. If there was an element of muddle about the writings of the Munich professors, they exerted an influence which spread abroad, as is shown by the recollections of Montalembert and Wiseman, who knew them.

Finally, the theological school at Tübingen, with Drey and Moehler, contributors to the *Theologische Quartalschrift*, appealed to the Romantic movement by proclaiming the spiritual and organic unity of the Church, and by re-emphasising the idea of a living community and a doctrinal continuity; certain historians have seen these efforts as a prefiguration of modernism, but in fact they represented rather attempts to give the concept of revelation its full value. According to Moehler, doctrine, like faith, was not a dead thing, frozen in a *ne varietur* formula, but a perpetual effort inside the Church to translate the life of faith into intellectual terms; dogma was a permanent process of creation by the Holy Ghost in the Church, a living organism, an incarnation of the Son of God; and heresy was nothing other than the work of contemplatives who disregarded the mystical life, individuals who cut themselves off from everything, retrogrades who harked back to the static Church of the first centuries, when in fact the Church represented the inner life and the intimate union of the Divine and the Human.

Now the new faith found it difficult to tolerate State interference and tried, by using the weapons which the Concordats had given it, to revise the Josephine laws. The chief bone of contention in this matter of the emancipation of the German Church was the question of mixed marriages. In spite of the papal brief of March 1830, the Prussian episcopacy had shown considerable complaisance towards the government, and even the Archbishop of Cologne, Mgr. Spiegel, had pledged himself by the 1834 agreement to demand no promise from the parents as to the religion in which their children were to be brought up. But this attitude suddenly changed when the see of Cologne was occupied by Mgr. von Droste-Vischering, an aged prelate, who was an absolute stickler for purity of doctrine. Trained in the Münster circle, he showed a determination to apply canon law on this point in all its rigour. He had shown the same rigour in his hostility towards the theologian Hermes, whose ideas had spread from Bonn throughout his diocese. The Prussian government, considering that this was a case of breach of faith, then made the mistake of having him arrested, as well as the Archbishop of Posen, Mgr. Dunin, who had adopted a similar attitude (1837). The affair aroused a storm of emotion throughout Germany, as well as a wave of protests, of which Görres's *Athanasius* was the most eloquent. Succeeding to the Prussian throne in the meantime, Frederick William IV thought fit to beat a retreat, arranged with the Pope for the appointment of a new archbishop for Cologne, Mgr. Geissel, and set up a Catholic department in the Ministry of Ecclesiastical Affairs.

The Cologne affair had none the less shown that the Catholics were now determined to escape from the tutelage of the State. By forcing the Berlin government to give way, they had won for their church that independence which had been taken from them by either the Protestant bureaucracy or the Josephine laws. By renewing relations with Rome and calling themselves Ultramontanists, they showed their determination to organize religious life themselves. The 'forties were characterized by the development of the Roman tendencies which were advocated by Mgr.

Geissel in Cologne and Mgr. Reisach in Munich, and which were accompanied by the revival of Thomist studies, an increase in Jesuit activity, and the appearance of a suspicious orthodoxy which did not hesitate to resort to denunciations to Rome. The Church also tried to extend its influence over the masses: by means of processions, feast-days and missions, it encouraged popular superstition and aroused the enthusiasm of the common people whom it hoped to wean away from subversive ideas in this way. It should be noted that this revival of Catholicism did not take place, as in Belgium and France, under the aegis of liberalism; in Germany Catholicism remained attached until a late date to the political and social ideas of Romanticism, and the Menaisian ideas about the separation of Church and State were given a cool reception. In his *Athanasius*, Görres came out in favour of a Christian monarchy in which the Church, free in matters of discipline and education, would imbue the laws with its morality and its precepts. From 1838 onwards there appeared in Munich a journal entitled *Historisch-politische Blätter* which, edited by Görres's son Guido, published rules of conduct laid down by two converts, Jarcke, a member of the Austrian Chancellery, and Professor Phillips of Munich University. Both doctrinaires, in the sense in which the word was understood during the Restoration, convinced by their friend von Lassaulx that they were living in a period of decadence, pessimistic as to the future of western culture, and struck by the thirst for emancipation and the materialism of their period, they attributed this sorry development first to the Reformation, which had destroyed the unity of the Church, and then to the philosophy of the Enlightenment, which had led to the French Revolution. Against the absolutist or liberal State, which ignored the bonds between one man and another, they set the Germanic Christian Church, founded on hierarchy, loyalty and obedience; and the *Blätter* even criticized the Irish and the Belgians for basing their struggle for independence on democratic claims.

However, it was impossible for the German Catholics to maintain indefinitely a completely negative attitude to liberalism and to ignore the economic and social means by which the latter was conquering the State. It was the commercial and industrial Rhineland, where Catholicism was in no way incompatible with a rational attachment to the institutions born of revolutionary and imperial France which realized the need for Catholicism to revise its attitude to constitutional questions. In 1847 a Cologne jurist, Peter Reichensperger, who had been roused by the Cologne affair to the point of providing a French friend called de Failly with material for an indictment of the Prussian government, but whom the conciliatory attitude of Frederick William IV had later brought back to more moderate sentiments, published his *Agrarfrage*, in which, wishing to establish a compromise between the historical attitudes of Catholicism and the demands of the modern world, he advocated the convening, in addition to the provincial Diets, of a national Parliament elected on a corporate basis. This does not mean that the Catholics of this shade of opinion rallied to liberalism, which by its origins was too closely linked to the Protestant Reformation and the rationalism of the Enlightenment to appeal to them; but, on the tactical level, they agreed to go with it a little way.

On the eve of the 1848 Revolution, a serious blow was likewise dealt to the *Staatskirchentum* in the Duchy of Baden, where Friedrich Buss, a professor at the University of Freiburg and a member of the *Landtag*, led a vigorous movement in favour of freedom for the Church, though not without arousing violent hostility from a clergy that remained extremely attached to the Josephine traditions. But this clergy could count on the growing support of the rural masses which, conscious of the social obligations of religion, it had tried to help during the terrible economic crisis of the years 1845-47. In Rhenish Hesse the struggle against Caesaro-papism was waged along lines laid down in the *Katholik* by Canon Lennig, a friend of Montalembert: even more than Munich, which was too dependent on the person of a mad sovereign, Mainz represented in 1848 the hopes of German Catholicism.

These few examples should not lead us to assume that there existed an organized Catholic party in Germany. The fact remains that on all sides the necessary weapons were to hand; contact was made between leaders and masses; the theory of the 'political party' was in the air. What was still lacking in most of the States was use of the right of association and assembly, which made it possible to mobilize the faithful; consequently far from holding aloof from revolution, the Catholic leaders would try to use it as much as possible, in order to obtain for the Church that freedom of action without which its influence and its spiritual authority would remain a dead letter. However, matters were not so far advanced in Austria, where the Josephine laws remained in force, with the consent of a large section of the upper clergy, but where there likewise existed, around the theologian Guenther and the former disciples of the Redemptorist Hofbauer, a whole group of young ecclesiastics who sought the revival of the Church, not in increased State aid, but in the development of its inner vitality.

In England the awakening of the Catholic Church was only beginning. But this awakening too was brought about by a movement of protest within the Anglican Church against its subjection to the State and against the religious indifferentism which resulted.

The powerful intellectual movement which revived the life and thought of the Church of England in the first half of the nineteenth century did not spring from the Catholics of that country. The object of a mission led by apostolic vicars dependent on the Congregation of Propaganda, Catholic England, in spite of the Emancipation Act, led a wretched and almost clandestine life about 1830. The efforts of the English Catholics were confined to obtaining tolerance for themselves, by playing down their attachment to Rome and keeping their faith intact by retiring within themselves; they turned to the past more than to the present and *a fortiori* to the future; they lived 'on memories and not on hope'. However, after 1830 two completely different centres, the University of Oxford and the English College in Rome prepared a revival of astonishing scope and brilliance. For in Rome there was a priest who was sufficiently English to understand his fellow countrymen and make himself understood to them, yet sufficiently detached by his personal upbringing from the habits of mind of the English Catholics to have neither their timidity nor their shortsightedness: this was Nicholas Wiseman. Trained at Douai and then in Rome, Wiseman became Rector of the English College in Rome in 1828. After 1835, when he heard Lacordaire preaching from the pulpit of Notre-Dame, he gave in London a series of 'Lectures on the principal doctrines of the Catholic Church', intended for Protestants as well as his fellow Catholics. In these lectures he avoided irritating controversies and used simple, intelligible arguments: several Anglicans were converted, like the architect Pugin, while others lost some of their prejudices. In agreement with O'Connell he founded in the same year the *Dublin Review*, which was to reveal 'the spirit of Christianity in its Catholic form', by dealing with vital questions belonging to the present day.

However, it was from the Oxford Movement that the decisive impulse would come. There can be no doubt that about 1830 the Church of England was swept by a wave of panic. Divided into three parties—the Low Church, with its puritanical tradition, in which the Evangelical Movement had tried to revive the apostolic spirit; the

Broad Church, which was latitudinarian and antidogmatic; and the High Church, which was conservative and sympathetic towards Catholicism—it felt itself to be threatened with doctrinal dissolution, at a time when it had just been shaken by the passing of the Reform Bill and the abolition of ten bishoprics in Ireland. However, far from sharing their colleagues' despondency, a group of young Oxford clergymen decided to take advantage of this crisis to reanimate the Church of England which was dying from inanition. The disease affecting it, they maintained, did not come from outside but from within; it should not count on political action but, rejecting what had warped and perverted it, should recover 'its supernatural titles' and its sense of mission. This was the theme of John Keble's sermon on 'National Apostasy' in July 1833, a rallying-call to the faithful and the clergy to unite against State interference and to devote themselves to the cause of the apostolic Church. An Oxford Fellow, the vicar of the University church, John Henry Newman began his campaign of tracts which lasted several years, and soon shook his readers out of their torpor and roused widespread public interest. Newman had no intention of urging his readers towards Rome, still less of moving in that direction himself: extremely attached to his church, which he would not abandon without a real 'agony', and still full of prejudices against Popery, which he repeatedly attacked, he for his part kept to the *via media*, half-way between Protestantism and Catholicism, upholding against the former the authority and tradition of the Fathers of the Church, and reproaching the latter with apparently novel doctrines. This middle way he saw as the true line of belief, which linked his conviction to the origins of Christianity and guaranteed its apostolic nature. He also taught that the contemporary Catholic Church consisted of three branches —Anglican, Orthodox and Catholic—'the sin of schism consisting of turning altar against altar, bishop against bishop, in the same diocese, after the fashion of the Donatists': a church did not lose its status as a church as long as it did not lose the apostolic succession, as long as it did not make common cause with heresy.

However, in the long run neither the theory of the *via media* nor that of the 'branch church' struck him as tenable. A study of Monophysitism and of the Council of Chalcedon showed him in fact that the Arians had preceded him in this *via media*. And an article on Donatism by Wiseman in the *Dublin Review* drew his attention to a text by St. Augustine dealing with the Universal Church. The condemnation of Tract 90, in which he had maintained that the Thirty-Nine Articles could be interpreted in a Catholic sense, and the pastoral letters published against him by the bishops showed that the breach was imminent. He began to have doubts : could the Anglican Church call itself a church? Gradually he became convinced that the Roman Catholic Church was the true church of the Apostles, and that the Roman innovations in matters of dogma were legitimate and necessary; and this law of growth, whose workings he traced in his *Essay on the Development of Christian Doctrine*, struck him as an additional argument in favour of the Catholic Church. In November 1845 he resigned his fellowship; a few days later he was received into the Roman Church by a Passionist father. He had been preceded in this course of action by a friend called Ward, who had drawn upon himself the wrath of the University authorities with his book *The Ideal of a Christian Church considered in a Comparison with Existing Practice*. His conversion was to be followed by a whole series of others, such as that of the future Oratorian Father Faber, while some of his old Tractarian friends, such as Keble and Pusey, remained in the Church of England and continued their efforts to re-catholicize Anglicanism. As for Newman, after offering Wiseman the homage of his conversion, he went to Rome, took Holy

Orders there, and entered the community of the Oratory. Later he returned to England to establish a similar community first in Birmingham and then in London.

This influx of university teachers and ecclesiastics of notable ability perceptibly raised the intellectual status and the vitality of the Catholic Church in England. It grew numerically as the result of the incursion, after the great famine of 1845-47, of large numbers of Irish immigrants, who settled mainly in the industrial areas, and whose Celtic exuberance and enthusiastic piety contrasted strongly with the secretive attitudes of Old English Catholicism. Wiseman, who was Apostolic Pro-Vicar of London from 1847, had a real job on his hands. There could be no doubt that Catholicism was emerging from its torpor and obscurity. Already the problem had arisen of the organization of an ecclesiastical hierarchy, which Wiseman himself favoured, though not without encountering considerable opposition from the old school of Catholics, who were still suffering from the timidity induced by centuries of persecution. However, it would be a mistake to exaggerate the extent of the revival: only after Manning's conversion in the 1850's would the movement towards Rome gain impetus, and among the people of England hostility towards 'Popery' still remained very deeply rooted.

The efforts made by the Catholics in the great European States to reconcile their Church with the principles governing the modern world came up against the indifference of popes who had thrown in their lot with absolutism and the counter-revolution. However, it was thought that the situation might change after the election of Cardinal Mastai, the Bishop of Imola, whom the Conclave chose, after brief deliberations, in preference to the reactionary Cardinal Lambruschini. Many people, in fact, praised the liberal tendencies of Pius IX, whose election was greeted with a tremor of hope. Sure enough, in the Roman sphere, he promptly granted an amnesty to political prisoners. But there was no reason to suppose that, even if he knew Gioberti's writings, he had given his support to the Neo-Guelfian programme; his so-called liberalism came down in fact, on the one hand to a generosity of soul which led him to think that it was better to disarm the revolutionary spirit by mildness than to try to conquer it by force, especially when the sovereign was also a priest, and on the other hand to a sincere desire to tackle the abuses of the papal administration and, in an authoritarian way, introduce certain reforms. If he showed greater sympathy than his predecessor to Montalembert and the struggle being waged in France for freedom of education, he had published on his accession (November 1846) the encyclical *Qui pluribus*, based on a text by Lambruschini, which condemned the two contrary excesses of rationalism and fideism in the same terms as those used by Gregory XVI, and incidentally denounced liberalism, 'that appalling system of indifference, which abolishes every distinction between virtue and vice, truth and error.' In spite of appearances, this was in no way a new era which was opening in the history of the Church.

Even more than the Catholic Church, the Protestant Churches took the demands of the modern world increasingly into account and tended to keep authority at a distance. By 1848 only the Lutheran Church in the Germanic countries would retain a resolutely conservative character.

In the wake of the great revolutionary upheavals, European Protestantism, profited by an ardent, mystical longing for faith as strong as Catholicism; it too reacted against rationalism and unbelief. In Germany this movement had been linked for a long time with Pietism and Romanticism: Schleiermacher, 'the second Reformer', had sought to define religion as the immediate awareness of the infinite, as the soul's profound desire to make contact with God:

in other words, it was not rooted in books and tradition, but in the heart. Schleiermacher's subjectivism was to have considerable influence on the evolution of Protestant thought, for it was taken up by disciples of merit, such as the theologians Neander and Tholuk, and what has been called the school of the 'peace-makers'. The religious movement known in the Western States as the 'revival' was born in Switzerland, in the milieu of the Geneva Academy, as a sign of protest against lukewarmness in the faith; it arose through, among other things, the activity of a Wesleyan missionary, the Scot Haldane, and it resulted in the foundation of independent churches in which the theologians Malan and Gaussen reaffirmed Calvin's teaching. The 'revival' spread to France, thanks to Charles Cook, a Methodist whose itinerant ministry awoke the moribund Protestant churches of the 'desert'; in Paris he enjoyed the support of notabilities such as the Duchesse de Broglie, Madame de Staël's daughter, and formed the independent church of the Rue Taitbout.

In fact, there were also present in the Protestantism of this period rationalist tendencies which were sometimes referred to by the name of liberal Protestantism. The Nîmes minister Vincent reminded the Huguenots that free inquiry was the very essence of Protestantism. But the revival of exegetical studies was chiefly a German phenomenon: while Strauss published his *Leben Jesu* (1835) depicting Christ as a sort of popular myth, the incarnation of the Messianic ideas of his time, Karl Baur, who taught in the Faculty of Protestant Theology at Tübingen, made considerable contributions to Biblical criticism and reduced Christianity to a conflict between two tendencies, one Judaizing and the other Pauline. These ideas were to have widespread influence in France through the University of Strasbourg.

However, the chief phenomenon remained the tendency of the Protestant churches to break away from the Church.

The powerful national churches, doctrinally united and allied to the State, had greatly assisted Protestantism in its early stages but had since become a source of weakness: hence, during the Protestant revival in the nineteenth century, the speeding-up of the 'disestablishment' movement. The revival of spiritual life with its inevitable controversies made things more and more difficult for State churches which were both authoritarian and devoid of religious life. Yet this development was more easily discerned among the Calvinists than among the Lutherans. England had for a long time given an example of powerful non-conformist communities: Parliament granted them, as well as the Catholics, religious equality (1828) by abolishing the Test Act of 1673. In 1836 the Whigs moved in the direction of the separation of Church and State by recognizing a Non-Conformist marriage ceremony performed by a registrar. However, State control still weighed heavily on the official Church, as was shown by the government's appointment, against the wishes of the High Church, of an unorthodox theologian, Dr. Hampden, as Bishop of Hereford. In Scotland a number of ministers who criticized the submissiveness of the Presbyterian Church towards the lay patrons seceded, and in response to an appeal by Chalmers founded a Free Church of Scotland in 1843. The French-speaking Calvinist communities were greatly influenced by Pastor Vinet, who as early as 1825, for the benefit of the French Society of Christian Ethics, had described the complete separation of Church and State as the only system calculated to guarantee the dignity of religion and the sincerity of the faithful. This development of ideas was much less marked in the Lutheran countries. For a long time the Scandinavian churches dealt harshly with the more or less non-conformist 'revivalists'. The Prussian monarchy remained attached to the principle of State Church: in 1817 Frederick William III had imposed an 'evangelical union' on the Lutherans and Protestants, whom he rather oddly obliged to adopt a common liturgy laid down in an official handbook. His successor Frederick William IV remained faithful to the idea of the Christian State, of which Stahl was the theorist, thus linking the Lutheran Church with the idea of social and political conservatism, and in spite of the meritorious efforts of certain evangelists like Wichern, the founder of the Spiritual Mission, making it impossible for it to have any effective contact with the modern world. There was no lack of superior intellects in German Protestantism about 1848 to note the changes taking place: V. A. Hüber in particular, the publisher of the review *Janus* and a protégé of Frederick William IV who had brought him to the University of Berlin, was well aware of the ineluctable character of the industrial revolution, which he had studied in England; but he was counting on the financial efforts of the State and the aristocracy to lay the foundations of Christian social action. Conservative Protestant thought, because of its social and ideological origins, was too respectful of State authority and the established hierarchies to have much influence on public opinion; in this respect it was a long way behind that of the Catholics.

Chapter IX

INTERNATIONAL RELATIONS

The conflict between the supporters of the Ancien Régime and those who favoured the national liberal movements was bound to be reflected in the history of international relations between 1815 and 1848. Hence the ideological character which the struggle between the great powers often assumed. The attempt made within the framework of Metternich's 'system' to stifle national aspirations towards liberty and unity came up against opposition, especially after 1823, from England, which posed as a liberal State and, in connection with the revolt of the South American colonies and then of Greece, succeeded in breaking up the monarchist coalition of 1815. The 1830 Revolution was to bring France into the camp of the liberal States and, notably in connection with Spanish affairs, to produce a new alignment of the powers. However, the somewhat precarious understanding between the liberal States succumbed before the persistence of imperialist rivalry, especially in the Mediterranean; and on the eve of the 1848 Revolution France, ruled by a despotic sovereign, sought to rejoin the camp of the conservative Powers.

The initial period, from 1815 to 1830, witnessed the organization and then the disintegration of the forces of oppression.

The results achieved by the diplomats gathered together at the Congress of Vienna (1815) had not been without merit. They had been inspired by the desire to rebuild Europe on a fairer foundation and to obtain respect, in the new determination of territory, for the consent of its proprietors. The term 'legitimacy' used by France's representative, Talleyrand, had not been an entirely empty word, and the Tsar, in spite of everything, had had to take it into account. Moreover, although the final Treaty of Vienna had not been given a general guarantee, it represented a collective contract in the interests of general peace. True, it was scarcely possible to talk of limiting State sovereignty in favour of an international organization, although this idea had been clearly expounded by certain innovators, such as the Pole Czartoryski and the Frenchman Saint-Simon. None the less, the results achieved at Vienna were inspired by a certain concept of international relations which excluded the use of force and which consequently represented a considerable advance on the 'highway robbery' of the eighteenth century and the revolutionary era. It was ultimately the idea of a balance of power between the European States which determined the basic concepts on which the new Europe was established. From the point of view of general policy, the fate of Europe remained in the hands of five great States which were roughly equal. The result was that the final Treaty of Vienna, in spite of the Tsar's aspirations to hegemony, looks very like an instrument of the English policy of the balance of power.

However, in practice the Treaties of Vienna were regarded by contemporaries as products of the Ancien Régime, because they achieved equilibrium while respecting dynastic arrangements. According to the accepted notions of politics they took account only of the facts of power, and divided peoples into lots, like an inheritance. The 1815 treaties ignored the moral forces which first the French Revolution and then Romanticism had unleashed in Europe. They were concluded without reference to the principle of nationalism. As a result of this outdated concept of what a nation was, the diplomatic achievement of Vienna, intended to rebuild the European order on legal foundations, was, so to speak, out of true: hence the hostility which the progressive parties showed towards it; hence the resentment it aroused; and finally, hence the moral position of France, whose chief interest was to obtain the revision of the treaties which had been imposed on her and which she resented for a long time as a humiliation.

For the time being, the Powers which had defeated France found themselves faced with two systems which were intended to ensure the maintenance of peace in Europe, and which were the result of the rivalry between Russia and England: the Holy Alliance and the Quadruple Alliance. In September 1815, in Paris, Alexander I had drawn up the Treaty of the Holy Alliance, which, slightly altered by Metternich, was submitted to the Christian Sovereigns for signature; placed under the invocation of the Holy and Indivisible Trinity, it created, between the signatories, sovereigns who were 'all members of a single Christian nation', a 'real fraternity', in conformity with 'the words of Holy Writ which command all men to regard one another as brothers'; it invited them to consider themselves members of a single family, whose head was 'God, our divine Saviour Jesus Christ, the Word of the Most High, the Word of Life'.

This document, which Metternich described as a 'high-sounding nothing' and Castlereagh as 'a piece of sublime mysticism and nonsense', is generally regarded as a mere whim of the Tsar's mystical cogitations; to explain its meaning, emphasis has been laid on the influence of Madame de Krüdener and the Frenchman Bergasse. But in spite of everything such an interpretation of the Holy Alliance remains inadequate. Alexander I was a complex character, difficult to grasp. Suffering from megalomania, he wished to attach his name to a great work and to appear as the leader of a regenerated Europe. But if he was sometimes carried away by mystical fervour, he never lost sight of his country's immediate interests; the Treaty of the Holy

Alliance therefore tended to introduce into an international organization all the Powers, including the maritime and colonial States, and consequently to use them against England. The latter naturally refused to join the Holy Alliance; and two months later Castlereagh set against it the Quadruple Alliance, by means of which Napoleon's four victors —England, Austria, Prussia and Russia—renewed the Treaty of Chaumont, formed a permanent league of surveillance, and arranged for the periodical calling of international conferences. For English diplomacy it was a question not merely of ensuring the material and moral disarmament of France but also of excluding the maritime Powers from the Concert of Europe, on the one hand in order to maintain the undisputed command of the seas, and on the other hand in order to halt the extension of Russian power on the Continent, an advance which was also against the interests of the Germanic States. Thus the Holy Alliance would enable the Tsar to set against England the counterweight of the maritime nations, while the Quadruple Alliance would enable England to set against Russia the counterweight of the Continental Powers. The rivalry of the two opposed coalitions made it possible for the French Foreign Minister, the Duc de Richelieu, the punctual executor of the obligations imposed on France by the second Treaty of Paris, to obtain from the Congress of Aix-la-Chapelle (1818) the evacuation of French territory and the readmission of France to the Concert of Europe : without the Treaty of Chaumont being denounced, the Quadruple Alliance turned into a Quintuple Alliance.

The continuance of the rivalry between England and Russia enabled Chancellor Metternich to acquire a dominant influence on the Continent. In his hands the Congress System, which had been tried out at Aix-la-Chapelle, became an instrument directed against national emancipation. Convinced, not without reason, that Austria was particularly threatened by the progress of liberal and national ideas, and considering that the European *status quo* was a vital necessity for his country, he wanted the monarchs to join together closely to save society from impending ruin. As it was governments which were ultimately responsible for revolutions, they should not shrink from taking the necessary preventive measures. According to Metternich, the sovereigns should not only agree between themselves and meet frequently in congresses to discuss what measures should be taken, but they should also be able to intervene in neighbouring countries to restore order when it was threatened. They should form themselves into a supreme political court to police Europe against revolution. Thanks to him, the Holy Alliance would therefore be turned into an international police system against innovators. In short, it was Metternich who, banking on the growing feeling of solidarity which since 1815 had united the former governing classes, would stamp the European alliance with its anti-revolutionary, anti-liberal character, and turn it into a powerful weapon in the hands of the Habsburgs. Between 1820 and 1822 the Metternich policy of intervention would achieve a whole series of successes.

At the Congress of Aix-la-Chapelle, English diplomacy had succeeded in preventing discussion of the question of European intervention against the Spanish American colonies which had revolted against their mother country. But when disturbances occurred in Spain—a revolt by the Cadiz regiments under Major Riego against Ferdinand VII—and in the Kingdom of Naples—a rising of the Carbonari against Ferdinand I—the question of intervention was raised once more. By means of the note of 5 May 1820 Castlereagh was able temporarily to prevent intervention in Spain. In the case of Naples, which was considered more serious, Metternich obtained recognition of the need for a military expedition to restore order threat-

ened by the liberals; he would doubtless have preferred
a purely Austrian intervention, but he finally accepted the
idea of a European Congress, as proposed by the Tsar. It
was therefore at the Congress of Troppau (autumn 1820),
that in spite of England's opposition, the principle was
established of intervention by the European alliance in any
State where a revolution had broken out, a principle which
contemporaries regarded as the triumph of Metternich's
' system '. At the Congress of Laibach (January 1821), at
which Ferdinand I appeared, Metternich obtained permission to act alone in Italy: it was Austrian troops who
restored the absolutist régime in Naples and who in Piedmont wiped out the liberals who had risen against the
lawful government. At the cost of its traditional influence
in Italy, French diplomacy had allowed Austria to wreak
her will.

On the other hand, it was France that took the initiative,
at the Vienna conferences and then at the Congress of
Verona (autumn 1822), of intervening in Spain, whose
sovereign kept appealing to the great Powers. In spite of
the Prime Minister, Villèle, who was in favour of peace,
the French representatives at the Congress, Montmorency
and Chateaubriand, the former out of sympathy for the Holy
Alliance, the latter in order to restore the prestige of the
Bourbons by a victorious war, sought to involve France in
intervention against liberal Spain. In spite of England's
opposition, but with Russia's support, France was entrusted
with command of the punitive expedition. This ended, after
the taking of the Trocadero at Cadiz by the Duc
d'Angoulême's troops (August 1823), with the restoration
of Ferdinand VII's absolute power. In spite of France's
desire to see a constitution granted to Spain, her intervention
represented a fresh triumph for the counter-revolution.

The victories of the Ancien Régime Powers had been
possible only because of England's virtual abstention.

Castlereagh had admittedly laid down the principle of non-intervention, but he had been forced to give up hope of imposing it on the Continent. He was too closely associated with the statesmen beside whom he had waged war against Napoleon to break with them now. Deeply concerned about the maintenance of peace, he did not use the forceful language required to move and satisfy public opinion, which in any case, as a diplomat of the old school hostile to 'generalizations', he tended to despise. Worn out by the debates in Parliament, and exposed to continual attacks by the Opposition, which demanded active non-intervention, he committed suicide in August 1822.

Canning, who succeeded him, was regarded for a long time as Castlereagh's living antithesis; the Conservative minister who was the least insular of English statesmen was supposed to have been succeeded by a radical eager to protect those peoples who wished to free themselves. In fact there was not such a profound difference between them. Canning did not wish to propagate revolution any more than his predecessor; a Tory like Castlereagh, he was attached to the principle of constitutional monarchy, and he thought it necessary to protect the treaties of 1815. But he was to show himself more contemptuous than his predecessor of the idea of European collaboration. Hostile to the Congress System, and determined to reduce the European alliance to its component parts, he wished not only to thwart the policy of intervention, but also to shatter the isolation in which, at the Congresses of Troppau and Laibach, English diplomacy had been placed. In support of his policy, he had decided to call on public opinion, if necessary against the King himself. Hence his resounding declarations, which aroused the enthusiasm of the British people, as also of liberals the world over. His policy would be applied first of all to the affair of the Spanish colonies, then to the question of Greek independence, and would finally bring about the collapse of Metternich's 'system' on the Continent.

At the time that the Congress of Verona opened, Spanish authority had been overthrown throughout Latin America : the problem facing the European Powers was whether or not to recognize the rebel States. Until then the British government, in spite of pressure from business circles, had hesitated to follow the example of the United States, which in 1822 had begun the process of recognition : it disapproved of the republican system and was afraid of setting a bad example to Ireland. But Canning, aware of the advantages which English trade would derive from the emancipation of America, and afraid that the principle of intervention might be extended by France, in accordance with Chateaubriand's views, to the rebel colonies, and that independent monarchies might be set up in that part of the world under the sceptre of the Bourbons, decided to come to an agreement with Washington with regard to the possibility of European intervention in South America. Negotiations were accordingly begun between Canning and the United States Ambassador Rush. But they were forestalled by President Monroe's decision to make known the guiding principles of his country's policy in a message to Congress. While the United States undertook not to intervene in European affairs and recognized the existing European colonies, it henceforth forbade the European States to extend their influence in the New World. By this declaration, Monroe stated his opposition to the threats of the Holy Alliance, as well as to the Tsar's intentions to monopolize the trade on the north coast of the Pacific; and he avoided acting as a satellite of England, on whose help he could count in any case. However, Canning had not waited for the American decision to neutralize the possibility of French intervention in the course of conversations he had with the French Ambassador Polignac, who agreed to sign a promise of abstention. After the defeat of the last Spanish troops, Canning decided, in January 1825, to grant official recognition to the American republics. This was the end of the 'European police system', and was a bitter blow to Metternich: 'Nobody wants to listen to me,' he complained; 'I am in the midst of chaos, like a man who at the approach of the flood finds himself alone on a desert island.'

However, it was the Greek insurrection which fatally compromised the monarchical alliance. Planned by rich Greeks living in foreign ports and grouped together in a secret society called the Hetairia, the Greek rebellion had broken out in March 1821. The instigator, Ypsilanti, one of the Tsar's *aides-de-camp*, who had shortly before set up the headquarters of the Hetairia in Odessa, thought that he could count on the support of the Greeks in the Danubian principalities; but he came up against the hostility of the Rumanian population, which in any case was roused to revolt against the landlords by Vladimirescu, and was promptly disavowed by Alexander. However, the movement spread to the Greeks of Hellas, who seized control of Attica and the Peloponnese; on 10 January 1822 the assembly at Epidaurus proclaimed the independence of Greece and elected Mavrocordato regent. Characterized by savage massacres, the struggle grew fiercer when Sultan Mahmud appealed for help to the Pasha of Egypt, Mehemet Ali. Mehemet made Navarino his bridgehead for the reconquest of the Morea, and Missolonghi and Athens fell in succession (1826-27).

At first the great Powers had regarded the Greek affair, not from the point of view of independence, but in the light of their personal interest. At Laibach, the Tsar had readily adopted Metternich's point of view, namely that the Greeks were merely rebels and should be abandoned to their fate: hence his disavowal of Ypsilanti. But on his return to Russia he had fallen under the influence of his close adviser, the Corfiote Capo d'Istria, as well as of the Orthodox clergy, who had been horrified by massacres of Greeks in Constantinople; he had accordingly sent a threatening note to the Sultan, calling upon him to restore the destroyed churches and to ensure freedom of worship. Soon, however, falling under other influences, he broke with Capo d'Istria, let it be known that he placed the unity of the monarchical cabinets above the cause of the Greeks, and refused to receive their delegates at the Congress of Verona. In January 1824, as a solution of the Greek question, he laid before the chancelleries a plan which would have divided Greece into three principalities enjoying a certain autonomy within the framework of the Turkish State, and over which he would have found it easy to establish his influence; but this plan came up against the opposition of Mavrocordato, who spoke of the 'hospodarization of Greece', as well as the hostility of Austria and England. The St. Petersburg conferences held to restore peace to the peninsula also came to nothing, so that Alexander I died without having achieved anything for Greece.

However, in 1826 three new circumstances altered the international situation completely. First of all, the growth of the Philhellenic movement obliged the diplomats to bow to the imperious voice of public opinion. The memory of classical antiquity, the romantic taste for exoticism, the longing for adventure among soldiers who had been idle ever since the fall of Napoleon, the development of liberal ideas, and the recollection of the Christian Crusade against Islam were so many factors—often contradictory as it happened—which aroused universal sympathy for the Greek cause, in democratic as well as in conservative and Catholic circles. The publication of Lamartine's *Dernier chant du pèlerinage de Childe Harold*, of Chateaubriand's *Note sur la Grèce*, and then of Hugo's *Orientales*, as well as the death of Byron at Missolonghi (1824) helped to stimulate the general enthusiasm, which from 1821 onwards found expression in a flood of volunteers and countless subscriptions raised by the Geneva banker Eynard. Paris, where the Philhellenic Committee met under the chairmanship of Chateaubriand; Munich, where King Ludwig I showed sympathetic interest; and Geneva, where Capo d'Istria was installed, were, like Boston in the United States, the chief centres of Philhellenism. Finally the Europeans living in the Middle East, originally somewhat suspicious of the Greeks, whom they criticized for their piratical actions and their lack of unity, had now been turned in their favour by Turkish violence: sailors and consuls alike warned their governments of plans to transfer whole populations, notably from the Morea to Egypt. However the Philhellenic movement would not have been sufficient to save the Greeks, if on the one hand the new Tsar, Nicholas I, had not been much more sensitive than his brother to the problems created by Russian expansion in the Balkans, and if on the other hand the Greeks had not cleverly turned for help to Canning, who in 1825 recognized their status as belligerents.

In fact, the question of the Danubian principalities interested the Tsar much more than the Greek question. As for England, she feared nothing so much as an increase in Russian power which would enable that country to lay her hands on Constantinople. But Canning considered that in the existing circumstances, instead of thwarting Russia, it was wiser to associate with her in the Balkan peninsula: this offered the best means of applying the brake in good time when necessary. The result was the signing of the agreement of April 1826 which prescribed for Greece a considerable measure of autonomy within the framework of the Ottoman Empire, to which she should pay taxes. The French government, which had supported the Turks for a long time (largely in order to curry favour with Mehemet Ali, who was then reorganizing Egypt and could reasonably be expected to be the Sultan's successor), but which had been obliged by the pressure of public opinion to revise its Balkan policy, now came on the scene. After lengthy negotiations, during which Greece's situation greatly deteriorated, the agreement of 4 April 1826 became the Anglo-Franco-Russian treaty of 6 July 1827. This stated that the three Powers would offer their mediation, that in the event of rejection by the Turks they would establish commercial and consular relations with the Greeks, and that if an armistice was not concluded they would under-take military intervention, though without themselves taking any part in hostilities. Timid though this treaty was, it none the less obliged all three Powers, by sending their fleet into the Mediterranean, to get caught in the toils. And it was thus that without any declaration of war, Admiral Codrington and Admiral Rigny, interpreting the treaty as a decision to intervene in favour of the Greeks, destroyed the Turco-Egyptian fleet in Navarino Bay (October 1827).

The Battle of Navarino, which was regarded in London as 'a regrettable incident', nearly proved fatal to the Greeks. On the one hand it led the Sultan to declare a holy war against the Christian States, whose ambassadors had to leave Constantinople, and on the other hand it sowed discord between the allies. While Russia declared war on Turkey (April 1828), England took fright at the advance of Russian power towards the Straits. An armed conflict between Russia and England seemed a possibility, but France acted as a mediator between the two Powers. The French Foreign Minister La Ferronays managed to persuade both the Tsar and Aberdeen, who had succeeded Canning in a cabinet led by the Duke of Wellington, to agree that Russia should intervene only on the Danube, while the Western Powers acted in the Mediterranean (July 1828). It was therefore the French who negotiated with Mehemet Ali for the evacuation of the Egyptian troops in the Morea. As for the Russians, after a difficult war, they succeeded in imposing on Turkey, by the Treaty of Adrianople

(September, 1829), the following terms. Serbia was to be autonomous under Miloch Obrenovich, as were the Danubian principalities, which would be governed in future by Rumanian hospodars appointed for life. These principalities, however, were to be occupied by the Russian army until a heavy indemnity had been paid. The terms further included freedom of trade in the Straits, the surrender of the mouths of the Danube, and important territorial concessions in Armenia and the Caucasus. However, as far as Greece was concerned, the Treaty of Adrianople, as a conference of ambassadors had decided in London a few months earlier, merely granted Greece autonomy under Turkish suzerainty, setting its limits along the Arta-Volo line: the English had shown little eagerness to see the Greeks established opposite the Ionian Isles. In fact, a year later, the second Treaty of London recognized Greece's total independence, in return for a slight reduction in territory.

From the European point of view, the result of these events was the complete collapse of Metternich's ' system '. Extremely hostile to the rebels, he had been unable to prevent European intervention, the formation of a triple alliance against Turkey, or the Russo-Turkish War. Indeed the Greek affair led to a fairly close rapprochement between Russia and France, a rapprochement which Chateaubriand had advocated as early as 1822, and even more insistently during his Roman embassy (1828). Polignac, called to power in August 1829, got Bois-le-Comte, a high official at the Ministry of Foreign Affairs, to draw up a ' grand plan ' which, based on an alliance between France, Russia and Prussia, and providing for an extensive scheme of territorial adjustments, would have given France authority to annex Belgium. The Treaty of Adrianople allowed no scope for these negotiations, but it was largely Russian support which enabled Polignac, when he organized the Algiers expedition, to ignore England's protests.

Thus by 1830 nothing remained of the monarchical alliance. England, by supporting the South American colonies, and Russia and France, by helping in the liberation of Greece, had ruined a policy which was built on the European *status quo*. Metternich had been right in predicting that the collapse of the league of conservative Powers would make the task of the revolutionaries easier: Latin America and Greece would serve as examples to other nations and encourage the oppressed peoples to revolt before long, without the Austrian Chancellor's being able to use the Holy Alliance to halt the progress of liberal and national ideas.

One might have thought that the French Revolution of 1830 would immediately reunite the coalition of the conservative Powers: in 1818 the Allies had in fact undertaken an obligation to uphold the Restoration government. However, though ill received by the Concert of Europe, Louis-Philippe promptly afforded proof of his peaceful intentions. A man of the eighteenth century, in favour of the European balance of power, and closer to Vergennes than to the ideology of the Revolution, he had felt that his crown needed recognition from the legitimate monarchs of Europe. The military missions which he sent to the various capitals immediately after his accession gave assurances that France had no intention of extending her frontiers and wanted peace; he would not consider taking action except where French interests were directly involved. He was accordingly recognized by all the Powers, first of all England and last of all Russia.

However, as a result of the 1830 Revolution, an element of uncertainty would linger on in international relations. This was because the July Revolution struck contemporaries primarily as a national revolution, an outburst of protest against the diminution of France's role in the Concert of

Europe. The political group connected with the *National*, and which included such men as Thiers, Mignet and Carrel, not only claimed the left bank of the Rhine for France, but also insisted that it was France's duty to promote revolution in Europe against the established governments. A large section of French public opinion, and particularly the Left, was led to demand revision of the 1815 treaties and imagined that this revision would be made possible by rousing the oppressed nations to revolt. Hence the idea of France's mission in Europe to liberate the other peoples, an idea which Louis Blanc expressed as follows in his *Histoire de dix ans* : ' Nothing like it had ever been seen in history. The proudest Powers were attracted : it was as if the nations could no longer live henceforth without France's help and permission.' The Napoleonic Legend which took shape after 1830 and which depicted the Emperor as the defender of national independence and the personification of the revolutionary spirit naturally strengthened in France the aspirations we have just described. In 1839, Louis Napoleon Bonaparte's *Idées napoléoniennes*, expounded the dual thesis that the Emperor's conquests had been imposed on him by England and that they had been simply a prelude to a rational re-organization of Europe. Finally, the French had assimilated the Messianism of the foreign refugees—particularly the Poles—who had poured into the country since 1830 : Michelet and Quinet described France as the apostle of the nations, and destined to become the centre of universal freedom. Michelet in particular likened France to ' the pilot of the ship of humanity '. Thus, first of all in France, and then throughout Europe, it was recognized that France was the repository of modern civilization, and that it was her duty to help the victory of the ideas of freedom and nationalism outside her frontiers.

It is essential to realize how much France disquieted

the absolute monarchs if one is to understand foreign reactions towards her in the years following the 1830 Revolution.

It was the Belgian revolution that produced a new regrouping of the Powers based on an ideological conflict of views : in face of the absolutist Powers (Austria, Prussia, Russia), the first *entente cordiale* between the liberal Powers England and France came into being.

The status of the Low Countries had been determined by the Constitution of 1814 granted by William I. Although, like a true enlightened despot, he had counted on educational progress and the economic system, which favoured Belgian industry, to win the allegiance of his new subjects, William I had been hampered in his policy of assimilation by certain serious grievances : the preponderance of Dutch elements in the civil service and Parliament; the compulsory use of Dutch as the official language; an unfair allocation of taxes; as well as the intolerance of the clergy, over whom the King, who from 1824 to 1827 returned to Josephine methods, tried in vain to obtain control. The tardy concessions made by William I, who after opening a college of philosophy at Louvain for the clergy, signed a concordat with the Pope in 1827, could not prevent the development of criticism.

How far did economic factors contribute to this discontent? Some Walloon manufacturers, it is true, called for increased protectionism; but the Antwerp merchants were generally favourable to the existing tariff system, and the most enterprising manufacturer, Cockerill, was 'in partnership' with the royal government which gave him considerable credit. Rather than independence, business circles therefore favoured a personal system of union which would leave the economic unity of Belgium and Holland untouched. What was more serious was the growth of a Belgian national consciousness, which abolished the antagonisms between liberal Walloons and clerical Flemings. The transformation of liberalism, powerful in Brussels (de Potter) and at Liège (Lebeau, Devaux, Rogier), which agreed to subordinate its religious preferences to its political preferences, and the spread of Lamennais's ideas among the Catholics, resulted in 'unionism'—a rapprochement between the great Belgian opposition parties against the Dutch : hence the vast campaign of petitions which was launched in 1828. However, as yet it was not independence but an end to personal rule that the Belgians were demanding. But after the Brussels insurrection of 25 August 1830—an unexpected consequence of the events in Paris—and William I's vain efforts to regain control of the capital (23-26 September), a provisional government was formed which called for independence and summoned a National Congress.

The events in Belgium constituted the first breach made in the territorial system established in 1815. They therefore made it possible for France to alter her frontiers. The danger of this happening was all the greater in that democratic France had promptly displayed considerable enthusiasm for the rebels. True, Belgian public opinion, with the exception of a few industrial centres in the Meuse valley, did not favour union with France, and the clergy were firmly opposed to it; yet towards the end of September, the provisional government had sent one of its members, Gendebien, to ask its powerful neighbour for material support. The powers accordingly reacted sharply, and troops were mobilized. But Louis-Philippe's government adopted an attitude which was both firm and reassuring. Delighted at the breaking-up of the Low Countries, which he regarded as an engine of war aimed at France, the King declared that he had no territorial designs whatever on Belgium; refusing to interfere himself, he would not tolerate any interference from a third Power. In this way he anticipated the desires of England which, by the terms

of her previous declarations, was committed to enforcing
the principle of non-intervention, but which would not
have accepted any territorial expansion on the part of
France. Talleyrand, appointed French Ambassador to
London, collaborated skilfully with Palmerston in order to
bring together the views of the two governments. A conference of ambassadors which met in London at the beginning of November decided to recognize the independence
of the new Belgian State. Russia, then paralysed by the
Polish insurrection (see p. 185), was powerless to oppose
it. Franco-Belgian pressure was likewise exerted in favour
of Belgian neutrality, which was recognized by the conference in January 1831. For France, this had the advantage that henceforth Belgium could not be used as a
springboard for an attack on her, and thus ensured the
security of her north-eastern frontier; for England, it
meant that the coast of Flanders could not serve as an
offensive base for a continental army.

It proved much more difficult to settle the question of
Belgium's territorial frontiers, and that of the choice of her
sovereign. On the first point the desire of the Belgian
Congress to include Luxemburg, Limburg and Zealand
Flanders in the new State was thwarted by the Conference,
which declared in favour of the 1790 frontiers. On the
second point, difficulties arose when the Congress chose
as King the Duc de Nemours, Louis-Philippe's second son
(February 1831). In the face of Palmerston's protests,
Louis-Philippe, although he had sponsored his son in order
to exclude the son of Eugène Beauharnais favoured by the
people of Brussels, decided to beat a retreat, and in the
end it was the English candidate, Leopold of Saxe-Coburg,
who was chosen (June 1831). But the favourable territorial
conditions granted to Belgium under the Treaty of the
Eighteen Articles provoked a violent reaction on the part
of William I, who invaded his defenceless former provinces. Louis-Philippe promptly despatched an army which

obliged the Dutch to give way and later drove them out of Antwerp. The fact remains that Belgium had to accept the Treaty of the Twenty-four Articles (October 1831), which deprived her of the contested territories, and which moreover was not ratified by Holland until eight years later, in 1839.

In the diplomatic sphere, the affair of Belgian independence had confronted the absolutist Powers with the Anglo-French *entente*. No doubt this *entente* had been possible only because Louis-Philippe had ignored the demands of the national party in France, because he had turned his back on the popular origins of his power, and because he had shown greater concern for European equilibrium than for material conquests. At the risk of compromising his popularity, he had refused to engage in a war of adventure; he had renounced the idea of acquiring France's ' natural ' frontiers, which he might have been able to obtain, either by annexation or by placing his son on the Belgian throne. But, at the price of these sacrifices he had dismantled the defence system established in 1815 against France. This result had been obtained with the agreement of England, which, realizing that the treaty was a dead-letter, had accepted the independence of Belgium, on condition that that country was neutralized. From the sympathy felt by both governments for the principles of liberalism there sprang an *entente* of which Palmerston said in March 1831 that it was going to govern relations between the two countries. However, England continued to show suspicion of France, especially on the entry of French troops into Belgium, and she refused to conclude an alliance with France, as Louis-Philippe had asked her to after the renunciation by the Duc de Nemours.

The successes of the liberal Powers in Belgium could only be obtained at the price of their non-interference in the other rebellious countries, where the absolutist monarchs were left at liberty to pursue a policy of merciless reaction.

In the case of Poland, France merely offered her mediation, which was refused. In the case of Italy, the rising in the Romagna had led to two successive interventions by Austria, which occupied Bologna. In February 1832, Louis-Philippe sent a regiment to Ancona as a spectacular, if not very effective protest against Austria's activities. Casimir Périer had let it be understood in his ministerial declaration that he was not prepared to act as the disinterested champion of the oppressed peoples: 'At home, order, without sacrificing freedom; abroad, peace, without sacrificing honour.'

For several years the *entente cordiale* between England and France made possible the peaceful solution of a certain number of conflicts. This *entente* was based on the similarity of the two political systems—the revised Charter of 1830, the Reform Act of 1832—on the personal contacts which Louis-Philippe had in London and the connection he had established with Queen Victoria through the Coburg family, and on the extent of English financial investments in French industry. The Duc de Broglie, who had been Foreign Minister since October 1832, wanted, partly out of distrust of Austria, and partly for personal reasons—he was Madame de Staël's son-in-law and had a great many connections with the world of English liberalism —to turn the *entente* with England into a solid instrument which would counterbalance the conservative Powers of Eastern Europe. He had the good sense to realize that an alliance should not be based only on political understanding but on permanent economic interests, notably the lowering of customs tariffs between the two countries. But in this sphere the Duc de Broglie, though supported by the Chambers of Trade of the great French ports and the encouragement of the English economist Bowring, came up against the opposition of the protectionist manufacturers, who exerted a decisive influence on a large section of Parliament. Besides, it may be doubted whether he was prepared to buy a diplomatic alliance at the price of important trade concessions, as Palmerston seemed to be urging him to do. In any case, the latter would not consider entering into an engagement of a general character which would be binding on English diplomacy for a long time. England had no objection, he explained, to treaties with specific and immediate objects, but had no liking for treaties concluded with regard to undefined and unforeseeable circumstances.

The rapprochement between France and England was revealed on the occasion of the first Egyptian crisis, and then in connection with the civil war in the Iberian peninsula. In 1832, the revolt by the Pasha of Egypt, Mehemet Ali, against the Sultan Mahmud, the collapse of the Turkish armies in Syria and Asia Minor, and the threat to Constantinople had led the Russians to anchor their fleet in the Bosphorus. Anglo-French diplomacy succeeded in avoiding the worst by reconciling the Sultan with his Pasha, who by the Treaty of Kutahia received the whole of Syria (May 1833), but it could not prevent Russia from following up her advantages with the Sublime Porte. The Treaty of Unkiar Skelessi (July 1833) obliged Turkey to close the Dardanelles to all foreign fleets : it was a treaty of immense significance, since it established a sort of Russian protectorate, with Russia herself out of danger in the Black Sea, and free, in the event of war, to occupy the Straits, if not to go through them, according to her political interests. The conflict between Turkey and Egypt also underlined the ideological regrouping of the Powers. Dissatisfied with the attitude of the western Powers, Nicholas I endeavoured at the Münchengrätz meetings (October 1833) to recreate with Austria and Prussia a sort of Holy Alliance, which tried to revive the principle of intervention in the defence of threatened crowns.

By way of a gesture, Broglie suggested a defensive treaty of alliance to Palmerston; the suggestion was turned down,

but Broglie succeeded in interfering in the affairs of the
Iberian peninsula, where ever since the death of Ferdinand
VII (1833) Palmerston had posed as the champion of the
liberal monarchs: in Portugal he had promised his support to young Doña Maria, and in Spain to Queen Isabella
and the Regent Maria Christina, against the Carlist pre-
tenders, Dom Miguel and Don Carlos, who were supported
by Metternich. It was this which made possible the signing
in April 1834 of the Treaty of the Quadruple Alliance,
which was in fact confined to Iberian questions. In the
eyes of Europe, which incidentally exaggerated the treaty's
importance, the Quadruple Alliance was the reply of the
liberal States to the Münchengrätz agreement, and the representatives of the three absolutist courts left Madrid together as a mark of protest. It really looked as though
ideological reactions to the Spanish civil war had divided
Europe into two camps.

In fact, although the *entente* lasted until 1840, it proved
artificial and unfruitful after 1834. Nobody was really in
favour of it on either the French or the English side: in
Paris, Thiers, Broglie's successor, could as a historian feel
little sympathy for Napoleon's enemy. As for Palmerston,
he distrusted France, whose expansionist ideas he had
always suspected ever since he had taken part, at the Admir-
alty, in the struggle against Napoleon; he had drawn closer
to France simply in order to keep a tighter rein on her and
above all to separate her from Russia. Despite all his pro-
testations, he remained faithful to the spirit of the 1815
alliance. In liberalism he saw above all else a sign of weakness in others, and he used it as a means of ensuring the
supremacy of England, whose interests were his sole pre-
occupation. Though he possessed undeniable qualities of
loyalty and a remarkable sense of his responsibilities, he
was dictatorial and offensive at the conference table, for-

ever trying to satisfy personal spites and showing no consideration for others. The opposition between France and England first came into the open in Spain, where the former supported the *moderados* under Martinez de la Rosa, and the latter the *exaltados* under Mendizabal, while the head of the Espartero Ministry, once victory over the Carlists had been achieved (1839), openly favoured Britain and authorized English companies to buy the property of the confiscated religious communities cheap. But colonial conflicts, especially in North Africa, where the English seemed to fear a French attempt at expansion from Algeria towards Morocco and Tunisia, and finally the maintenance of protectionist laws by France, provided arguments on both sides for those who advocated a weakening of the *entente*.

In reality Louis-Philippe, who wanted to obtain forgiveness for the origins of his power, was tending, with the support of Thiers and Molé, to draw closer to the absolutist States. In the affair of the Cracovian Republic, and in that of the Swiss refugees, he modelled his policy on Metternich's. He was unable to obtain the hand of an archduchess for his son, the Duc d'Orléans, but he succeeded in breaking the 'matrimonial blockade', and the Duc d'Orléans finally married the daughter of the Duke of Mecklenburg-Schwerin, who was related to the Prussian royal family. In 1838 Molé concluded negotiations with Metternich for the simultaneous withdrawal of the occupying forces from Ancona and Bologna. But at bottom in the absolutist courts, suspicion of France lingered on; while the Anglo-French *entente* was in the process of becoming a dead letter, it was none the less impossible for France to enter into a new system of alliances. She was to discover the full measure of her isolation in the course of the 1840 crisis.

It was the second Turco-Egyptian War which was to reveal the extent of the existing rivalries. Since 1834

Palmerston's policy with regard to the Eastern question had been based on a few simple principles. First of all, he was determined to win back from Russia the influence she had acquired in Constantinople by virtue of the Treaty of Unkiar Skelessi. True, he did not share the fears and hostility with regard to Russia felt by his fellow countrymen, who were beginning to be affected by intense Russophobia; and he did not approve of the excesses of his diplomatic agent Urquhart, who carried his hostility towards Russian policy to the point of monomania, trying to compromise Nicholas I's government by publishing secret documents taken from the Grand Duke Constantine in his journal *The Portfolio*. But he was determined not to allow the St. Petersburg government to make use of the privileges it had acquired in 1833. Even more than Russia, he feared the expansionism of Mehemet Ali, France's ally, whom he suspected of wishing to create a great Arab State capable of dominating the eastern Mediterranean, and whose ambitions could compromise the safety of communications with India. Consequently in 1838, he had concluded a trade agreement with the Sultan Mahmud directed against the Egyptians, and in 1839 he had obtained the cession of Aden to England.

The crisis was started by an attack launched by Mahmud against Syria, which resulted in his complete discomfiture; his sudden death left the Porte at the mercy of the Pasha of Egypt (June 1839). To begin with, Palmerston tackled the most urgent problem, namely the prevention of independent Russian intervention; taking advantage of the conciliatory attitude of the French government, which accepted the idea of an international solution of the crisis, he arranged for the sending of a note from the five Great Powers (July 1839) which established the collective tutelage of Europe over the Ottoman Empire. There remained the problem of settling the conditions of the Turco-Egyptian peace, which engaged the attention of a conference of ambassadors meeting in Vienna; but on this point there immediately appeared a fundamental difference of opinion between France, which opposed any coercive measures against Mehemet Ali, and England, which wanted the Powers to insist on the Pasha's returning the Turkish fleet and relinquishing Syria. Palmerston did not hesitate to enter into negotiations with Russia, while Russia for her part grasped the opportunity to create a split in the *entente cordiale*. In fact French public opinion wanted the settlement of the crisis to be favourable to the Pasha, and therefore made it a matter of principle that his possessions should be regarded as hereditary and that the whole of Syria should remain his. To Palmerston's proposals for a sort of partition of Syria, the French Foreign Minister, Marshal Soult, had sent a negative reply. Thiers, on succeeding him in March 1840, further stiffened France's position and hoped to arrange a direct agreement between Mehemet Ali and the Porte, convinced that for the sake of peace and quiet the Powers would finally give way. Pointing out the contradiction between these efforts and the note from the five Great Powers, Palmerston got Russia, Austria and Prussia to sign the London Convention (July 1840), which offered Mehemet Ali hereditary rule of Egypt and the Pashalik of Acre for life, in return for immediate submission.

The French government, informed after the event, interpreted the London Convention as a sign of the determination of the Great Powers to humiliate France, and even to reconstitute the 1814 Coalition against her. There seemed to be a danger of war, all the more so in that in France, where public opinion was at fever pitch, there was talk of 'playing the revolutionary game'. There were also suggestions of reconquering the Rhine frontier (which in turn provoked a revival of German national feeling against France, of which the most obvious manifestation was the Rhineland poet Becker's *Der deutsche Rhein*), and Thiers embarked on a policy of military bluff. However, after the bombardment of Beirut and the recall of the consuls in Alexandria, it became clear that the Powers were determined to enforce the decisions taken in London. Louis-Philippe did not want to be dragged into war by his 'little minister', and after he had refused to countersign a bellicose speech, he replaced Thiers with Guizot, then French Ambassador in London, who had disapproved of the policy pursued so far. Moreover, on the appearance of a fleet off Alexandria, Mehemet Ali had capitulated unconditionally. Palmerston would doubtless have wished for the complete humiliation of the Pasha, but in this he was supported by neither his colleagues nor Metternich: Mehemet Ali accordingly kept Egypt on a hereditary basis. As for France, anxious to be readmitted to the Concert of Europe, she joined in signing the Straits Convention (July 1841), which closed the Straits to all warships. Thus the crisis ended triumphantly for England. She excluded Russia from the Straits and France from the Nile, and ensured a dominant position for herself in the Mediterranean. However brutal and discourteous Palmerston's diplomatic methods might be, there can be no doubt that he was one of the great promoters of English power in the world.

Was there going to be a return to the *entente cordiale*? Engaged in a policy of expansion all over the world (notably in Afghanistan, China and British Columbia), England continued to favour a balance of power on the Continent. Lord Aberdeen, who in August 1841 had succeeded Palmerston at the Foreign Office, wished to resume relations with France, chiefly in the hope of keeping Russia isolated in the Middle East. Now Guizot, a great admirer of British constitutional government, to which he had devoted an important part of his historical studies, and who because of his Protestant origins had many friends in England, was likewise in favour of a resumption of the *entente cordiale*. He saw it as a guarantee of fruitful economic collaboration, particularly in the building of railways in France. The new *entente* was essentially based on relations between the two Ministers, who were both friends of Princess Lieven, as well as on the links which had been established between the two reigning families: in 1843 and 1845 Victoria visited Louis-Philippe at Eu, while he in his turn visited the Queen at Windsor in 1844. The absolute sovereigns naturally took umbrage over this cordial relationship; but a visit which the Tsar paid to London in June 1844 had no practical results. The *entente cordiale* made it possible to reach an amicable solution of certain difficult problems: the abolition of the right to search slave ships, and the settlement of the Pritchard Affair (the case of the British consul at Tahiti, whose political activities had led to his expulsion, but to whom Guizot agreed to pay an indemnity). However, in the long run the lack of mutual understanding compromised the *entente*, which the continuing economical and political rivalry of the two Powers in Spain finally turned into a conflict. Possibly Guizot was thinking of enrolling Spain in a Bourbon league, of Paris, Naples and Madrid, as part of a vast Mediterranean policy of which the Franco-Piedmontese trade agreement of August 1843 would have been another part. On the other hand, England seemed unwilling to see France, already in control of Algeria, obtain a preponderant position in Spain, which would enable her to dominate the western Mediterranean. It was the question of the 'Spanish marriages' which provided the focal point for Anglo-French rivalry: would Queen Isabella marry a Coburg, one of Queen Victoria's first cousins, or one of Louis-Philippe's sons? In 1843, on the occasion of the meeting at Eu, the two countries had agreed on a policy of 'mutual inaction'; but in 1844 Guizot proposed a marriage between Isabella's sister Louisa to the Duc de Montpensier, admittedly after the birth of a royal heir. This was enough to make Palmerston, who had returned to power, seize the chance to revive the Coburg candidature, whereupon Guizot considered himself free to retract his promise and to negotiate the simultaneous marriage of Isabella and Louisa, to which the government of Madrid agreed a few months later. Palmerston took the opportunity afforded by the affair of the ' Spanish marriages ' to turn English public opinion against France, and to communicate to Thiers and members of the French parliamentary opposition documents calculated to compromise Guizot.

The collapse of the *entente cordiale* left considerable freedom of movement to the absolutist States : in 1846, Metternich decided to annex the Republic of Cracow to Austria without arousing any protests. Moreover, since the break with England, Louis-Philippe's government, following its natural bent, had once again moved closer to the conservative Powers. The rapprochment of Guizot and Metternich, based on their common anxiety with regard to the growth of Prussian power in Germany, would be intensified in the course of the *Sonderbund* War.

In Switzerland the radicals had been planning to turn the Federation into a centralized, unified State, contrary to the provisions of the 1815 treaties; and in June 1847, as a warning, Metternich had called upon the Powers to enforce observance of the Swiss Constitution, as well as of the Catholic liberties. Without answering this call, Guizot had suggested, in opposition to the government of Berne which had ordered federal action to be taken against the Catholic cantons of the *Sonderbund*, concerted action by the Powers, in which England would be invited to participate. Palmerston showed his cunning by accepting this invitation in principle, while at the same time putting forward an alternative scheme, in order to gain time in which the Catholic cantons could be crushed. The Swiss government was accordingly able to reject the offer of European mediation. It was in vain that in January 1848 the European

Powers, with the exception of England, protested against the illegality of the Berne government's operations and announced measures which the 1848 revolutions prevented from being taken.

Guizot's policy was not strictly speaking a reactionary policy. He tried to act as a mediator between the revolutionary movement sweeping across Europe, and the counter-revolutionary movement led by Austria. He hoped for moderate reforms which would respect the established order—a policy which he had outlined to Metternich, first by sending him a personal envoy, the German Klindworth, then in a personal letter of May 1847. This was the policy which he tried to apply in Italy, where Austrian troops had occupied Ferrara in response to revolutionary agitation, but where the French government, while trying to restrain Austria in her policy of intervention, kept urging the sovereigns, particularly the Pope, to introduce administrative reforms: this was the special responsibility of the French Ambassador in Rome, Pellegrino Rossi. It was a difficult policy to pursue, because it came up against both the hostility of the French nation and the mistrust of the absolutist Powers: whereas he wanted to be the guide of European liberalism, kept within reasonable bounds, Guizot was regarded as the tool of the reactionaries. It was much easier for Palmerston to send out agents to make contact with revolutionary elements everywhere—agents such as Lord Minto, one of his colleagues in the Cabinet, whom he sent to Italy—and to pose as the protector of the oppressed nationalities against reactionary Austria.

By breaking with France in 1846 and forcing Louis-Philippe to make advances towards the camp of the absolutist Powers, England helped to bring about the revolution of February 1848. Everywhere, indeed, by stirring up national feeling and liberal agitation, she prepared to overthrow the Europe established by the 1815 treaties. But whether she tried, as Castlereagh did, to use the sup-

port of the Powers which had defeated Napoleon, or
whether, as in Palmerston's day, she allied herself with
the revolutionaries, her object was always to divide and
weaken the Continent. After the brilliant, bloodless victories which she obtained, first on the Atlantic front and
then in the Mediterranean region, she went on advancing
her interests throughout the world, in the face of a Europe
which lacked any inner element of stability.

Conclusion

THE CAUSES OF THE
1848 REVOLUTIONS

Except for Greece and Belgium, the map of Europe, in 1848, had not changed since the Congress of Vienna. But the moral upheaval which had taken place during those thirty years had been considerable; and in 1847 feeling was at such a pitch that it can be said without fear of exaggeration that the old Europe of the 1815 treaties was no longer anything but a worn-out façade, and that the political equilibrium was extremely precarious: The proof of this can be seen in the disproportion between the immediate causes of the various revolutions, which were generally insignificant incidents, and the extent of the upheaval represented by these revolutions, which were obviously due to profound causes.

It has been rightly remarked that the 1848 revolutions were due to the conjunction of an economic crisis and political discontent. As in 1789 and 1830, the political crisis coincided with an economic one. Any one-sided explanation of the revolutionary movement would therefore come up against insuperable difficulties; but it is still necessary to establish a fair estimate of the respective importance of the two factors.

Historians are agreed on the importance of the cyclical crisis of 1847 and on its dual character—an agricultural crisis of the old type, and a credit crisis of a new type— but they disagree as to the importance of these two phenomena. Some regard the crisis as essentially an agricultural crisis which gradually affected the overall economy of the country; it originated in a food shortage produced by the potato disease which destroyed the entire potato crop, especially in Ireland, Flanders, the Netherlands and Germany. The following year, the same disaster affected the grain harvest: a sudden drought and exceptional heat destroyed the crops, and there were no stocks left over from the previous year. In western and central Europe, the food shortage made itself felt as early as the spring of 1847.

The effects of this shortage, which was accompanied throughout Europe by riots and disturbances, were particularly serious in the country areas whose economy was based on a combination of agriculture and industrial work, for domestic industry was already suffering from competition with the machine. The textile industry was soon hard hit, and this in its turn led to complete or partial unemployment. The other forms of industrial labour were rapidly affected, while at the same time, because of the crisis, credit and State aid ceased to be available for great national undertakings such as the railways, which had inspired a wave of speculation since 1841. By forcing the banks and the government to buy large quantities of foreign corn, the agricultural crisis had emptied the country's coffers. Bankruptcies multiplied, while the cash holdings of the great national credit institutions diminished, in spite of the general rise in the discount rate.

However, against this traditional view of the crisis, certain historians have pointed to the primary importance of financial factors which, they claim, offer a complete explanation of the profound changes which took place. In the first phase, characterized by confidence and rapid development, investment, especially in railways and industry, steadily increased, while the liquid assets of banks and undertakings fell considerably. Agriculture itself was affected by the attraction of industrial profits, which were far higher than agricultural profits; landowners were led to place a large part of their capital in stocks and shares instead of investing it in their land. However, in the second phase, excessive investments, which incidentally were often ill advised and even purely speculative, produced a disproportion between fixed capital and circulating capital, the latter gradually diminishing. The result was an increasing shortage of liquid assets; in order to obtain them, companies issued masses of shares, which fell in value. Loss of confidence, producing financial crashes, was rapidly followed by a fall in the price of goods, resulting from the general sluggishness of business. Industrial and commercial bankruptcies multiplied, and the depression spread to the agricultural sector, by way of the fall in prices, the rise in debts, and the lack of liquid assets. Thus the agricultural crisis was not the cause but the consequence of the general crisis, as the *Journal des Économistes* pointed out in 1847; and the events of 1845-47 can be seen as the prelude to the great crises of modern times, dominated by speculation and the abuse of credit facilities.

However, whatever the order in which these various factors are placed, it would seem that the 1848 revolutions occurred, not at the height of the crisis, but during the period of slow recovery which followed the crisis. In 1848, prices, which had risen by 100 to 150 per cent between 1845 and 1847, were keeping steady, while wages were generally low. If the causes of the revolutions had been purely economic, the revolutions would have broken out a year earlier. Poverty rarely produces anything more than riots. The fact remains that the wave of high prices and the accompanying hardships swept over Europe like a flood, and like a flood ebbing away, it left behind it a whole population in distress, with their savings gone. What is more, it prepared the ground for subversive propaganda by undermining the authority and the credit of the State. The crisis, it has been said, 'revived every grievance'; it intensified and unified discontent.

Now this discontent was essentially political in character. It was the absence of liberty which, in one form or another, was most deeply resented by the peoples of Europe and led them to take up arms. In France the hopes of 1830 had turned into reaction : the French had dreamt of a sovereign who would lead them towards universal suffrage and of a monarchy which, in the famous phrase, would be the best of republics; but they had to endure a king who opposed any move towards political emancipation and who refused to recognize anything but the *pays légal*, ignoring the *pays réel* and the Opposition's demands for electoral and parliamentary reform. In Germany, where the Diet was nothing but a police department bent on harrying the liberal press, discontent was chiefly aroused by the practice of absolutism, by hatred of the bureaucratic police State, and by the feeling of personal insecurity which afflicted every citizen; there was growing impatience with the close supervision of intellectual life and the arbitrary measures of which the most progressive elements of the nation were daily victims. There was even more impatience with the reaction in Austria, where the bureaucratic, old-fashioned system under Metternich depended for its existence on the censorship and the secret police. Finally, in Italy, absolutism went hand in hand with espionage, favouritism and informing.

Faced with the forces of reaction, the liberal elements became aware of their solidarity. When Louis-Philippe had refused to become the advocate and champion of liberal demands in Europe, public opinion had taken on that role in his stead. Not only the republicans, but the whole of the Left, and even men like Thiers, regarded the prestige of their country as bound up with the victory of the revolutionary ideas; Paris had become the capital of European liberalism, the refuge of Polish, German and Italian exiles, and the school in which hundreds of foreign teachers and students were educated, while French, still the language of good society, spread a system of liberal ideas as far as the Balkans. It was in Paris that the League of Exiles was founded in 1834, Mazzini's *Young Europe*, in 1844, and the *Annales Franco-Allemandes*. It was Paris that sheltered most of the Polish emigrants, who were to be found in all the revolutionary attempts of the 1830s and the 1840s. If there was no international conspiracy in 1848, there was a revolutionary cosmopolitanism and a sense of solidarity among all liberals.

Inseparable from these liberal aspirations was the hope which inspired the peoples of Europe of seeing States established on a national basis. In support of the nationalist principle, Romanticism, although it had originally adopted a reactionary attitude, had now taken on a revolutionary character. Michelet saw France as the Nation *par excellence*, destined to summon the other peoples of Europe to independence and unity, and he expected nationalist fervour to result in universal peace and harmony; in *Le Peuple* (1846) he wrote that 'patriotism is the necessary initiation for universal brotherhood.' In his lectures at the Collège de France, where he addressed an audience from all parts of Europe, he extolled the idea of nationalism and gave France the mission of leading Europe in that direction: 'France,' he said, 'possesses the divine genius of society ... She is the pilot of the ship of humanity.' Among the European élite, the conviction had steadily grown that France was the repository of modern civilization; and it was regarded as her duty to obtain victory for the ideas of liberty and nationalism on which all civilization was built. 'France,' wrote another historian, Edgar Quinet, 'can no longer halt but a thousand foreign tongues promptly shout in her ear: *Onwards! Onwards!*' And in a pamphlet published in 1847, *De la France, de son génie et de ses destinées*, Henri Martin would write that 'the nationalities have never imposed such a strain on the political structure which they are trying to reform. There are unmistakable indications that before many years have passed, the question of nationalism, linked, as it will be, with the social question will over-shadow all others on the Continent, and that those States which do not make the principle of nationalism their *raison d'être* will be transformed or broken up.' In the eyes of the theorists of the idea of nationalism, such as Mazzini, the nation's work did not end at the nation's frontiers, but embraced the concept of mankind; 'Mankind,' he cried, ' is an association of all countries; mankind is an alliance of all nations to carry out, in peace and love, their mission on earth.'

Such were the ideas which produced the revolutionary movements of 1848, and which won the unanimous support of all those who wanted the destruction of the territorial and political system created by the Congress of Vienna. True, most of the men of '48 saw these essential changes in an idealistic light, and often in complete ignorance of political realities and power politics; they had an other-worldly concept of international relations and cherished fond hopes of universal brotherhood. The fact remains that the aspirations of the peoples of Europe were so manifest and powerful that the established authorities, as soon as they were attacked, were obliged either to disappear, or to grant important concessions.

However, these aspirations, whether political or national in character, appear in a very different light according to the degree of economic maturity and the social structure of the countries under consideration. Consequently the causes of the 1848 Revolution could not be the same in France, where the bourgeoisie had long since carried out its revolution and wielded real power, and in the countries of central Europe, where the Ancien Régime had been only partially abolished and where the old governing classes were still in control.

In France, the fundamental cause of the Revolution is to be seen in the isolation of the *haute bourgeoisie* which had completely identified itself with the régime. As de Tocqueville wrote in his *Souvenirs*: 'In 1830 the triumph of the middle class had been so complete and final that all political power, every franchise, every prerogative, the whole government of the country, were enclosed and so to speak piled up inside the narrow limits of that class, to the exclusion in law of everything which was below it and in fact of everything which had been above it. Not only was it thus the sole ruler of society, but it may be said that it became the framer of society, the particular spirit of the government; it dominated foreign policy as well as home affairs . . . Supreme master as no aristocracy had ever been and perhaps ever will be, the middle class which had become the government took on the appearance of a private industry; it soon shut itself up in its power and shortly afterwards in its egoism, each of its members thinking far more of his private affairs than of public affairs, and of his pleasures than of the nation's greatness.'

However, in 1848 this *grande bourgeoisie* found itself an object of suspicion to the *petite bourgeoisie*, which considered that the former had become a monopolistic class. It had become common practice for socialist authors to stress the dangers to the workers presented by big business and industrial concentration, especially as the government refused to apply the combination law to combinations of capital. Even in the *grande bourgeoisie* agreement was not complete; only the financial aristocracy, as Marx observed, was entirely satisfied, and industrial circles, disturbed by the excessive growth of speculation, began to move closer to the Opposition.

But above all the proletariat had come into existence, and had become the 'rising' class: a united proletariat which combined the factory workers and the suburban craftsmen, and no longer as in the eighteenth century a scattered proletariat; a united proletariat in which signs of class consciousness could already be distinguished. For what was new was not so much the appearance of the working class, but that the working class should become aware of its poverty and its power: socialism, and even communism, were the order of the day. Here again de Tocqueville's comments (in a speech made on 27 January 1848) are highly significant: 'Look at what is happening inside the working classes, which at the moment, I admit, are quiet. It is true that they are not tormented by political passions to the extent that they were in the past. But can you not see that their passions, from being political, have become social? Can you not see that opinions and ideas are gradually spreading among them which are not only going to overthrow certain laws, a certain ministry or a certain government, but society itself, knocking it off the foundations on which it rests today? Can you not see that it is being increasingly said among them that the division of goods as practised so far is unjust, and that property rests on inequitable foundations? And do you not suppose that when such opinions penetrate deep into the masses, sooner or later they lead to the most fearful revolutions?' Thus the social conflicts taking place in 1848 can be seen as a triangular class struggle between two sections of the middle class (the *grande bourgeoisie* and the *petite bourgeoisie*) and the lower class. It was against the *grande bourgeoisie* that the February Revolution would be directed; admittedly the two sections of the middle class, united by fear, would in their turn later isolate the proletariat, but the fact remains that the 1848 Revolution in France was carried out to extend the *pays légal* to cover the entire nation.

In Germany, where industrialization had not been so extensive and the old governing classes retained a dominant influence, the middle class engaged in trade and industry still had to win its place in the sun. It was therefore the bourgeoisie which brought about the Revolution. On the eve of the events of 1848, liberalism was a force to be reckoned with, and the economic crisis had provided it with a favourable opportunity which it turned to good advantage. The Rhenish upper middle class in particular had shown a political maturity in the united *Landtag* of 1847 which had not failed to impress foreign observers : it held views on the future of the German nation which were both consistent and carefully considered. In a united, constitutional Germany, the middle class could hope to keep that dominant position which its wealth, activity and intelligence conferred upon it. But to carry out the revolution which would have given it a dominant role in the government of the country, this upper middle class would have needed the support of the lower classes. In fact, it found itself confronted with a hostile working class whose activities, even before the revolutionary period, had caused it grave anxiety, and with which it refused to co-operate. In short, as ill luck would have it, Germany, whose economic development had been slowed down by territorial divisions, was unable to advance its liberal institutions until the very moment when industry was faced by a threatening proletariat. All would have been well if the lower classes had been sufficiently educated in 1848 to understand the significance of the industrial revolution; but as yet Germany did not possess a united working class aware of its objectives. Its centre of gravity consisted of an anxious artisan class which was threatened with proletarianization but still felt itself attached to the bourgeoisie, and looked for a solution to the crisis less in the organization of industrial society than in the restoration of corporate links; in other words it looked to the past rather than to the future, and was therefore unwilling to accept the position to which economic development relegated it, and which it regarded as humiliating. The description of society contained in the *Communist Manifesto* was simply a vision of the future. In the social sphere, the 1848 Revolution can therefore be seen as an attempt by the upper middle class to obtain the political power which, since the creation of the *Zollverein*, its economic situation conferred on it; but, in view of the difficulties created on its left by the threat of social agitation, it was inclined to come to a compromise with the old ruling classes, and its object in 1848 seemed to be a division of power rather than the conquest of power.

In a country such as Hungary, where national feeling was particularly strong, but where the virtually non-existent middle class was incapable of taking control of the movement for emancipation, the role of the Third Estate fell to the minor nobility, which, aware of the crisis in the feudal economy, called for the abolition of an outdated economic system based on serfdom. But it also had to rely on its left on an aristocratic plebs, many members of which had been to university and formed a sort of intellectual proletariat : it was this class which had produced Kossuth. Fighting valiantly against the imperial régime and the aristocrats who defended it, Kossuth tried to convince the bulk of the nobility that it was by adopting a democratic system that it would take control of the new nation-state. Thus Hungary, like the other European States, had reached a point in her development where the destruction of the existing framework could be seen as a necessity, but where fear of radicalism paralysed any attempt at reform.

It follows from these observations that underlying the 1848 revolutions there was a strong social factor, and that the struggle was directed against the selfishness of the governing classes, whether, as in central Europe, it was a question of a world which was still essentially feudal in character, or, as in France, of an upper middle class which had refused to share its power since 1830. In the eyes of the men of '48, there can be no doubt that political and national emancipation was bound up with the destruction of a social system which was itself bound up with absolutism and particularism. However, the structure of society remained a serious handicap for the revolutionaries. Divisions, in fact, appeared among them as soon as the question was raised of the workers' participation in any revolutionary activity. It is here that we come up against the ambiguous attitude of the *petite bourgeoisie*, which formed an essential yet unreliable element in the Revolution. Immediately after the events of 1848, Engels wrote about this class: ' Its intermediary position between the capitalists in trade and industry, the bourgeoisie proper, and the working class or proletariat, determines its special character. It aspires to the position of the bourgeoisie, but the slightest financial set-back plunges its members into the proletariat. . . . Constantly torn between the hope of raising itself to the level of the richest class and the fear of being reduced to the level of the proletariat or even to complete destitution: divided between the hope of advancing its interests by obtaining a share in the control of public affairs and the fear of provoking by untimely opposition the wrath of a government which could dispose of its very existence . . . and possessing limited resources as insecure as they are paltry, this class vacillates wildly in its opinions. Meek and ignobly submissive under a feudal government or a powerful monarchy, it inclines towards liberalism when the bourgeoisie is in the ascendant; it has fits of democratic fervour as soon as the bourgeoisie has established its own supremacy, but it subsides into profound discouragement as soon as the class below it, the proletariat, attempts independent action.' In short, the predominant feeling actuating this important section of the community was fear of proletarianization. No doubt the basic problem for the men of '48 and the fundamental cause of their failure lay in the fact that the revolutions, inspired by the unanimous determination of the peoples of Europe to obtain liberty and nationhood, took place at a time when the economic and social structure, still strongly marked by the forms of the Ancien Régime, did not allow the disinherited classes to make common cause against the classes in possession and to take up the banner of social revolution.

MAPS
BIBLIOGRAPHY
INDEX

The Formation of the Zollverein 1828–1848

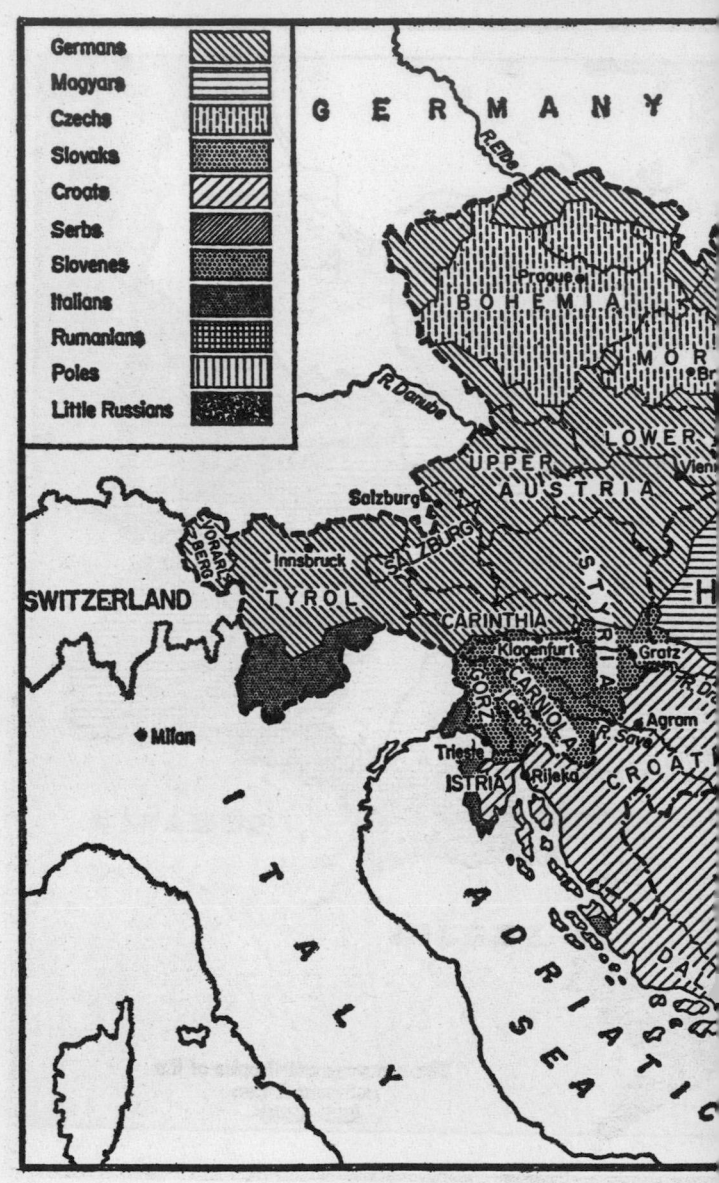

The Language and Peoples of the Habsburg Empire 1815–1848

SELECT BIBLIOGRAPHY

I. General Works

In England, the *Cambridge History*, which enjoyed a considerable reputation in its time, has been replaced by the *New Cambridge History*, in which, for the period in question, see vol. x, J. P. T. BURY, *The Zenith of Europe 1830-1870* (1960). Two stimulating shorter histories of the period are:— E. HOBSBAWM, *The Age of Revolution: Europe, 1789-1848* (1962), and J. L. TALMON, *Romanticism and Revolt: Europe 1815-1848* (1967).

In France, the most recent series is 'Peuple et civilisations', in which see vol. xv, F. PONTEIL, *L'idée des nationalités et le mouvement libéral 1815-1848* (1960). For a bibliography and the present state of research, see the volume in the series 'Clio' by J. DROZ, L. GENET and P. VIDALENC, *Restaurations et Révolutions 1815-1871* (1953), as well as the volume in the series 'Nouvelle Clio' by J. B. DUROSELLE, *L'Europe de 1815 à nos jours* (1964). See also, in the series 'Histoire générale des Civilisations', R. SCHNERB, *Le XIXe Siècle* (1955), which gives considerable space to economic and social questions.

In Germany see the 'Propyläen Weltgeschichte', vol. VIII of which is entitled *Das 19. Jahrhundert* (1960), as well as vol. x of the series 'Historia Mundi', *Das 19. und 20. Jahrhundert* (1961).

In the United States several general studies have been published. In W. LANGER'S series 'The Rise of Modern Europe', see vol. XIV, F. ARTZ, *Reaction and Revolution 1814-1832* (1934) and W. LANGER, *Liberalism, Nationalism and Socialism 1832-1852* (1935). In the series 'The University of Michigan History of the Modern World', each volume is devoted to a separate region or country.

On the history of Europe, for the present state of historical research, see in particular the series edited by M. BELOFF, P. RENOUVIN, F. SCHNABEL, F. VALSECCHI, *L'Europe du XIXe et du XXe Siècles*, vols. I and II: 1815-1870 (1959).

Finally mention must be made of the thought-provoking work by J. PIRENNE, *Les grands courants de l'histoire universelle*, vol. IV *De la révolution française aux révolutions de 1830* (1951) and vol. V. *De 1830 à 1904* (1953).

Several general economic histories have appeared, especially in the United States. Among the most useful general economic histories are H. HEATON, *Economic History of Europe* (London, 1930); S. B. CLOUGH and C. W. COLE, *Economic History of Europe* (Boston,

1940); G. LUZZATTO, *Storia economica dell'eta moderna e contemporanea*, vol. II (1948); *Cambridge Economic History of Europe* vol. VI parts I and II (1965).

For a general history of demography see L. CHEVALIER, *Démographie générale* (1951) and M. REINHARD, *Histoire de la population mondiale de 1700 à 1948* (1949).

The general evolution of political, economic and social ideas has been the object of numerous studies. See the classic work of H. MICHEL, *L'idée de l'Etat, Essai critique sur l'histoire des théories sociales et politiques en France depuis la Révolution* (1896), which goes beyond its stated subject. The most useful work is now P. TOUCHARD, *Histoire des idées politiques*, vol. II *Du XVIIIe Siècle à nos jours* (1962). In English the classic work is G. H. SABINE, *A History of Political Theory* (1950), and in German W. THEIMER, *Geschichte der politischen Ideen* (1955). Socialism in the period in question has been the object of a composite study: E. HALEVY, *Histoire du socialisme européen* (1948). Economic doctrines have been studied by C. GIDE and C. RIST, *Histoire des doctrines économiques*, vol. I *Des physiocrates à John Stuart Mill* (1947), by E. JAMES, *Histoire des théories économiques* (1950), and lastly by G. MYRDAL, *The political element in the development of economic theory* (1953).

II. History of International Relations

The only recent large-scale work dealing with the whole field of international relations, regarded as something more than a mere summary of diplomatic history, is P. RENOUVIN, *Histoire des relations internationales*, vol. V *Le XIXe Siècle. De 1815 à 1871. L'Europe des Nationalités et l'éveil des nouveaux mondes* (1954). This book introduces the study of the 'underlying forces' which situate and explain the work of the statesman. See also J. DROZ, *Histoire diplomatique de 1648 à 1919* (1959) and F. L'HUILLIER, *De la Sainte Alliance au Pacte Atlantique*, vol. I. *1815-1898 L'hégémonie européenne et la formation des nationalités* (1954).

In England, *The Cambridge History of British Foreign Policy 1783-1919*, edited by A. W. Ward and G. P. Gooch, deals with our subject in vol. II. For a Marxist treatment of the subject, see V. POTIEMKINE, *Histoire de la diplomatie*, vol. I, *De l'Antiquité à 1871* (1947).

For the period under study, see first of all the now classic works by two great English historians, C. K. WEBSTER, *The Foreign Policy of Castlereagh 1815-1822* (1925) and H. TEMPERLEY, *The Foreign Policy of Canning* (1925). On the Congress of Vienna, see C. K. WEBSTER, *The Congress of Vienna* (1934) and K.

GRIEWANK, *Der Wiener Kongress und die Neuordnung Europas* (1942). On the Holy Alliance, see J. H. PIRENNE, *La Sainte-Alliance*, 2 vols. (1946) and 1949), and M. BOURQUIN, *Histoire de la Sainte-Alliance* (1954). On Metternich's diplomacy, see H. RIEBEN, *Grundlage und Diplomatie in Metternichs Europapolitik 1815-1848* (1942) and P. W. SCHROEDER, *Metternich's Diplomacy at its Zenith 1820-1823* (1962). G. BERTIER DE SAUVIGNY, *Metternich and His Times* (1962).

M. S. ANDERSON, *The Eastern Question* (1966) provides a clear introduction to European diplomacy in the Near East during this period. On the diplomatic consequences of Greek Independence see also E. DRIAULT and M. LHERITIER, *Histoire diplomatique de la Grèce de 1821 à nos jours*, 5 vols. (1925-1926) and C. W. CRAWLEY, *The Question of Greek Independence* (1930).

For the period 1830-1840, see R. GUYOT, *La première Entente cordiale* (1926), F. CHARLES-ROUX, *Thiers et Mehemet Ali* (1951), A. de RIDDER, *Les projets d'union douanière franco-belge et les puissances européennes 1836-1843* (1933); and S. MASTELLONE, *La politica estera del Guizot 1840-1847. L'unione doganale. La lega borbonica* (1957). The principal work remains C. K. WEBSTER, *The Foreign Policy of Palmerston 1830-1841* (1951). On the affair of the Spanish marriages see E. J. PARRY, *The Spanish Marriages* (1936). The part played by the *Sonderbund* War in international affairs has been studied by W. NAEF, *Die Schweiz in Metternichs Europa* (1940).

III. History of The Church

There is no entirely satisfactory history of the Church for the period 1815-1848. In the series 'L'Histoire de l'Eglise' edited by A. Fliche and V. Martin, see the volume by J. LEFLON, *La crise révolutionnaire 1789-1846* (1949); and for the early years of Pius IX's pontificate, see the remarkable work by R. AUBERT, *Le Pontificat de Pie IX 1846-1878* (1952). There are a great many manuals of ecclesiastical history such as J. HERGENROETHER, *Handbuch der allgemeinen Kirchengeschichte*, vol. IV (1925). The history of the Papacy has been written by J. SCHMIDLIN. *Papstgeschichte der neuen Zeit*, vols. I and II (1933-1934).

The history of the Church in the different countries of Europe is better served. For France, see A. DANSETTE, *Histoire religieuse de la France contemporaine. De la révolution à la IIIe République* (1948) and above all A. LATREILLE and J. R. PALANQUE, *Histoire du catholicisme en France. La période contemporaine* (1962). For Germany, see the old but indispensable work by G. GOYAU, *L'Allemagne religieuse. Le catholicisme*, vols. I and II (1905-

1909) and above all F. SCHNABEL, *Deutsche Geschichte im 19. Jahrhundert,* vol IV. *Die religiösen Kräfte* (1937). W. LIPGENS, *Graf Spiegel. Kirche und Staat, 1789-1835* (1965). KARL BUCHHEIM, *Ultramontanismus und Demokratie. Der Weg der deutscheh Katholiken im XIX. Jahrhundert* (1963). W. O. SHANAHAN, *German Protestants Face the Social Question: The Conservative Phase,* 1815-1871 (1954). For England, P. THUREAU-DANGIN, *La renaissance catholique en Angleterre au XIXe Siècle* remains indispensable.

For the Protestant churches, the reader now has at his disposal a general study: G. LEONARD, *Histoire générale du protestantisme,* vol. III *Déclin et renouveau* (1964). There are a great many works on the Oxford Movement and Newman, including C. F. HARROLD, *J. H. Newman. An expository and critical study of his mind, thought and art* (1945.

IV. History of the Principal Countries

GREAT BRITAIN: The principal general history is *The Oxford History of England,* in which see vol. XIII: E. L. WOODWARD, *The Age of Reform 1815-1870* (1960). In the series 'A History of England' see vol. VII: D. BEALES, *From Castlereagh to Gladstone 1815-1885* (n.d.), and in the 'Pelican History of England' see vol. VIII, D. THOMSON, *England in the Nineteenth Century 1815-1914* (1957). None of these works can replace the work of the French historian E. HALEVY, *Histoire du peuple anglais au XIXe Siècle,* vol. I *L'Angleterre en 1815* (1912); vol. III *Du lendemain de Waterloo au Reform Bill 1815-1830* (1923); vol. III *De la crise du Reform Bill à l'avènement de Sir Robert Peel 1830-1841* (1923); vol. IV *Le milieu du siècle 1841-1852* (1946). The best economic history is that by J. H. CLAPHAM, *Economic History of Modern England* vol. I 1820-1850 (1930). See also W. W. ROSTOW *and* D. GAYER, *The Growth and Fluctuation of the British Economy 1790-1830,* 2 vols. (1953).

Among the general works covering our period, see in particular: A. BRIGGS, *The Age of Improvement 1774-1874* (1959); J. R. M. BUTLER, *A History of England 1815-1918* (1932); G. M. TREVELYAN, *British History in the Nineteenth Century and After 1782-1919* (1945).

There are few works on the pre-Victorian period, apart from A. S. TURBERVILLE, *The House of Lords in the Age of Reform 1784-1837* (1958). On the other hand, the political history of the Peel era has been studied by N. GASH, *Politics in the Age of Peel*

(1953) and *Mr. Secretary Peel* (1960). See also N. MCCORD, *The Anti-Corn Law League* (1958).

On British political institutions in general, there are a great many works, of which the acknowledged classic is W. ANSON, *Law and Custom of the Constitution*, 2 vols. (1922 and 1935); but among which mention must be made of D. L. KEIR, *The Constitutional History of Great Britain 1485-1937* (1948). A useful work is J. REDLICH, *The History of Local Government in England* (1958).

There are a great many works on the history of the various parties. A classic study of Radicalism is E. HALEVY, *La formation du radicalisme philosophique*, 3 vols. (1901-1904), of which vols. I and II concern our period; see also S. MACCOBY, *English Radicalism*, vol. II *From Paine to Cobbett* (1955). On Chartism and the working-class movement, see first of all the works of G. D. H. COLE, particularly *A Short History of the British Class Movement 1789-1937* (n.d.) and *Chartist Portraits* (1941). For a French work on the subject see E. DOLLEANS, *Le Chartisme* (1949). A useful work is D. WILLIAMS and J. FROST, *A Study in Chartism* (1938). On the Conservative Party, see K. G. FEILING, *The Second Tory Party 1714-1832* (1938) and R. H. HILL, *Toryism and the People 1832-1846* (1929).

On Ireland, see the classic study by E. CURTIS, *A History of Ireland* (1945). D. GWYNN has written a work entitled *Daniel O'Connell* (1947). Among recent works, see R. B. MCDOWELL, *Public Opinion and Government Policy in Ireland 1801-1846* (1952) and R. D. EDWARDS and T. D. WILLIAMS, *The Great Famine. Studies in Irish History 1845-1852* (1956).

FRANCE. For the period as a whole, see S. CHARLETY, *La Restauration* and *La Monarchie de Juillet*, vols. IV and V of 'L'Histoire de la France contemporaine' (n.d.). The only reliable general work is F. PONTEIL, *La Monarchie parlementaire 1815-1848* (1949). P. BASTID has made a study of *Les institutions politiques de la monarchie parlementaire française 1814-1848* (1954). The best work on the Restoration is G. BERTIER DE SAUVIGNY, *La Restauration* (1955); the best general study of the July Monarchy is P. VIGIER, *La Monarchie de Juillet* (1962), although mention must be made of P. THUREAU-DANGIN, *Histoire de la Monarchie de Juillet* 7 vols. (1884-1892).

For local history, see J. VIDALENC, *Le département de l'Eure sous la Monarchie constitutionnelle 1814-1848* (1952), and also the introductions to the important recent theses on the 1848 Revolution in France, such as P. VIGIER, *La Seconde République dans la région alpine* (1959).

An important work on the political history of the period is the thesis by C. H. POUTHAS, *Guizot sous la Restauration* (1923), which is the starting point for the numerous studies of constitutional monarchy by this historian. A more recent significant study is D. JOHNSON, *Guizot, Aspects of French History 1787-1874* (1963). On Ultra-Royalism, see G. BERTIER DE SAUVIGNY, *Un type d'ultra-royaliste: le comte Ferdinand de Bertier 1782-1864 et l'énigme de la Congrégation* (1948). So far, there are no reliable studies of the political personalities of the July Monarchy, apart from C. ALMERAS, *Odilon Barrot, avocat et homme politique* (1948). On the history of the various political parties, see the major work by R. REMOND, *The Right Wing in France from 1815 to de Gaulle* (1966); as well as G. PERREUX, *Au temps des sociétés secrètes. La propagande républicaine au début de la Monarchie de Juillet* (1931). Useful information is to be found in the old work by G. WEILL, *Histoire du parti républicain en France 1814-1870* (1900). See also L. GIRARD, *La Garde nationale* (1964).

The economic history of France, dealt with by A. L. DUNHAM, in *The Industrial Revolution in France 1815-1848* (1955) has been shown in a new light by B. GILLE in *La Banque et le crédit en France de 1815 à 1848* (1959). For a demographic study see C. H. POUTHAS, *La Population française pendant la première moitié du XIXe Siècle* (1956). For the social history of France, see R. BEAU DE LOMENIE, *La responsabilité des dynasties bourgeoises: I. De Bonaparte à Mac-Mahon* (1943), which should be treated with caution, and the more recent work by J. LHOMME, *La Grande Bourgeoisie au pouvoir 1830-1880* (1960). Two thought-provoking studies are L. CHEVALIER, *Classes laborieuses et classes dangereuses à Paris pendant la première moitié du XIXe Siècle* (1958) and *Le choléra* (1958). A. DAUMARD has studied *La bourgeoisie parisienne de 1815 à 1848* (1963) and A. J. TUDESQ *Les grands notables en France* (1840-1849), 2 vols. (1964). The reader cannot afford to neglect B. GUYON, *La pensée politique et sociale de Balzac* (1947.

The political and social ideas of this period are examined in the now classic work by M. LEROY, *Histoire des idées sociales en France* vol. II *De Babeuf à Tocqueville* (1950). On certain special aspects, see J. B. DUROSELLE, *Les débuts du catholicisme social en France 1820-1870* (1951) and R. GARAUDY, *Les sources françaises du socialisme scientifique* (1948). As yet there is no satisfactory history either of the working-class movement or socialist thought in the period under study. Apart from the rather old-fashioned work by E. DOLLEANS, *Histoire du mouvement ouvrier*, vol. I *1830-1870* (1947), see the thought-provoking work by J. BRUHAT, *Histoire du mouvement ouvrier français* vol. I (1952). Saint-

Simonism and positivism have been studied in several works; see particularly H. GOUHIER, *La Jeunesse d'Auguste Comte et la formation du positivisme*, 2 vols. (1941).

GERMANY. The classic work remains F. SCHNABEL *Deutsche Geschichte im 19. Jahrhundert*, 4 vols. (1954), which replaced the great work, now completely out of date, by H. TREITSCHKE, *Deutsche Geschichte im 19. Jahrhundert* 5 vols. (1886-1895). The reader may consult other general works, such as H. HERZFELD, *Die moderne Welt 1789-1890* (1957) and G. MANN, *Deutsche Geschichte des neunzehnten und zwanzigsten Jahrhunderts* (1959). In English, see J. PASSANT and W. O. HENDERSON, *A Short History of Germany 1815-1945* (1959). A. RAMM, *Germany 1789-1919. A Political History* (1967) and in French, J. DROZ, *Histoire d'Allemagne* (1958), which does not supplant the classic work by E. VERMEIL, *L'Allemagne. Essai d'explication* (1939).

On the *Vormärz* in particular see the (stimulating) work by T. S. HAMEROW, *Restoration, Revolution, Reaction. Economics and Politics in Germany 1815-1871* (1958), as well as R. H. THOMAS, *Liberalism, Nationalism and German intellectuals 1822-1847* (1951). Liberalism itself has been the object of a great many studies, particularly L. KREIGER, *The German Idea of Freedom. History of a political tradition* (1957) and F. C. SELL, *Die Tragödie des deutschen Liberalismus* (1953). D. G. ROHR, *The Origins of Social Liberalism in Germany* (1963). Certain regional aspects of liberalism have been studied separately. For the Rhineland, see J. DROZ, *Le libéralisme rhénan 1815-1848. Contribution à l'histoire du libéralisme* (1940). JOHANNA KOESTER, *Der rheinische Frühliberalismus und die soziale Frage* (1938) and for Hesse, P. WENTZKE and W. KLOETZER, *Deutscher Liberalismus im Vormärz. Heinrich von Gagerns Briefe und Reden 1815-1847* (1959). For Schleswig-Holstein, W. CARR, *Schleswig-Holstein, 1815-1848. A Study in National Conflict* (1963). For German politics as a whole, see L. BERGSTRAESSER, *Geschichte der politischen Parteien in Deutschland* (1960). The history of elections in Germany is beginning to interest German historians; see H. BOBERACH, *Wahlrechtsfragen im Vormärz. Die Wahlrechtsanschauungen im Rheinland 1815-1849 und die Enstehung des Dreiklassenwahlrechts* (1959). For the development of Prussian conservatism in the period, H. J. SCHOEPS, *Das andere Preussen* (1952), T. H. VON LAUE, *Leopold von Ranke* (1950) GORDON CRAIG, *The Politics of the Prussian Army* (1955). On the democratic movements A. H. J. KNIGHT, *Georg Büchner* (1951) E. M. BUTLER, *The Saint-Simonian Religion in Germany* (1926).

It is impossible to separate the political history of Germany from Prussia's efforts to organize the country's economic unity. See P. BENAERTS, *Les origines de la grande industrie allemande.*

Histoire du Zollverein 1833-1866 (1832). Also on the development of the *Zollverein* W. O. HENDERSON, *The Zollverein* (2nd Ed. 1959); A. H. PRICE, *The Evolution of the Zollverein* (1949). Certain aspects of the social evolution of the period have been analysed in a symposium, *Staat und Gesellschaft im Deutschen Vormärz 1815-1848* (1962). The best general economic history of the period is F. LUETGE, *Deutsche Sozial—und Wirtschaftsgeschichte* (1960). On Social history, a good collection of essays is to be found in W. CONZE (ed) *Staat und Gesellschaft im deutschen Vormärz, 1815-1848*, vol. I (1962). An unusually charming picture of life in the 'Biedermeier Era' can be found in P. E. SCHRAMM, *Neun Generationen, Dreihundert Jahre deutscher Kulturgeschichte im Lichte der Schicksale einer Hamburger Bürgerfamilie*, 2 vols. (1963 and 1964). The principal aspects of the economic history of Germany have been studied by J. KUCZYNSKI, in various works, particularly his *Geschichte der Lage der Arbeiter in Deutschland* vol. I *Von 1800 bis 1932* (1947) and are the object of important studies in eastern Germany. There are, of course, a great many studies on the origins of German socialism and particularly the young Karl Marx and his comrade-in-arms Friedrich Engels; apart from the studies by F. MEHRING, see in particular A. CORNU, *Karl Marx et Friedrich Engels*, 3 vols (1958-1962).

ITALY. There now exist several important Italian series of historical studies. In the F. Cattaneo series, see vol. III *Dalla Pace di Aquisgrana all'avvento di Cavour* (1959), a symposium; and in G. Candeloro's *Storia dell'Italia moderna*, see vol. II *1815-1848* (1958), a Marxist study. The best English work is R. A. CARRIE, *Italy from Napoleon to Mussolini* (1950); in French, apart from M. VAUSSARD, *De Pétrarque à Mussolini* (1961), there is an excellent general work by P. GUICHONNET, *L'unité italienne* (1961).

The Risorgimento itself has aroused impassioned controversies in Italy. See A. GRAMSCI, *Il Risorgimento* (1955); A. OMODEO, *L'Età del Risorgimento italiano* (1952); and *Difesa del Risorgimento* (1951). On political thought in general, see the remarkable work by L. SALVATORELLI, *Il pensiero politico italiano dal 1700 al 1870* (1949).

There are a great many works on the leading figures of the 'idealistic' period of the evolution of Italian unity. On Mazzini, see in particular M. DELL'ISOLA and G. BOURGIN, *Mazzini, promoteur de la République italienne et pionnier de la Fédération européenne* (1956) *and* E. E. Y. HALES, *Mazzini and the Secret Societies* (1956), which do not supplant the very old work by G. SALVEMINI, *Il pensiero religioso, politico, sociale de G. Mazzini* (1905). On Gioberti, see A. OMODEO, *V. Gioberti e la sua evoluzione politica* (1941); on d'Azeglio, see A. M. GHISALBERTI, *Massimo d'Azeglio, un moderatore realizzatore* (1953.

The regional aspects of the Risorgimento should not be overlooked. For northern Italy, see in particular K. R. GREENFIELD, *Economics and Liberalism in the Risorgimento. A Study of Nationalism in Lombardy 1815-1848* (1934). The personality of Charles Albert of Piedmont has given rise to fierce controversy; see A. OMODEO, *La Leggenda di Carlo Alberto nella recente storiografia* (1940).

Here again, political history cannot be separated from economic history. See G. LUZZATTO, *Storia economica dell'età moderna e contemporanea* vol. II (1948); R. ROMEO, *Risorgimento e capitalismo* (1959). The social repercussions are studied in L. BULFERETTI, *Socialismo risorgimentale* (1949).

AUSTRIA. For a full understanding of the development of this multinational State, see the recent histories of Austria, particularly H. HANTSCH, *Die Geschichte Oesterreichs* vol. II (1959) and E. ZÖLLNER, *Geschichte Oesterreichs* (1961), which are superior to A. J. P. TAYLOR, *The Habsburg Monarchy 1815-1918* (1942). Some interesting opinions are to be found in R. A. KANN. *The Habsburg Empire. A Study in Integration and Disintegration* (1957).

Only very brief mention can be made here of the works dealing with the different constituent parts of this monarchy. For Bohemia, apart from the old work by E. DENIS, *La Bohême depuis la Montagne blanche*, vol. II (1903), see H. MUENSCH, *Böhmische Tragödie. Das Schicksal Mitteleuropas im Lichte der tschechischen Frage* (1949). For Hungary, apart from J. SZEKFU, *Etat et nation* (1945), see the important work by C. A. MACARTNEY, *Hungary* (1934). There is no satisfactory general study of the nationalities problem in this period; but some interesting opinions are expressed in H. HANTSCH, *Die Nationalitätenfrage im alten Oesterreich* (1953). For an attempt at a synthesis, see J. DROZ, *L'Europe centrale. Evolution historique de l'idée de Mitteleuropa* (1960).

The administration of the monarchy cannot be separated from the personality of Metternich, of whom a new view is given by H. *von* SRBIK, *Metternich, der Staatsmann und der Mensch*, 3 vols. (1952 and 1954), in complete contrast to V. BIBL, *Metternich, Der Dämon Oesterreichs* (1936). For Metternich's domestic policies and political attitudes, A. G. HAAS, *Metternich, Reorganization and Nationality, 1813-1818* (1963). E. L. *Woodward, Three Studies in European Conservatism* (1929). On the literature about Metternich, P. W. SCHROEDER, 'Metternich Studies since 1925' *Journal of Modern History* (1961). On Friedrich von Gentz, G. MANN, *Friedrich von Gentz. Geschichte eines europäischen Staats-*

mannes (1947). The principal political tendencies have been studied by F. VALJAVEC, *Der Josefinismus* (1945), as well as by E. WINTER, *Die geistige Entwicklung A. Guenthers* (1931) and *B. Bolzano und sein Kreis.* (1933). See also K. EDER, *Der liberalismus in Altöster-reich. Geisteshaltung, Politik und Kultur* (1955). There are few studies as yet of the economic and social history of Austria. See J. BLUM, *Noble Landowners and Agriculture in Austria 1815-1848. A Study in the Origin of Peasant Emancipation* (1948).

RUSSIA. The classic general study in Russian is M. V. NECKINA, *History of the USSR*, vol. II *Russia in the Nineteenth Century* (1949). Among the studies in western languages see in particular M. T. FLORINSKY, *Russia, A History and an Interpretation* (1959); V. GITERMANN, *Geschichte Russlands*, vol. II (1944); P. N. MILIOUKOV, C. SEIGNOBOS, L. EISENMANN, *Histoire de la Russie*, vol. II (1932); B. NOLDE, *L'Ancien régime et la Révolution russe* (1935); B. PARES, *A History of Russia* (1949); B. H. SUMNER, *Survey of Russian History* (1944); M. C. WREN, *The course of Russian History* (1958). The essential work on the economic history of Russia is P. I. LYASCHENKO, *History of the National Economy of Russia to the 1917 Revolution* (1949); see also B. GILLE, *Histoire économique et sociale de la Russie du Moyen-Age au XXe siècle* (1949).

The main outlines of the revolutionary movement in this period can be studied in M. SLONIM, *De Pierre le Grand à Lénine* (1933) and above all in N. BERDIAEV, *Les sources et le sens du communisme russe* (1938) and J. DANZAS, *L'itinéraire religieux de la conscience russe* (1935). For a large-scale study of political activity under Nicholas I, see A. KOYRE, *La philosophie et le problème national en Russie au début du XIXe Siècle* (1929). See also P. LABRY, *A. I. Herzen 1812-1870. Essai sur la formation et le développement de ses idées* (1928); C. QUENET, *Tchaadaev et les lettres philosophiques. Contribution à l'étude du mouvement des idées en Russie* (1932); and A. GRATIEUX, *A. S. Chomiakov et le mouvement slavophile* (1939). The Decembrist movement has been the object of a great many studies, as can be seen from the *Soviet Encyclopedia*; see A. G. MAZOUR, *The First Russian Revolution 1825. The Decembrist Movement, its origins, development and significance* (1937). On Bakunin before 1848, see in particular B. P. HEPNER, *Bakounine et le panslavisme révolutionnaire* (1950).

The history of Russian society in the period under study has yet to be fully elucidated. However, see D. S. MIRSKI, *Russia. A social history* (1931). For details of recent works published in the Soviet Union on these problems, the reader is referred to the specialist periodicals, especially the *Slavonic Review* and *Le Monde slave.*

On Poland, see *The Cambridge History of Poland from Augustus II to Pilsudski 1697-1935* (1951). On Czartoryski and Polish emigration, see the essential work by M. KURIEL, *Czartoryski and European Unity 1770-1861* (1955).

INDEX

Fontana Press

Fontana Press is a leading paperback publisher of non-fiction. Below are some recent titles.

- ☐ PATRIOTS AND LIBERATORS Simon Schama £9.99
- ☐ THINKING ABOUT SOCIAL THINKING Antony Flew £5.99
- ☐ THE RUSSIAN REVOLUTION Richard Pipes £12.99
- ☐ LATE VICTORIAN BRITAIN J. F. C. Harrison £5.99
- ☐ HISTORY OF THE SOVIET UNION Geoffrey Hosking £7.99
- ☐ THE RISE AND FALL OF BRITISH NAVAL MASTERY
  Paul Kennedy £7.99
- ☐ SEX, DEATH AND PUNISHMENT
  Richard Davenport-Hines £7.99

You can buy Fontana Paperbacks at your local bookshops or newsagents. Or you can order them from Fontana, Cash Sales Department, Box 29, Douglas, Isle of Man. Please send a cheque, postal or money order (not currency) worth the price plus 24p per book for postage (maximum postage required is £3.00 for orders within the UK).

NAME (Block letters)_____

ADDRESS_____

_____